GLACIER CLIMBING & CREVASSE RESCUE

Essential Skills for Snow Travel

Ian Nicholson

To Greg Shaw and in memory of Paula Shaw—
with infinite thanks for their lifelong influence

MOUNTAINEERS BOOKS is dedicated to the exploration, preservation, and enjoyment of outdoor and wilderness areas.

1001 SW Klickitat Way, Suite 201, Seattle, WA 98134
800-553-4453, www.mountaineersbooks8org

Printed in China
Distributed in the United Kingdom by Cordee, www.cordee.co.uk

First edition, 2025

Design and layout: McKenzie Long, Cardinal Innovative
Illustrator: John McMullen
All photographs by the author unless credited otherwise
Cover photographs, front: *A team ascends Radio Control Tower on Peak 12,200 (Lisa Peak) in the Alaska Range.* (Photo by Brooke Warren); back, *Tino Villanueva demonstrates rappel-to-ascension methods in a crevasse in Washington's North Cascades.*
Frontispiece: *Sam Marjerison stares into an enormous crevasse on the Sulphide Glacier on Mount Shuksan in Washington's North Cascades.*

Leave No Trace Seven Principles © Leave No Trace, www.LNT.org

Library of Congress record is available at https://lccn.loc.gov/2024060220.
Ebook record available at https://lccn.loc.gov/2024060221.

Mountaineers Books titles may be purchased for corporate, educational, or other promotional sales, and our authors are available for a wide range of events. For information on special discounts or booking an author, contact our customer service at 800-553-4453 or mbooks@mountaineersbooks.org.

Printed on FSC-certfied materials

ISBN (paperback): 978-1-68051-644-9
ISBN (ebook): 978-1-68051-645-6

An independent nonprofit publisher since 1960

GLACIER CLIMBING & CREVASSE RESCUE

Essential Skills for Snow Travel

CONTENTS

CHAPTER 4
Tools of the Trade

CHAPTER 5
Moving on Snow and Ice

CHAPTER 6
Rigging the Rope and Travel Techniques

CHAPTER 7
Snow and Ice Anchors

CHAPTER 8

Belaying on Snow and Glaciers

CHAPTER 9

Crevasse Rescue and Mechanical Advantage

CHAPTER 10

Self-Rescue

CHAPTER 11

Rappelling, Rappel Anchors, and Lowering

CHAPTER 12

Glacier Travel and Crevasse Rescue for Skiers and Snowboarders

CHAPTER 13

Overnight and Expeditionary Glacier Travel Hazards

CHAPTER 14

Preparation and Practice

Opposite: *Danny Spreafico on the Cosmique Arête on the Aiguille du Midi in the French Alps*

The Art of Climbing Glaciers

More than two and a half decades ago, at age sixteen, I walked into the ranger station on the south side of Mount Rainier to get a climbing permit. My fifteen-year-old friend Jaya Sa and I had paid our friend John Graham, a senior in high school, an hourly rate to drive us down from Seattle, drop us off, and then pick us up three days later.

Jaya and I knew you had to be eighteen to climb Rainier without a parent accompanying you, but we felt we could pass as a few years older—what teenager doesn't? When it was our turn to talk to the ranger, we walked up confidently. The ranger quizzed us about crevasse rescue, a skill we'd learned by reading Andy Selters's guide to glacier travel and then diligently practiced on my deck in Seattle in the weeks leading up to the trip. He continued to ask us about our gear and experience, which at the time included a few ascents of Mount Hood, an ascent of both Mount Adams and Colchuck Peak, and a few other relatively moderate glaciated climbs. Our answers were satisfactory, but then came the moment we'd been dreading.

"How old are the two of you?" he asked.

"Eighteen," we hurriedly replied.

"Can I see your driver's licenses?" he responded.

Ian Nicholson in the Japanese Couloir on Mount Barille at age eighteen, the Alaska Range. (Photo by Graham McDowell)

"We don't have any," Jaya and I both said nervously.

"Well, how did you get here?"

I told him that our friend had dropped us off, to which he fired back, "Well, then what year were you born?"

Doing the math in my head quickly to subtract a couple years, I fired back, "Uh, uh, 1981."

The ranger looked at us and said bluntly, "Well, you two seem like you know what you're doing, but if you have any problems, find a guide or a ranger and tell them you need help."

Jaya and I went on to climb the Disappointment Cleaver on Mount Rainier over the next few days, and our ascent went off without a hitch. Now, I'm not recommending that anyone ever lie to rangers, but all our preparation for glacier travel had paid off, giving us the skills and confidence to navigate this often-hazardous environment. Had one of us fallen into a crevasse or down a steep slope, we knew that we possessed the knowledge to save our bacon. That is where *Glacier Climbing & Crevasse Rescue* comes in. Writing this book has allowed me to share the knowledge I've amassed and honed throughout my several decades of climbing and guiding since that life-changing Rainier ascent.

THE DANGERS OF ICE-COVERED MOUNTAINS

Alpine glaciers exist on all seven continents (if you group New Zealand with Australia). Though mountaineering and alpine routes do not always require crossing glaciers, being proficient at traveling across snow-covered landscapes remains an integral part of climbing mountains. On smooth, relatively low-angle glaciers, the dangers are frequently hidden. Unlike rock or waterfall ice climbing, where you can feel the exposure beneath your feet, the dangers of crevasses are often invisible. If a member of a rope team breaks through a snowbridge and falls into a crevasse, they are instantly transported from a relatively benign environment to a very vertical, often very cold one.

The fallen climber's companions will likely be the ones building and using complex rope systems to extract them. Thus, while moving across even a low-angle, mostly snow-covered glacier can appear simple, performing crevasse rescue is more technical than most situations you will encounter while climbing rock or waterfall ice.

Climbing glaciated mountains is about planning, navigating, and moving over snow. Here, Chris Marshall crosses through a crevasse near the top of the long, technical North Ridge of Mount Baker, North Cascades, Washington. (Photo by Chris Marshall)

AN AMALGAM OF SKILLS

Climbing glaciers is about far more than simply preparing for crevasse rescue, though that is no doubt an important technique to master. Climbing in this challenging environment requires an amalgam of skills. Before you embark on your trip, you need to plan your route and be proficient enough to navigate in a whiteout. You need to be able to smoothly and effectively climb over snowy, icy, variably angled terrain while wearing crampons and using an ice axe. You need to know when and how to rig the rope to travel across low-angle stretches of glacier, as well as how to build and use a belay anchor in the snow.

You need to be familiar with techniques for descending a glaciated peak, which can range from simply walking downhill to building rappel anchors in snow or ice. You need to be confident about tying various knots and hitches and know how to ascend a rope to self-rescue. And, lastly, you need to know how to build technical systems that use mechanical

A group navigates complex glacial terrain on their way to the high camp for Alpamayo and Quitaraju in the Cordillera Blanca, Peru. (Photo by Jonathon Spitzer)

Keith Sidle enjoys feeling small in a big, glaciated world.

advantage to haul a fallen climber out of a hidden crevasse.

Luckily, climbers do not need to master all these skills at once. You could start by climbing snowy mountains that may not even have glaciers and then build up to peaks with relatively small glaciers that may have only a few crevasses and are easy to navigate. Then you could ascend more-complex glaciated routes with steep snow that require pitching the climb out—the difficulty grows from there. As with all disciplines in climbing, it's wise to start in a low-risk environment as you build your skills, practice applying what you learn, and gain confidence with your technical systems. The skills and techniques presented in this manual reflect that progression. If you study and practice these techniques and then apply your skills out in the field with mentors, you'll be well on your way to a lifetime of adventure on glaciers.

Next page: *The massive northwest face of the 8,000-meter Himalaya peak Cho Oyu* (Photo by Dallas Glass)

CHAPTER 1

Understanding Glaciers and Their Hazards

A persistent mass of ice that slowly moves downhill under its own weight, a glacier forms when the accumulation of seasonal snow exceeds its ablation (the melting or transport of seasonal snow) over many years and often centuries. As the snow breaks down, it becomes ice; over the years, the ice mass grows, forming—or becoming integrated into—the glacier. As a glacier moves downhill, it abrades and gouges rock and moves sediment, creating landforms like cirques, moraines, and fjords.

Climbing many mountains around the world requires crossing snow and glaciers. Being proficient with techniques for snow, ice, and glaciers integral to climbing mountains. There are approximately seven thousand glaciers on our planet, covering around 10 percent of Earth's total land mass. Collectively, these glaciers contain around 69 percent of Earth's fresh water and enough water that if all the glaciers on Earth melted, the sea level would rise around 230 feet.

THE DYNAMIC ANATOMY OF GLACIAL TERRAIN

Just like the terms *ridge*, *gendarme*, *summit*, *horn*, *aiguille*, *buttress*, and *arête* describe parts of a mountain, similar terms describe the terrain characteristics of a glacier and the terrain immediately adjacent. Being familiar with common terms (fig. 1-1) will not only help you better understand how glaciers form but also how to communicate about them.

The accumulation zone of a glacier is the area where more snow accumulates through snowfall than is lost or where seasonal snow always covers the glacier's surface. Glacier ice is not consistently exposed in the accumulation zone. The ablation zone is the lower part of a glacier where more ice is lost through melting and other processes (like calving) than is gained through seasonal snowfall. The ablation zone is usually where a glacier experiences a net loss of ice mass.

A crevasse is a crack in the surface of a glacier created by stress on the ice mass, typically a result of its downward movement or some of the ice being forced to bend out of the plane of travel as the glacier moves. In other words, when a glacier turns up, down, or to either side, the different areas of the glacier move at different speeds, creating stress.

TENSION AND COMPRESSION ZONES

The classic and fairly accurate analogy of a glacier is the "Snickers bar," which refers to the tension (convex) and compression (concave) zones of the glacier. Think about the glacier in a vertical cross section, working upward from the bedrock beneath it to its surface. For

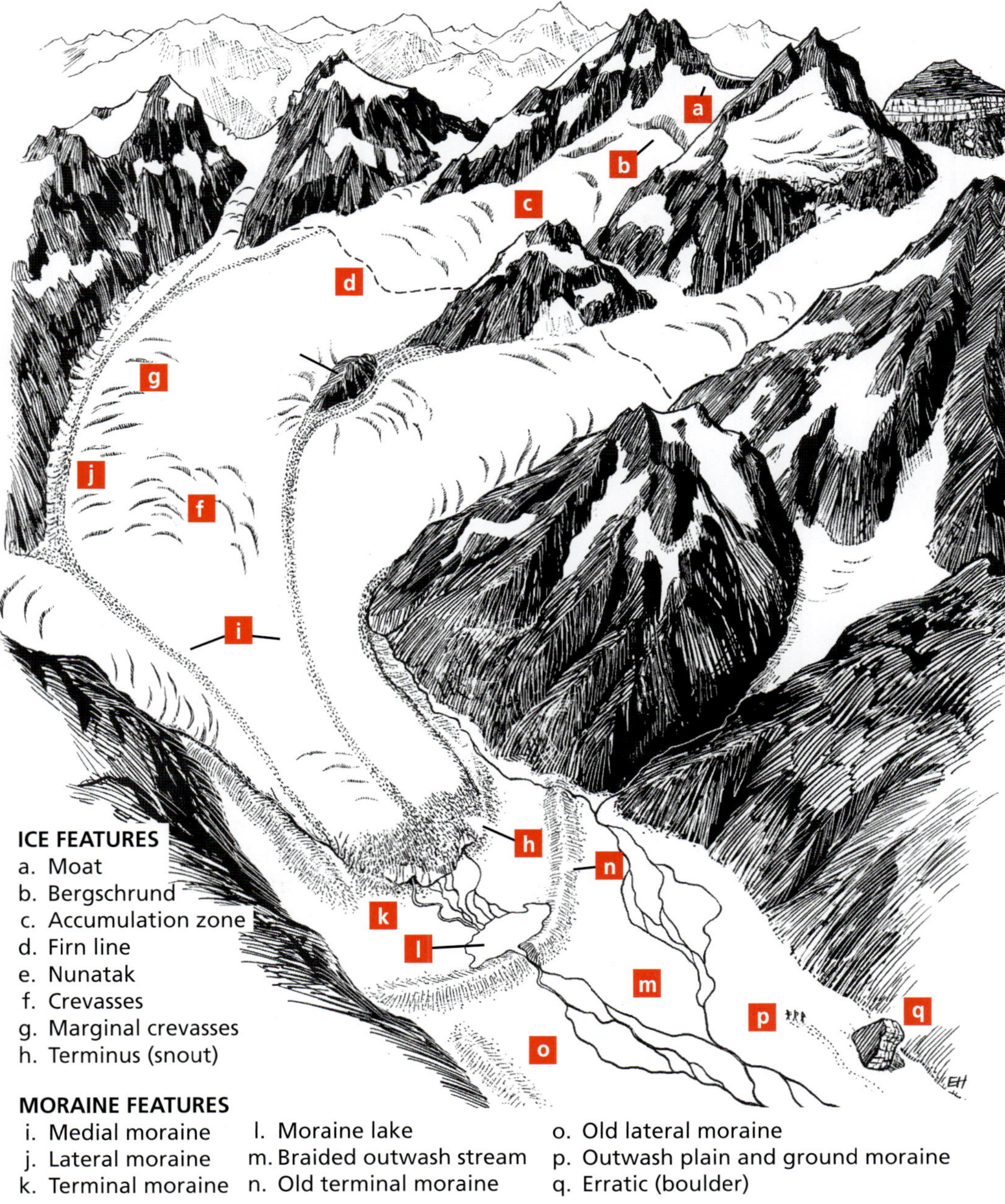

Figure 1-1. *Aerial view of glacier terrain features*

KEY GLACIOLOGICAL TERMS

Becoming familiar with these common glaciology terms will help you understand the shape and structure of glaciers and how they form and evolve.

ablation zone The area of a glacier where annual snowfall melts away during the drier, warmer months, exposing bare glacial ice; this is where the glacier recedes.

accumulation zone The area of a glacier where annual snowfall is equal to or greater than the annual melt rate; this is where the glacier "grows" from.

bergschrund Giant crevasses found at the upper limit of glacier movement, formed where the moving glacier breaks away from an ice cap or snowfield above.

crevasse A crack or chasm in a glacier.

firn Old snow in the process of becoming glacial ice. Firn is at least one year old and has survived for at least one melt season. As it gets buried again by the next season's snow, it gradually increases in density and slowly turns into glacial ice.

icefall Steep, jumbled section of a glacier.

lateral moraine Mounds of rock and debris deposited along the sides of a glacier.

moat Gap between snow and rock.

moulin Roughly circular opening in a glacier that meltwater flows through to channels below a glacier.

névé Granular snow that has melted, refrozen, and compacted; can become part of a glacier.

serac Tower of ice on a glacier.

snowbridge Arc formed by snow across a crevasse, creek, or other terrain gap.

tarn Lake or pond formed in a mountain cirque excavated by a glacier.

terminal moraine Mounds of rock and debris deposited at the toe or edge of a glacier.

example, as the glacier "rolls over" into steeper terrain, the surface of the glacier needs to move much faster and travel a greater distance to keep pace with the bottom of the glacier, which doesn't need to move as far. If the roll is steep enough (and it doesn't take much), the highest part of the glacier won't be able to keep pace with the lowest part, and the tension will literally break it apart, forming crevasses (fig. 1-2).

Sometimes a tension zone develops not because of a change to the angle of the glacier but because of the shape of the bedrock underneath the glacier. All glaciers are masses of ice pulled downhill by gravity, at whatever pace. If there is a "bump" or some other obstruction big enough to force the glacier to change its flow in any direction, it will generally be evidenced on the surface in the form of crevasses. Thus those "random" midslope crevasses are actually the result of features in the bedrock, which is why you must probe to confirm the presence or absence of a crevasse (with a thick seasonal snowpack, even probing may not be sufficient).

RADIAL CREVASSES

Radial crevasses form when a glacier significantly changes direction or turns a corner (fig. 1-3). As the ice turns a corner, different areas of the glacier move at different speeds; the portion closest to the outside of the turn must travel faster than the portion on the inside of the turn (as on a racetrack). When

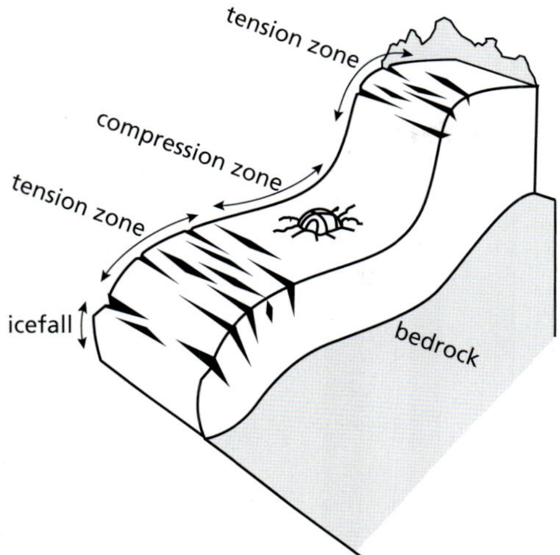

Figure 1-2. Comparing tension and compression zones and how they create crevasses. Compression zones tend to push the crevasses back together, making for better camping and break locations. Undulations in the bedrock can lead to irregular formations.

the portion of the glacier on the outside of the turn can't keep up with the ice mass on the inside, the tension pulls it apart, cracking it at roughly 45-degree angles back up the glacier. The inside of the turn can also form crevasses that radiate out from the inside wall, but these tend to be much smaller and narrower.

MARGINAL CREVASSES

Marginal crevasses (fig. 1-3) are like radial crevasses but form for different reasons and thus can form in different directions. If a glacier is flowing relatively straight, the ice in the middle is moving slightly faster than the ice along the outside edges. This is due to the glacier's mass and the added friction of the glacier's edge dragging along the sides. The stress from the ice in the glacier traveling at

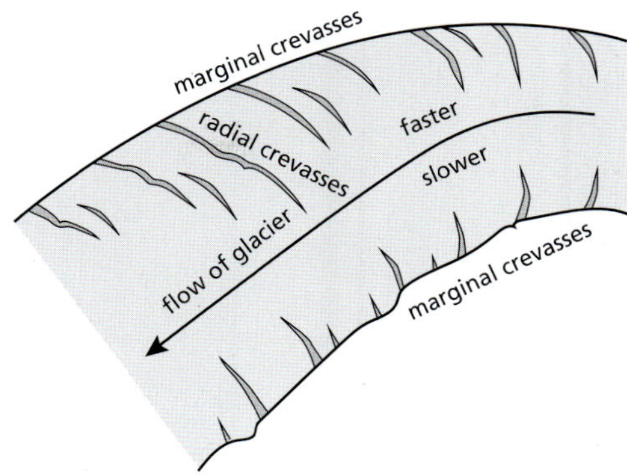

Figure 1-3. Radial and marginal crevasses form on its sides as a glacier turns a corner.

different speeds can cause crevasses to form in a herringbone pattern, generally fracturing around 45 degrees up-glacier from the valley wall—these are marginal crevasses.

Glaciers are dynamic features and can appear quite complex and chaotic. Figure 1-4 shows the different types of crevasses that form as the glacier flows in different directions over an erratically shaped bedrock surface.

BERGSCHRUNDS AND MOATS

Bergschrunds and moats present similar navigation problems to crevasses in that they are dark, often deep places you could fall into. Sometimes exposed and sometimes hidden, they are created and form in distinctly different places.

A bergschrund (fig. 1-5), a German word meaning "mountain cleft," and also commonly referred to by climbers as a "schrund," is found where the glacier moves away from stagnant seasonal snow or stagnant permanent snow or ice. Since bergschrunds generally have snow on both sides, they might look like crevasses but are not in fact cracks in the glacier

Figure 1-4. *The Boston Glacier in Washington's North Cascades shows the chaotic effects of dynamic motion.*

itself. They frequently form where steeper terrain exists above the glacier, and the glacier slowly pulls away or moves laterally across it. Depending on their size, bergschrunds can be easy to navigate or present a serious obstacle. They are frequently quite deep and often extend along the bedrock for the entire depth of the glacier (fig. 1-6).

Moats are gaps that form between a glacier and a rock. Because the rock is darker than the glacier, it absorbs more heat and subsequently melts the snow adjacent to it. While moats can be quite deep and are responsible for many deaths, they are generally not as deep or as big as most crevasses or bergschrunds. The danger of moats is that they can get undercut due to the heating-melting cycle, forming an unstable "diving board" of snow over an abyss. Approach moats with caution and use a belay from a thicker part of the glacier if you have any reservations.

OTHER TYPES OF GLACIERS

Climbers cross a few other types of glaciers that, while often smaller, have different characteristics and thus different hazards compared to more traditional glaciers.

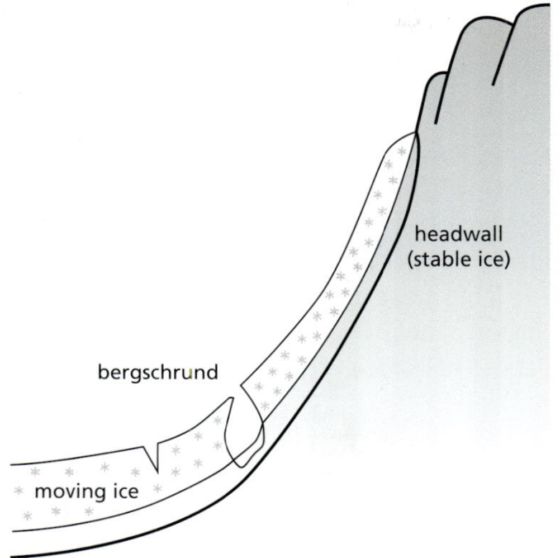

Figure 1-5. *A glacier can pull away from nonmoving headwall ice or a permanent snowfield to create a bergschrund.*

ROCK GLACIERS

Rock glaciers are former traditional glaciers that have become partially or completely overlaid by talus. Rock glaciers are often the last part of a slowly receding glacier but maintain some mass because they are in steep cirques or basins where the snow sliding off the walls accumulates to form ice. This process mixes rock and ice, and the glaciers' relatively low mass means they move relatively slowly; crevasses are therefore small to nonexistent. Examples include many of the remaining glaciers in the Rocky Mountains of Colorado and the Tetons and the Timpanogos Glacier in Utah.

HANGING GLACIERS

A hanging glacier starts high on a mountainside or the wall of a glacial valley and abruptly stops atop a cliff. Hanging glaciers

Figure 1-6. *The Park Glacier on Washington's Mount Baker is an excellent example of how bergschrunds form as the entire glacier slowly pulls away from the immobile headwall ice.*

Figure 1-7. *Climbers ascend the Forbidden Glacier below the hanging glacier on the Northwest Face of Forbidden Peak, North Cascades National Park, Washington.*

often produce icefalls at very irregular, unpredictable times. The ice that falls is rarely a result of temperature, solar radiation, or other weather inputs and is most frequently the result of glacial movement, which is impossible to predict. Approach these features from below with caution, and do not dally below them (fig. 1-7).

GLACIERS THROUGH THE SEASONS

Unlike rock climbs, glacier climbs change significantly throughout the seasons (fig. 1-8). For example, a given route over a given set of glaciers will present different challenges and hazards depending on the time of the year.

In the middle of winter, a significant amount of seasonal snow may hide all the crevasses, so you may need to consider avalanche hazards and use flotation—skis, a splitboard, or snowshoes—to avoid sinking into deep snow. Conversely, the very end of the "traditional" climbing season may not present any avalanche danger. This time of year, the glacier has large areas of completely bare ice, and all the crevasses are exposed, which removes the danger of hidden crevasses but complicates navigation.

WINTER

The winter season generally refers to the period during which seasonal snow creates a thick blanket on the glacier's surface. While it can be just a few meters thick, the winter snowpack is often much deeper. In more temperate and alpine regions (versus Arctic and

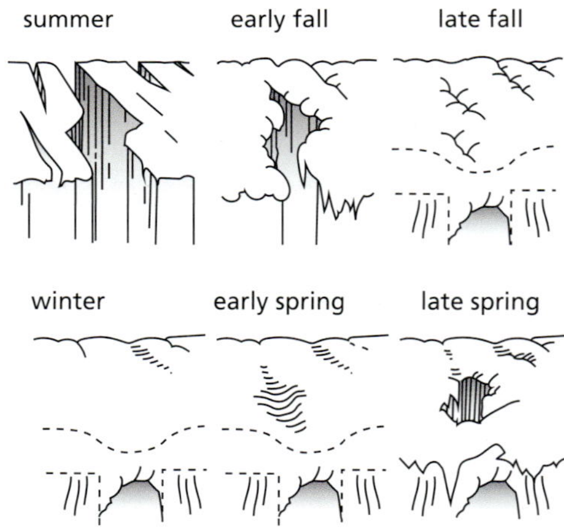

Figure 1-8. *The amount of seasonal snow on the glacier, which correlates with the thickness of snowbridges, varies across the seasons and impacts a climber's ability to travel directly through the terrain.*

FALLING THROUGH A CORNICE

BY GEORGE LOWE

After ten long days, we had become the first team to ascend the 9,000-foot Central Spur on the South Face of Mount Foraker in the summer of 1977. The route would eventually become known as the Infinite Spur, one of the most cutting-edge ascents of its day. As Michael Kennedy and I reached the summit at 4 p.m., the high wind dropped, but the –20° temperatures at 17,000 feet chilled us to the bone, and we both became concerned about frostbite. After the obligatory victory photos, we started down the long and complex Southeast Ridge.

The first section was so easy that we ran, losing a couple thousand feet in a couple hours. Each foot we lost energized us as the effects of altitude receded. We downclimbed some tricky sections, occasionally belaying each other, and then the weather once again changed abruptly. Big black clouds moved in from the north, south, and east; Foraker blocked the western view. We simply couldn't afford to sit out another storm. All went well until we hit a heavily corniced section of the ridge, apparently the crux of the route and the trickiest portion of our descent.

Having spent a lot of time in big mountains, we were both very leery of cornices and moved slowly and carefully around them. The next few seconds lasted an eternity. Thirty feet from the crest, I came across what appeared to be a small crevasse, probed it, and stepped across. I heard a dull cracking sound, and a fracture appeared and ran along the ridge for 100 feet. Then the cornice disappeared, taking me with it.

The rope came taut and jerked Michael off his feet across one side of the ridge. The rope pulled tighter, reeling Michael up to the crest; he later said he imagined himself shooting over the edge and the two of us falling helplessly to the chaotic glacier 8,000 feet below. But instead, Michael stopped 20 feet from the edge and rammed in a T-slot within seconds. Michael was sure that I was either dead or very seriously injured, in part because I was not responding to his shouts, as I couldn't hear him. Then the rope slackened and he began to pull up a few feet of rope, then another few feet, and another few, and then he put me on belay: miracle of miracles, I was in good enough shape to climb! We were soon reunited and set about gathering our shattered wits. I was bruised and shaken and had a cut on my nose, but that was it. We very cautiously traveled down the rest of the Southeast Ridge, eventually making our way back to Kahiltna Base Camp.

KEY TAKEAWAYS: Always give cornices plenty of space—they can break much farther back than you expect. Consider adjusting your travel techniques to best protect your group from a cornice fall. Falling through a cornice should be your primary concern, with a hidden crevasse second.

One of the most accomplished alpinists in the US, **George Lowe** is known for his bold first ascents, including the Infinite Spur on Mount Foraker and the North Twin Tower in the Canadian Rockies. A pioneer of alpine-style climbing, he made groundbreaking ascents in the Himalayas, including the first ascent of Everest's Kangshung Face and a legendary attempt and near success on the North Ridge of Latok I.

Figure 1-9. *A group unknowingly crosses a large hidden crevasse on the Emmons Glacier on Mount Rainier.* (Photo by Adam Frost)

Antarctic areas), glaciers form due to heavy seasonal winter snow.

All but the biggest crevasses in these regions will be covered, which often means more secure travel. But because the snow is colder "winter snow," it isn't as strong or dense as springtime or summer snow, so the odds of punching through snowbridges are higher, particularly in the early part of the winter when it is colder and the seasonal snow is thinner. During winter, the use of flotation aids like skis, a splitboard, or snowshoes is more likely to be required, and there's a higher risk of slab avalanches.

EARLY SEASON

During the early season—referring to late winter through late spring or very early summer—much less or no additional snow is added to the glacier's surface. There is still plenty of snow on the glacier, and the bridges are strong, as the seasonal snow is going

Figure 1-10. *A climber ascends a steep snow slope high on the North Ridge of Artesonraju, Cordillera Blanca, Peru. Climbing glaciated mountains often involves managing hazards beyond hidden crevasses.* (Photo by Jonathon Spitzer)

through melt-freeze cycles. At the start of this period, additional flotation, like skis or snowshoes, might be required but only until winter snow consolidates.

From the end of the early season into the midseason, these bridges can become thin enough to punch through and are more affected by temperature. For example, a snowbridge is safe in the morning when the snow is frozen but very weak in the day's heat. Slab avalanches are a possibility, but most avalanches are going to be tied to late storms or loose, wet snow.

MIDSEASON

From very late spring through summer, travel is still straightforward, and the snow surface tends to be dense enough to not require flotation aids. The snowbridges continue to thin, and in the later part of spring and into the early summer, many hidden crevasses remain, leading to the greatest tally of "hidden crevasse falls" of any season. As the midseason wears on, more crevasses reveal themselves, making them easier to spot, and the bridges slowly become more suspect.

Figure 1-11. *Travis Powell ascends very steep snow above the Tokositna Glacier on the upper slopes of the Harvard Route on Mount Huntington in Alaska.* (Photo by Connor Chilcott)

LATE SEASON

By fall, the late season, nearly all of the snow has melted off the glacier, leaving mostly bare ice. There are very few hidden crevasses, but a few suspect snowbridges may remain. Travel is challenging due to both the icy condition of the snow surface and the size of the crevasses—any crevasse that is too wide to step over will need to be end-run, making travel time-consuming or even impossible (fig. 1-9).

EARLY WINTER

As the first seasonal snow begins to fall onto the ice, travel becomes very difficult. Crevasses become covered by very thin bridges of recently fallen, very weak snow. Early winter conditions prevail even as the snow piles up a few meters on the glacier and flotation becomes required.

OTHER GLACIAL HAZARDS

While this book focuses largely on crevasses and managing steep snow and ice, a number of other hazards warrant the attention of the alpinist looking to climb in glaciated ranges (fig. 1-10).

SLIP-AND-FALL HAZARDS

While hidden crevasse falls can pose a significant risk, slips and falls lead to more injuries among climbers: chapters 5 and 6 will help you build a good foundation of skills to move securely on snow. Many people assume that walking on snow is easy, and it is, but walking on snow securely and efficiently takes practice and technique: Chapter 7, on building snow anchors, and chapter 8, on belaying, speak to navigating on steep terrain, where the risk and consequence of a fall are too great to climb unroped. Learning good snow- and ice-climbing skills, possessing the ability to efficiently build sound anchors, and being familiar with a wide range of belay techniques are essential for any mountaineer or alpine climber (fig. 1-11).

ICEFALL AND SERAC FALL

Icefall and serac fall (fig. 1-12) can be difficult to predict, as can the size of any potential release. While some icefall and serac hazards can be effected by warming temperatures and sunshine, others are tied to glacial movement, which is impossible to predict. Take breaks before entering areas of potential icefall or serac fall, then travel through as quickly as is reasonable to move continuously without stopping.

CORNICES

Cornices form other exposed features where wind can transport snow from one side of the feature to the other, usually on the lee side of a ridge, where the snow slowly builds up to form an overhanging lip. Cornices can range from barely half a foot of overhanging snow to the size of a high-rise apartment building, posing a hazard for climbers because it is nearly impossible to tell (without a probe) where the ridge ends and the cornice begins

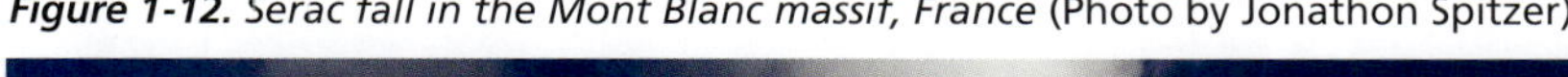

Figure 1-12. *Serac fall in the Mont Blanc massif, France* (Photo by Jonathon Spitzer)

Figure 1-13. *Cornices, such as this huge one on the final summit ridge of Denali, are another deceptive hazard that climbers must deal with.* (Photo by Brooke Warren)

as well as accurately assess the cornice's strength (fig. 1-13).

Cornices pose two primary hazards: First, the cornice itself can fall away, crushing the climber. Second, and even more dangerous, is the gap that forms as the weight of the cornice slowly pulls away from solid ground, creating a crevasse. Unfortunately, several well-known climbers have died falling through this gap. Often, these climbers did not die because the entire cornice collapsed but because they essentially ended up falling off a large cliff due to the exposed nature of the ridge. Give cornices the space and respect they deserve.

WHITEOUTS

Don't underestimate the ease of getting lost when the clouds roll in and the snow starts to fall. A dusting of snow or a light wind can cover your tracks, making it nearly impossible to figure out where you are and which way you should go without appropriate planning

Figure 1-14. *Whiteouts are common, making it essential to plan ahead and be able to use tools such as a map, compass, and a smartphone loaded with navigation data ahead of time.* (Photo by Bryce Hill)

REMEDIAL LESSONS ON MOUNT ROBSON

BY FOREST MCBRIAN

Robson still looked far away as we stood atop the Kain Face—it was humbling to think of Conrad Kain chopping steps in 1913 for his clients up the thousand feet of steep snow we had negotiated with running belays and two tools. But in twenty years climbing with my partner, David Moskowitz, I'd always striven to bring the right technique to bear on the terrain for what we needed, right then. How, then, should we proceed over an extremely corniced ridge up among the goblinesque serac bulges that guarded the route to the summit?

Much of the terrain looked easy—easy enough for walking, really, and I thought we could certainly stay below the large cornices we had noticed on our way up. For some reason, I thought of the many great alpinists who had perished on such terrain: Joe Puryear and Patrick Berhault came to mind. The snow was soft and good for self-arresting, but I also tied blocking knots in roughly 10 meters of rope that separated us, and we coiled off the rest; I hoped this configuration might not only offer some protection on the corniced ridge but also help save a transition once we got on more traditional glaciers up higher. David said his favorite line, "I'll follow you anywhere, Forest," which always both charms and horrifies me. I made him go first—it's relevant that I outweigh him by forty pounds.

Minutes after we'd rigged the rope, Dave disappeared up to his armpits, his feet dangling. Despite giving himself plenty of space, he had unknowingly crossed onto the wrong side of the cornice line! He crawled out of a trapdoor far above the Kain Face, both of us grateful for the rope.

KEY TAKEAWAYS: Give cornices plenty of room—and even when you think you have, do not be complacent near them. Using a rope to protect your partners in the same way you would during more traditional glacier travel can be the difference between shared laughter and something much, much worse.

Forest McBrian is an IFMGA mountain guide, writer, surveyor, and prolific explorer of the modern Cascades based in Snoqualmie, Washington.

David Moskowitz dips his toes in a thousand feet of air atop the Kain Face of Yuh-hai-has-kun, also known as Mount Robson. (Photo by Forest McBrian)

and navigation skills (fig. 1-14). See chapters 3 and 4 for in-depth information on foundational navigation skills, trip-planning tools, and mission-critical alpine tools—including GPS, map, and compass—to navigate on glaciers and snow above tree line.

HYPOTHERMIA, FROSTBITE, AND ALTITUDE SICKNESS

This book is not intended to provide in-depth information about the avoidance and treatment of hypothermia, frostbite, and altitude sickness; however, these are real hazards to the mountaineer that can be avoided in most cases with some basic preventive measures.

Hypothermia

Hypothermia occurs when your body loses heat faster than it produces it. Prolonged exposure to cold temperatures will eventually use up your body's stored energy. One key way to avoid hypothermia is to fuel yourself by eating and drinking plenty of food and water. Also, adjust your layers accordingly, and try not to let yourself get too sweaty—if you become damp, you need to switch to warmer clothing, even if this sounds inconvenient or unpleasant, or you are tired. If you are cold, don't "save your layer for later"—put it on until you get warm again.

Frostbite

Frostbite is a cold injury that, in the most severe cases, results in the freezing of the skin and underlying tissues, causing permanent damage (fig. 1-15). In the earliest stage, frostnip, when just outermost layers of skin are frozen, rewarming is time-consuming and painful. Frostbite occurs when skin is exposed to cold, such as when adjusting clothing layers. Avoid going bare-handed in cold temperatures and make sure your gloves or mittens are thick enough for the conditions and your activity. Make sure your gloves and boots stay dry or you dry them when possible, and cover your cheeks and nose and wear windproof clothing in windy conditions.

The risk of frostbite increases at below-freezing temperatures, particularly when there is potential for prolonged exposure during a typical summit push. However, the risk increases significantly as air temperature falls below 5°F (–15°C), even with low wind speeds. For colder or higher-elevation climbs, frostbite can occur in less than thirty minutes if the windchill falls below –15° F.

It sounds like a cliché, but the best treatment for frostbite is prevention. Check in

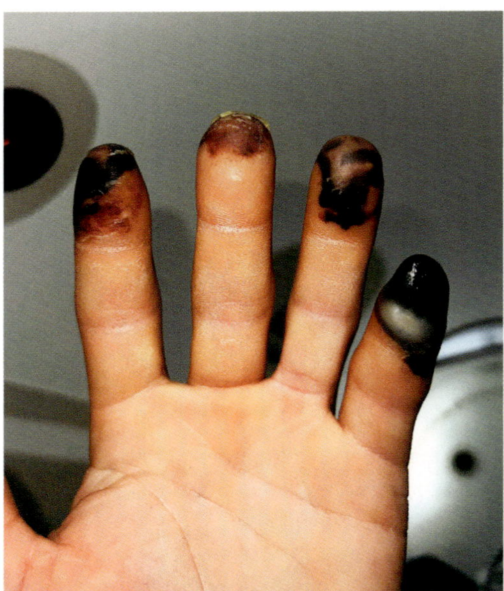

Figure 1-15. *Alan Rousseau's hand after making the first ascent of* Round Trip Ticket *on the North Face of Jannu in 2023—months later Alan would lose the tips of two of his fingers.* (Photo by Alan Rousseau)

Figure 1-16. *Climbers ascend the Lhotse Face at around 7,300 meters (24,000 feet) on Mount Everest. At such extremes in altitude, the human body struggles to adapt to lower amounts of oxygen and less atmospheric pressure.* (Photo by Dallas Glass)

with yourself. Can you feel all your fingers? All your toes? Touch the ends of your ears and nose. How do they feel? Are they numb? One of the easiest things you can do is wear the right clothing and keep yourself fed and hydrated. If your hands are cold, try aggressively doing windmills with your arms, using centrifugal force to "whip" blood into your extremities. Try wiggling your toes and gently rubbing your ears or nose. If the feeling doesn't return, then descend to a safe place where you can focus on rewarming the affected areas.

Altitude Sickness

As you ascend, the air gets thinner because atmospheric pressure is lower at higher elevations (fig. 1-16). Air molecules are more spread out, leading to less oxygen in a given volume. This reduction in air pressure, and a climber's subsequent inability to take in as much oxygen as they can at sea level, not only affects their performance but also causes various forms of altitude sickness.

Depending on the severity, symptoms can range from a mild headache and loss of appetite to acute, life-threatening conditions. Climbers can suffer from altitude sickness on mountains as low as 10,000 feet, and nearly all climbers will feel the effects if they live near sea level and ascend to 14,000 feet. See chapter 13 for more on the acclimatization process and signs and symptoms of altitude sickness.

Opposite: *Sharon Birchfield crosses the McAllister Glacier on the way to Dorado Needle, North Cascades National Park, Washington.*

CHAPTER 2

Rope Work: Knots, Hitches, Ratchets, and Tractors

While there is a nearly infinite number of knots and hitches, this chapter focuses on the ones used most often for glacier travel, including tips on tying them and their pros and cons for various applications. All climbers should practice these knots and hitches to the point where they can tie them correctly the first time, every time, and create them under the duress of a crevasse rescue.

FOUNDATIONAL TERMINOLOGY

To better understand knots, hitches, and the construction of technical systems, you must be familiar with a few foundational terms to be able to communicate their construction and various applications.

BIGHTS AND LOOPS

Bights and loops are commonly used by all who use ropes, from sailors to mountaineers to rope-access workers. A bight is like a "mouth" or a V, U, or C shape in the rope where the rope strands do not cross. A loop is created by making a circle where the strands cross once to complete the loop (fig. 2-1).

Figure 2-1. *A bight (left) is always open on one side, while a loop (right) forms a closed circle with the strands crossed once.* (Photo by Truc Allen)

KNOT VS. HITCH

A knot stands alone when tied in the rope, whereas a hitch needs to be tied around something—and when that something is removed, the hitch no longer exists. You are left with twists or loops of rope.

ATTACHING YOURSELF TO THE ROPE: KNOTS

While traveling on glaciers, climbers generally clip in to the rope (fig. 2-2), but they may choose to tie directly in to their harness in specific situations. Understanding different ways to attach to the rope, as well as some potential applications of different knots, will give you a well-rounded toolbox for solving more complex problems and choosing the best knot for your objective.

Figure 2-2. *While traveling on glaciers, climbers generally clip in to the rope with a knot and a carabiner rather than tying in directly, as is most common while rock climbing. The mountaineer's coil shown here is covered in more detail in figure 6-12.* (Photo by Sharon Birchfield)

FIGURE-EIGHT ON A BIGHT

A figure-eight on a bight (fig. 2-3) is a strong, easy-to-check knot tied in the middle of the rope. Climbers most often use it to attach themselves to the rope while on glaciers. However, it must be clipped to whatever it is being attached to (generally using carabiners) rather than tied in to directly. You cannot reasonably attach the climbing rope to your harness with a figure-eight on a bight without carabiners or some other attachment mechanism.

Figure 2-3. *A figure-eight on a bight is a strong, easy-to-check knot. It is among the most common knots climbers use to attach themselves to the rope while on glaciers.* (Photo by Truc Allen)

REWOVEN FIGURE-EIGHT

The rewoven figure-eight (fig. 2-4) is just as strong and easy to check as a figure-eight on a bight, but unlike that knot, a rewoven figure-eight is tied at the rope ends. This knot is also known as the figure-eight follow-through or figure-eight retrace. This is the most common knot for attaching a climber directly to the end of the rope, and with good reason: it is easy to tie, easy to check, won't come untied on its own, and is one of the strongest knots, maintaining around 75–80

Figure 2-4. *To tie a figure-eight follow-through:* **a**, *tie a figure-eight on the rope;* **b,** *then run the end of the rope back through each section of the figure eight, tracing each bend to create five sets of parallel strands.* (Photos by Truc Allen)

percent of the material it is tied with due to its shallow bends, and is even around 5–10 percent stronger than a bowline. Also, unlike a bowline, this knot does not need a backup knot—it's strong enough with a "fist's worth of tail," or around 3–4 inches.

Tip: To make a rewoven figure-eight easier to untie once it becomes weighted, ensure the knot is tightened and well dressed. Take the extra ten seconds to push the overlaps around so that all five "pairs" of ropes end up parallel and well cinched.

ALPINE BUTTERFLY

The alpine butterfly is a knot tied in the middle of the rope (figs. 2-5 and 2-6) that offers the advantages of loading slightly better inline on the rope than a figure-eight on a bight and being "shorter"—the knot rides higher, catching less frequently on your knees and crampons than a "longer" knot.

Its main application is in alpine climbing and glacier travel, for the middle members of the rope team to clip in to, where there is potential for the knot to be loaded in either direction. It's also the most common "stopper knot," tied

Figure 2-5. The alpine butterfly is another great knot to connect to the rope or use as a "stopper knot" in a rope on glaciers and snow.

between climbers to help arrest the group in the event of a crevasse fall by "jamming" into the lip of a crevasse and reducing the loads on the arresting members of the team.

OVERHAND ON A BIGHT

The overhand on a bight (fig. 2-7) is another knot that mountaineers and alpinists commonly use to attach themselves to the rope, mostly because it is quick and easy to tie and rides slightly higher than the figure-eight. It isn't quite as easy to untie as the figure-eight nor as strong, but it's still strong enough for climbing and crevasse-rescue purposes.

JOINING TWO ROPES

There will be times when you need to join two ropes, most commonly for long rappels. Here are three of the most common and useful knots.

FLAT OVERHAND

The flat overhand (fig. 2-8) is the most common knot for joining two ropes together

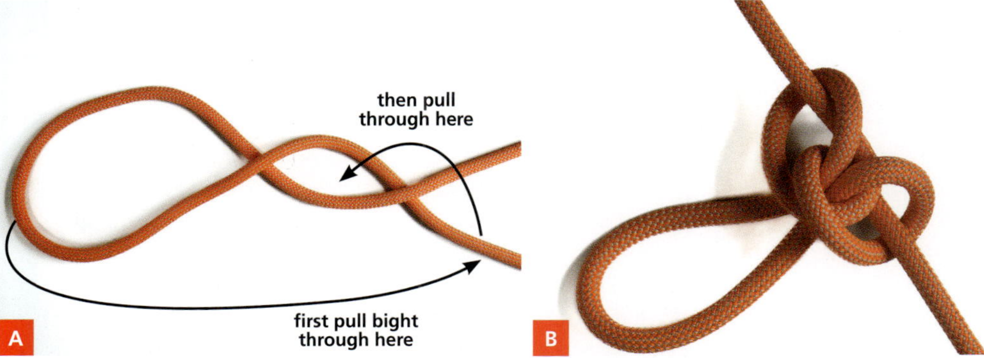

***Figure 2-6.** There are several ways to tie an alpine butterfly. For the method shown here, follow these steps:* **a,** *Take a bight of rope and flip it over twice, creating two twists. Pass the bight around the bottom of the lowest twist. Take the bight you just passed below the lowest twist and pass it up through the loop you created.* **b,** *Pull the knot tight.* (Photos by Truc Allen)

WHEN IT COMES TO CREVASSES, COMPLACENCY KILLS

BY CLINT HELANDER

As I skidded to a stop over a black hole in the glacier, morbid images filled my mind. Graham Zimmerman and I had skied this steep Alaskan pocket glacier numerous times on our trip, roped up at first, but seeing no signs of crevasses on our now well-worn trail had gradually lulled us into complacency. This day, after bailing from our would-be objective, I had remained at a narrow pass, taking photographs of distant mountains, while Graham had skied ahead toward base camp. Halfway down, his tracks ended at a dark abyss. I dropped to my knees.

"GRAHAM," I loudly whimpered.

The tightness in my chest eased somewhat when he screamed back, "I'm in a crevasse!"

We had packed for a technical alpine climb, and my crevasse-rescue kit was inadequate at best. After burying my backpack and skis as an anchor, I clipped into the rope, inched toward the crevasse, and was horrified by what I saw. Graham was 50 feet below the surface, wedged sideways in blue ice above eternal blackness. He was conscious but so stuck that he could move only one arm.

I quickly lowered a bight of rope with a Petzl Micro Traxion device, padded the lip with my ice tool, and built a basic 3:1 hauling system with carabiners and Dyneema slings. At first, all Graham could do was clip in to the shoulder strap of his backpack. Eventually he freed an ice tool from his pack to assist. Two hours later, he flopped onto the surface heaving with relief and exhaustion—his only notable injury a badly bruised thigh. We had narrowly escaped a fatal accident and learned a vital lesson: complacency kills.

Years later, while navigating the crevasse-ridden Ramen Icefall under Mount Hunter in the central Alaska Range, I asked my partner, August Franzen, to keep the rope taut as I prodded ahead in the flat light of early dawn. Suddenly, the snow gave way beneath my skis and I began to sink and then free-fall. My skis made violent sounds scraping against the ice, and I felt a dull pain as my body richocheted against the hard, blue walls. In those microseconds that seemed to stretch like minutes, I thought: *Still falling. I'm going to break my legs. Why hasn't August stopped me? I'm going to drag him in. We're both going to die. No one will ever find us.*

I jarred to a stop and looked up to see the rope threading out a narrow hole 25 feet above my head. I quickly pulled out my rescue gear and climbed the rope. A half hour later, I heaved myself out. "Well, let's keep going," I said to August. "But keep me extra tight from now on."

KEY TAKEAWAYS: Proper planning, carrying rescue equipment, and trusting your partners are incredibly important when it comes to preventing and recovering from crevasse falls. Crevasse falls can occur when you are complacent and when you are extra cautious. Rope up even when the terrain seems benign or familiar. Practicing self-extraction, partner rescue, and terrain navigation are essential to minimizing your risk.

Clint Helander has been climbing for more than two decades and has been on dozens of expeditions that established first ascents in the Alaska Range, Patagonia, and Himalaya. He lives in Anchorage, Alaska.

Figure 2-7. *After the figure-eight on a bight, the overhand on a bight is the next most common knot climbers use to clip in to on glaciers. While it is plenty strong, it can untie easier—use caution when clipping into the end of the rope for glacier travel with this knot.*

Figure 2-8. *To maximize the strength of a flat overhand, pull on each strand independently of the others.* (Photo by Truc Allen)

Figure 2-9. *A flat overhand is strong enough for rappelling—as long as you have around 30 centimeters (1 foot) of tail.* (Photo by Truc Allen)

when rappelling. Despite its nickname, the Euro death knot or EDK, this knot is quite strong, offering more than enough strength for joining two ropes of different diameters. The key to making the flat overhand strong is to individually tighten all four strands of rope emerging from the knot (i.e., avoid tightening them two at a time) and to leave around 30 centimeters (1 foot) of tail (fig. 2-9). Avoid making the tails too long, as accidents have occurred in which people mistakenly threaded one of the tails into their belay device instead of the main strands (the long ends).

The advantages of a flat overhand over a double fisherman's knot or Flemish bend include the fact that the flat overhand is easier to tie; it is far easier to untie; it has a far lower profile, meaning it is less likely to get stuck in

Figure 2-10. *A flat figure-eight looks familiar, but it is a lot weaker than either a figure-eight on a bight or a flat overhand.* ***Never*** *use it to join two ropes for rappelling.*

cracks, flakes, or other features; and it has the tendency to "stand up," allowing the bulk of the knot to stand above the rock rather than get dragged along the surface, reducing the likelihood of sticking.

While a flat overhand has many purposes, avoid tying the similar looking flat figure-eight (fig. 2-10). It is not as strong as a flat overhand and can fail below 2 kilonewtons of force (below 500 pounds). Climbers have died because they used a flat figure-eight to tie two ropes together.

A common misconception is that it is not okay to use a flat overhand with ropes of different diameters, but for the diameters of ropes most climbers are using (6–10 millimeters), this is not an issue (fig. 2-11). However, if you are using ropes that differ by more than 4 millimeters or using a Reepschnur rappel with a "rap line" and a "pull line," consider using a Flemish bend or a double fisherman's knot instead.

Tip: Do not use a flat figure-eight. It is not as strong as a flat overhand!

Figure 2-11. *Ian Nicholson rappels on 9.7-millimeter and 6-millimeter ropes tied together after attempting a new route in Torres del Paine, Patagonia.* (Photo by Graham Zimmerman)

FLEMISH BEND

The Flemish bend is best for joining ropes inline rather than for rappelling. While it is perfectly suitable for rappelling, it is extremely bulky, making it more likely to get hung up. While many rock climbers choose it to join two ropes in-line for toproping, it can also be a great tool for ski mountaineering, where skiers often carry multiple shorter, very skinny ropes among members of the group while skiing but then tie them together when they rope up. If you are familiar with the rewoven figure-eight, the Flemish bend is just a variation. Make your figure-eight skeleton as you would if tying in, but then run the second rope into it from the other side, with the long end on the opposite side (fig. 2-12).

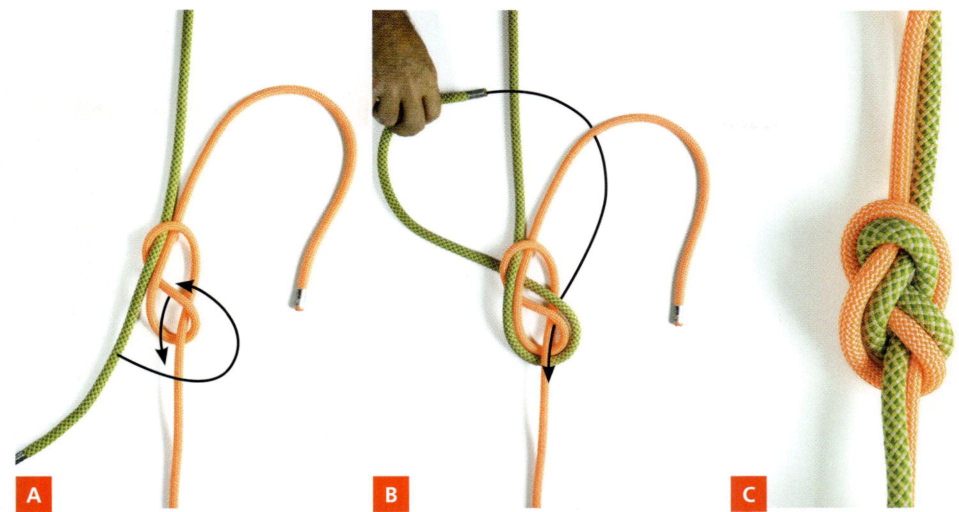

***Figure 2-12.** To tie a Flemish bend:* **a,** *Start with one rope (here, orange) with a figure-eight.* **b,** *Pass the second rope (green) through, retracing the other rope as if you were tying a rewoven figure-eight.* **c,** *Tighten the strands to dress the knot.* (Photos by Truc Allen)

DOUBLE FISHERMAN'S KNOT

The double fisherman's knot is a very strong, self-locking knot that can be difficult to untie when loaded. It is the preferred knot for joining two ends of cord that you don't intend to regularly untie (e.g., dedicated prusik hitches used for crevasse rescue; fig. 2-13) or for long topropes on routes where a single rope won't suffice. This knot is preferred over the flat overhand for topropes because it is stronger when pulled in-line.

To dress the double fisherman's knot appropriately, both Xs should be on the same side and the tails should be approximately double the length of the knot when tied. For smaller-diameter cords (6–7 millimeters), this means the tails should be around 5 centimeters (2 inches), and in glacier-travel applications, with dynamic 8- or 9-millimeter ropes, the tails should be around 9–14 centimeters (4–5 inches).

***Figure 2-13.** A double fisherman's knot is great for joining two cords you do not want to come untied.* (Photo by Truc Allen)

HITCHES

A hitch is different from a knot in that, with a hitch, the rope needs to be around something to hold its integrity, whereas a knot can be tied and will stay tied in the rope even if there is nothing in it.

CLOVE HITCH

Likely the most used hitch in all of climbing, the clove hitch is the most common way for a climber to secure themselves with a rope to

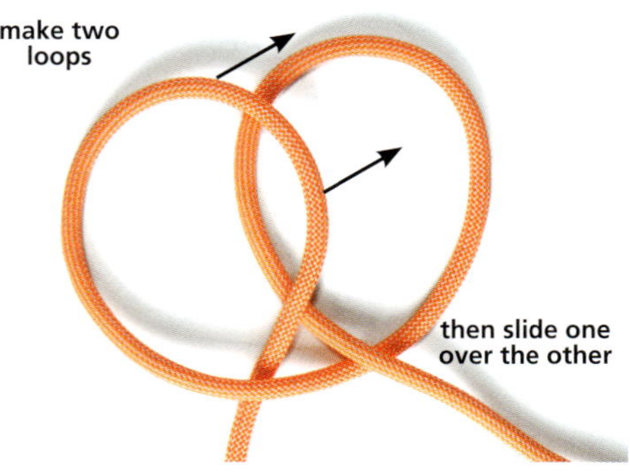

Figure 2-14. *To tie a clove hitch: Make two loops in the rope, with the rope ends on different sides of the main strand. Slide the loops together with the rope ends on the inside and tighten them.* (Photo by Truc Allen)

an anchor or to back up a technical system. This simple hitch (fig. 2-14) is strong and offers the primary advantage of being easy to adjust even after being loaded, after which you can pull on each strand to "lock it back down."

MUNTER HITCH

The Munter hitch is named after the famed Swiss mountain guide Werner Munter. It is also known as the Italian hitch due to the popularity it gained, at least initially, in Italy in the 1950s. Even today, HMS—short for *Halbmastwurfsicherung*, the hitch's name in German, meaning "half-clove-hitch belay"—appears on some locking carabiners. The versatile Munter can be "flipped over" and

Figure 2-15. *Forest McBrian belays someone out of a crevasse using a Munter hitch on the Quien Sabe Glacier, North Cascades National Park, Washington.*

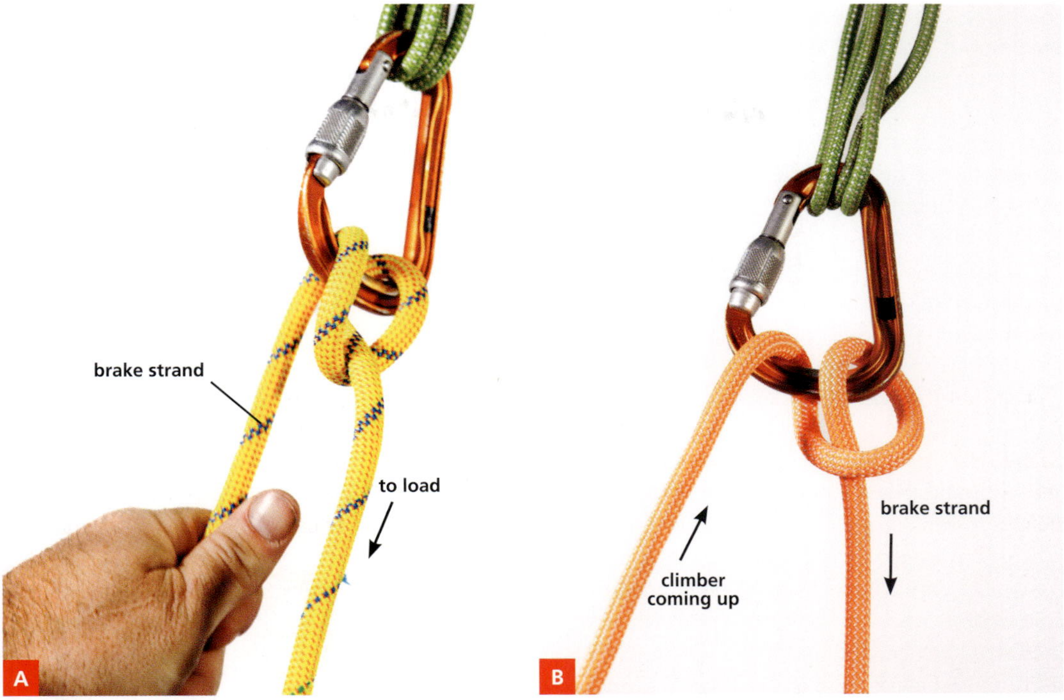

Figure 2-16. *The Munter can be flipped into:* **a**, *lower mode or* **b**, *belay mode.* (Photos by Truc Allen)

used in either direction, and it can be used for belaying, lowering, or in a pinch for rappelling short distances (fig. 2-15).

The Munter is strong enough for lowering (fig. 2-16a), but take care to minimize twists introduced into the rope as it passes through the hitch by holding the brake and load strands as parallel as possible. It is ideal for belaying as it provides a lot of friction (fig. 2-16b). For rappelling, keep in mind that twists are nearly unavoidable, so consider other techniques for all but the shortest rappels.

Figure 2-17. *The load strand goes toward the climber or load, either active or anticipated, and the brake strand is the side a belayer maintains control of in a given system.*

Understanding the difference between the load strand and brake strand (fig. 2-17) is critical to understanding technical systems that relate to belaying. The load strand is the side of the belay system (generally incorporating a belay device or Munter hitch) that goes from the climber or load to the belay system; if the climber weights the rope, this strand becomes taut. The brake strand is exactly what it sounds like—the side of the belay system to which friction is added to slow progress (in the case of lowering or rappelling or stopping the climber on the load strand).

MULE HITCH

The mule hitch is a blocking hitch, which means it stops progress from being lost. Its biggest advantage is that it can be released easily even after it has been placed under a tremendous load. The key is to "pinch the two load strands together" and make a loop that folds up and away from the two strands, and then just pass a bight through.

MUNTER MULE OVERHAND

The Munter mule overhand combines the mule hitch and the overhand and is the most common hitch used in rescue situations. This knot lets you belay or lower someone or something, tie off the system with a mule hitch, and back up those two hitched with an overhand knot to secure it (fig. 2-18).

To tie a Munter mule overhand:

1. Tie a Munter hitch on a locking carabiner, and then make a loop on either side of the load strand, keeping the loop folded outward (fig. 2-18a).
2. Take the rope from the other side of the load strand and pass a bight through the loop you just made so that the brake strand you are working with wraps around the load strand (fig. 2-18b).
3. Pull on the bight you just made to extend it (fig. 2-18c).
4. Finish the hitch with an overhand knot (fig. 2-18d).

FRICTION HITCHES

Friction hitches are hitches that can "grab" another strand or rope but can be quickly adjusted. There are countless friction hitches. Here are the three most common, plus best applications and pros and cons.

When using friction hitches, keep in mind that they work better when the difference between rope diameters is around 3–4 millimeters. Attempting to tie friction hitches where the difference is only 1–2 millimeters can be difficult, depending on the material, and will certainly require additional wraps. Meanwhile, if the difference in diameter is greater than 4 millimeters, then the friction hitches bite almost too well and can be difficult to release.

PRUSIK HITCH

A prusik hitch is so widely known and widely used that to some extent, a "prusik" is a generic term for all friction hitches, even among climbers (fig. 2-19a). The prusik does have a lot of advantages: It grabs predictably, it can be loaded in either direction, and it is moderately easy to open by pulling back on its "smiley face." Its main disadvantage is that it is slower to tie than other friction hitches, particularly if you are using longer pieces of material, and can be harder than other hitches to loosen when it bites hard, as is the case while ascending.

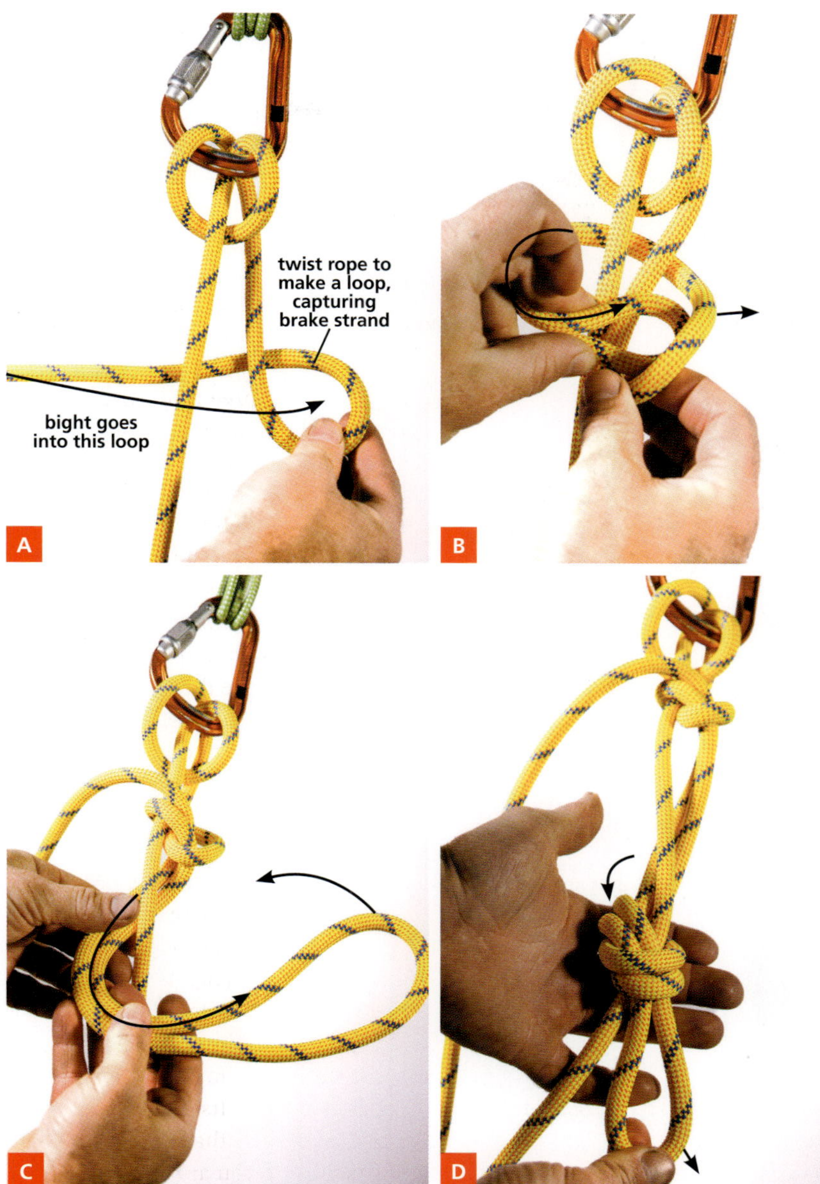

Figure 2-18. *To tie a Munter mule overhand:* **a,** *Tie a Munter hitch on a carabiner and make a loop.* **b,** *Take the rope from either side of the load strand and pass a bight through the loop.* **c,** *Pull on the bight to extend it.* **d,** *Tie an overhand knot on the load strand.* (Photos by Truc Allen)

Figure 2-19. *A prusik hitch is the most common friction hitch that you can think of as grabbing the rope:* **a**, *tying a prusik;* **b**, *a well-dressed prusik hitch.* (Photos by Truc Allen)

Figure 2-20. *A Klemheist is a good friction hitch if you have a long piece of material that you need to tie the friction hitch with. Unlike other friction hitches where you need to pass the entire piece of material through itself for each wrap, with the Klemheist, you only have to pass it through once regardless of the number of wraps.* (Photo by Truc Allen)

Figure 2-21. *An autoblock doesn't grab as strongly as a prusik but is easier to slide—for this reason, it's the most common choice for backing up rappels.* (Photo by Truc Allen)

The prusik hitch is tied with three complete wraps, and occasionally four if the materials are 1–2 millimeters different in diameter or are unusually slick (fig. 2-19b). It grabs most consistently with the wraps starting in the middle and working outward, which also offers the advantage of letting you "break" the prusik open by pushing outward on the outermost wrap—known as "the smile" or "smiley face."

KLEMHEIST HITCH

The Klemheist hitch (fig. 2-20) is easier and more efficient to tie than a prusik when you are using longer pieces of material because each wrap only goes around the rope rather than passing through itself. The Klemheist is also a good choice for ropes of similar diameters (at most 1–2 millimeters of difference), as it is easier and quicker to add wraps. However, the Klemheist generally takes a greater number of wraps to grab, and it certainly works far better in one direction (toward the "eye"—to get the Klemheist to grab effectively, make the eye as small as possible).

AUTOBLOCK

An autoblock hitch (fig. 2-21) is the quickest to tie of the friction hitches discussed here; however, with the same number of wraps, it offers the least "grabbing" power. If the autoblock

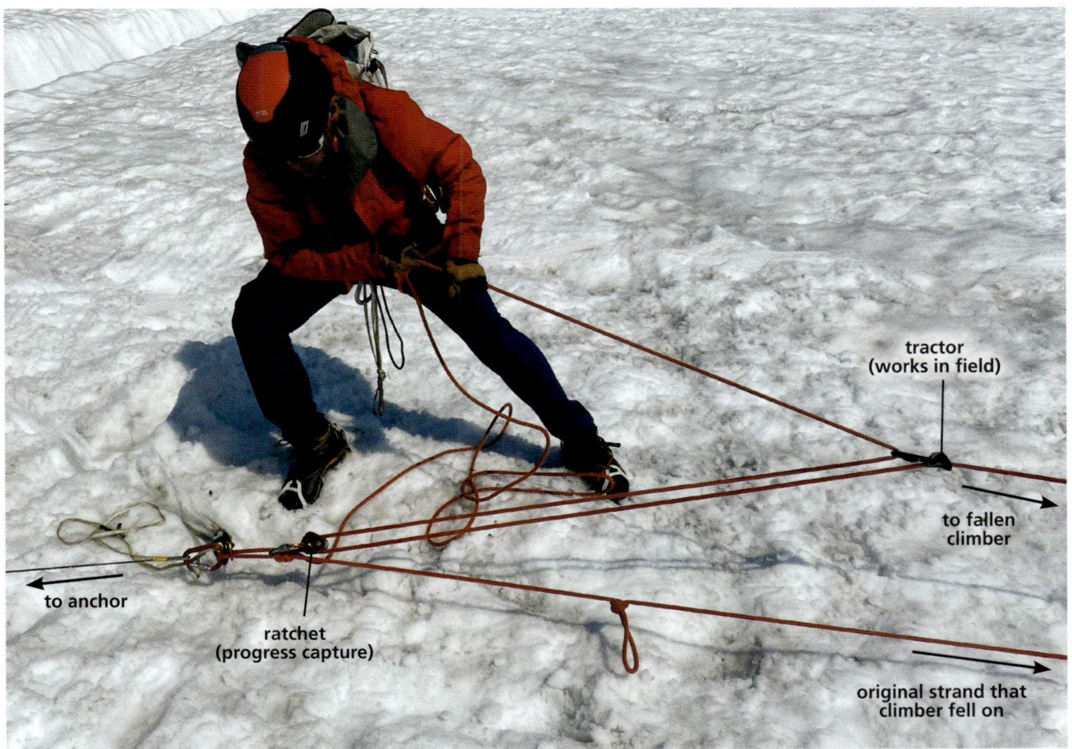

Figure 2-22. *The different parts of a hauling system: Grant Price performs crevasse rescue on the Inspiration Glacier, North Cascades, Washington.*

offers enough friction for a given application, then it is very easy to tighten and release. It is most commonly used as a "third hand"—a friction-hitch backup for rappelling—but it's occasionally used as a tractor in hauling systems. The autoblock also generally requires a greater difference in the diameter of the ropes compared to friction hitches with the same number of wraps.

RATCHETS AND TRACTORS

Familiarizing yourself with ratchets and tractors—as well as with a handful of mechanical (prefabricated) options—makes performing any sort of crevasse rescue easier (fig. 2-22). A ratchet is the progress capture in any type of hauling system. For example, when you haul your load two feet, the ratchet is what allows you to "capture" progress so that when you let go, the weight being hauled doesn't lower back down.

A tractor, on the other hand, works as a force increaser in the system, increasing mechanical advantage: the ratio of output force to input force in a system. The tractor, placed between the anchor and the load in most climbing-related systems, nearly always moves. Therefore, a good way to remember

Figure 2-23. *A Klemheist is one of the simplest ratchets to use, but be extremely careful so that it doesn't flip or slip through the anchor carabiner while hauling.*

Figure 2-24. *Putting a belay device in the carabiner where your ratchet attaches keeps the friction hitch from flipping through the carabiner.*

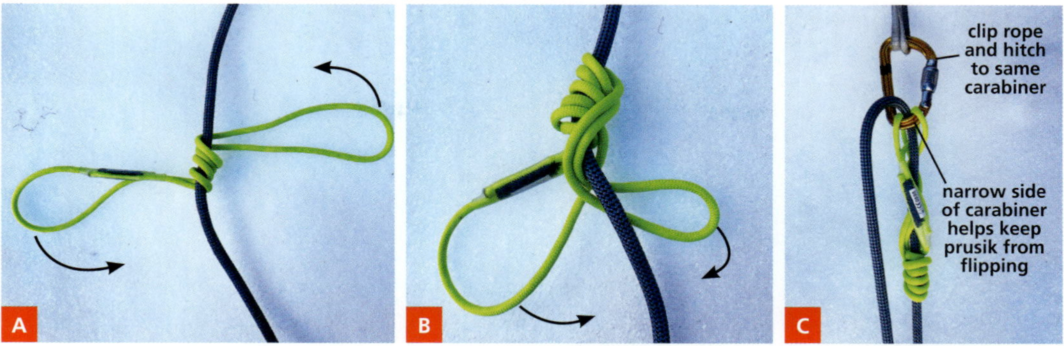

Figure 2-25. *To tie a VT prusik with a skinny carabiner:* **a,** *Start by making two complete wraps around the rope with your prusik material.* **b,** *Make Xs until you can't make any more and run out of material.* **c,** *Clip the two ends to a carabiner.*

the tractor is that "it works in the field" between anchor and load.

TRADITIONAL KLEMHEIST AS A RATCHET

The traditional Klemheist is a popular ratchet option because you can use a longer piece of material, giving you more throw (i.e., rope hauled between resets) during crevasse rescue. Keep in mind that the Klemheist has little chance of "self-minding" on the anchor: sliding when it needs to by opening up against an anchor, then tightening and holding the load when the hauling has ceased. Therefore, take care to ensure it does not get pulled through the anchor carabiner during an initial change in force direction, as this is extremely difficult to fix midrescue (fig. 2-23).

FRICTION HITCH WITH A BELAY DEVICE

An effective solution that eliminates the risk of a Klemheist, prusik, or other friction hitch from getting hauled through the carabiner at the initial change in direction is to use a belay device as a "minder" (to make it self-tending or self-minding). With this method, you do not set up your belay device in autoblocking mode, if it has that option; instead, rig it so both strands of rope come out parallel to each other through the holes in the belay device. With this technique, the belay device does not act as a progress capture on its own but lets the rescuer enjoy the very low friction of friction-hitch progress capture without the risk of it getting pulled through (fig. 2-24).

Tip: Don't use your belay device in autoblocking mode (a.k.a. guide mode) as a ratchet during crevasse rescue. You will already be working against a fair amount of friction in the system.

VALDOTAIN TRESSE PRUSIK

The VT prusik is widely used in the arbor and rope-access realms, but it has only recently become popular among climbers. It is one of the better options to ascend or descend a loaded line, but more importantly, it is an excellent self-tending ratchet to capture progress in complex hauling systems or during crevasse rescue (fig. 2-25).

Figure 2-26. To tie a Garda hitch: **a**, *With both carabiners in the same orientation, clip the rope across both of them.* **b**, *Wrap the brake strand, creating a loop, and clip it into the left carabiner.* **c**, *Tension the system.*

To tie a VT prusik:

1. Make two complete wraps with your prusik material around the rope you are tying the friction hitch around (fig. 2-25a). Keep the ends protruding from either side of the rope equal lengths.
2. Next, crisscross the prusik material, making as many Xs on either side of the rope as possible until you run out of material (fig. 2-25b).
3. Once you run out of material making Xs, clip both loops and the climbing rope through the anchor carabiner (fig. 2-25c). It is key that the Xs are tight to help the VT prusik self-mind and not flip through the carabiner if being used as a ratchet.

Tip: When you're using a VT prusik for a ratchet, make sure to also clip the rope in to the carabiner and orient the narrower side of the carabiner toward the load.

GARDA HITCH

The Garda hitch has many of the same rope-grabbing applications as other friction hitches, but it also works particularly well as a ratchet in a hauling system, when the rope exits in the opposite direction from where it enters, rather than staying inline. It also loses very little rope if tension is released, which means the hauler loses nothing during a reset. However, it is only effective in a single direction and functionally impossible to release when loaded—you need to unweight it to unload or take it apart. Thus, it works well for

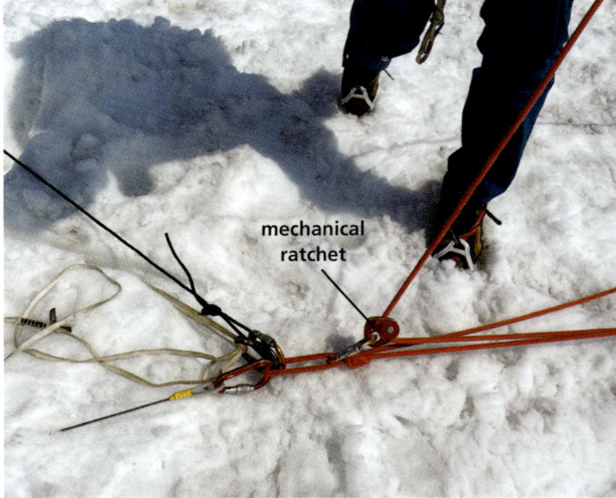

Figure 2-27. A number of ratchet pulleys, like the Petzl Micro Traxion shown here, are geared toward climbing and crevasse rescue.

Figure 2-28. *While perhaps less efficient than a mechanical ratchet, the prusik-minding pulley is still an effective way to capture progress.*

most crevasse-rescue techniques but poorly if you may need to reverse to lower.

To build a Garda hitch:

1. Hold two similarly sized nonlocking carabiners in the same orientation.
2. Clip the rope through both carabiners. The load strand will be on the left, and the brake strand will be on the right (fig. 2-26a).
3. Wrap the brake strand up and around to make a loop and clip only the "first" (left) carabiner a second time (fig. 2-26b).
4. Tension the system. The load will be designed to come into the first carabiner that is clipped in the system and exit on the other side (fig. 2-26c).

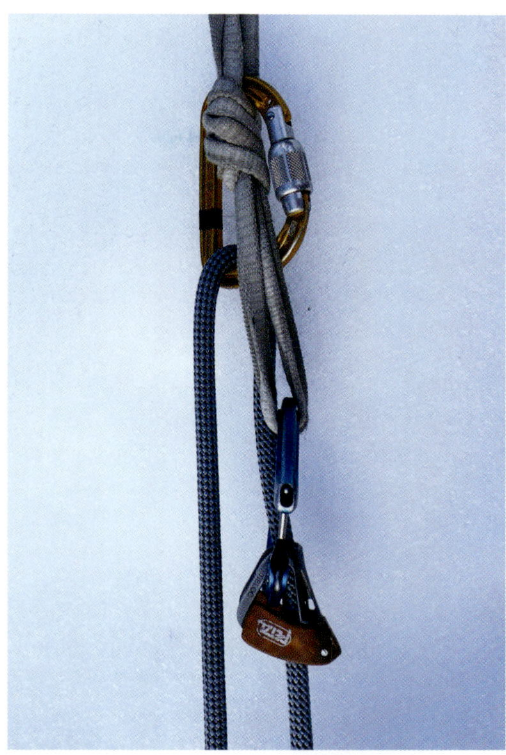

Figure 2-29. *The Petzl Tibloc, a mechanical prusik*

Tip: When using a Garda hitch, girth-hitch both carabiners together with a sling or other piece of material when attaching it to its given application.

MECHANICAL RATCHETS

There are a number of mechanical ratchets on the market, such as the Petzl Nano Traxion, Petzl Micro Traxion, or Edelrid Spoc (fig. 2-27). A mechanical ratchet combines a pulley and a rope clamp into one device weighing no more than a locking carabiner. The pulley drastically reduces friction, essentially enabling the rescuer (in both crevasse rescue and self-rescue) to pull a greater load with the same effort. The rope clamp is not only an extremely efficient ratchet, allowing almost no slippage with each haul, but it also can be used almost anywhere a traditional friction hitch is used. This means that these devices can be used for ascending and as tractors, and not just as ratchet-specific tools.

PRUSIK-MINDING PULLEY

A prusik-minding pulley is a pulley designed with a flat bottom edge so that, like a belay device, it is impossible for the friction-hitch portion of the ratchet to flip through the system and the edge helps open, or mind, the prusik. Thus, the rescuer can haul aggressively yet only lose the distance from the pulley to the point where the friction hitch comes taut.

This completely viable and often overlooked ratchet system isn't popular for one small but important reason: the location of the pulley, which ends up in a relatively inefficient spot without the benefits of a full-on ratchet, where you would not lose slack as the system becomes weighted (fig. 2-28).

Pulleys are more effective the closer they are to the person doing the hauling because the energy saved from efficient pulling is gained and passed down through the system—a trickle-down effect. Therefore, if you only have one pulley, it is most effectively used closest to the hauler.

MECHANICAL PRUSIKS

A mechanical prusik is a rope-grabbing device typically made of metal (fig. 2-29). Popular models include the Petzl Tibloc, Wild Country Ropeman, and CAMP Lift. They offer the advantages of being quick to place on the rope and easy to move, which is particularly useful while ascending. These easy-to-reset ratchets are also difficult to flip or to slip through the primary locking carabiner during hauling.

While there are a seemingly infinite number of knots and hitches, learning about a half dozen of the most common, as well as how to best apply them and their limitations, is a huge attribute for anyone climbing or skiing on glaciers.

Opposite: *Descending from the summit of Cotopaxi, Ecuador, on a stormy day* (Photo by Jonathon Spitzer)

CHAPTER 3

Navigation

Along with the forethought to plan your trip and bring the necessary equipment and skills, navigation is an essential part of your mountaineering tool kit. This process begins when you make a plan ahead of time (often called a "tour plan") on your computer and transfer that information to a smartphone or a traditional GPS. Being skilled with a map and compass is essential (fig. 3-1). Having strong navigation skills and preparing thoroughly lets you get where you need to go if you're ascending a less-traveled route without a clear, well-established path. Such skills become crucial when your route becomes obscured in snow or a whiteout.

Figure 3-1. *Maps are essential for alpine climbing and mountaineering. They can help you plan trips and navigate once you arrive.*

MAP BASICS

Understanding the information that various maps, including a GPS-based map app on a smartphone, provide is a foundational navigation skill to plan your tour and figure out your current location and desired destination. One advantage of using a smartphone app or other GPS tool is that it's easy to see your location, but you also need to know how to match that up with a physical topographic map, so keep the following fundamentals in mind.

TOPOGRAPHICAL MAPS

In this book, when I talk about maps, I am discussing topographical maps (except when talking about satellite imagery, which is another form of map). Topographical maps are the most useful type of map for climbers and mountaineers, as they use lines and colors in a two-dimensional diagram to represent the shape of the terrain as well as other important information, such as the location of trails, vegetation, glaciers, bodies of water, rivers, and so forth.

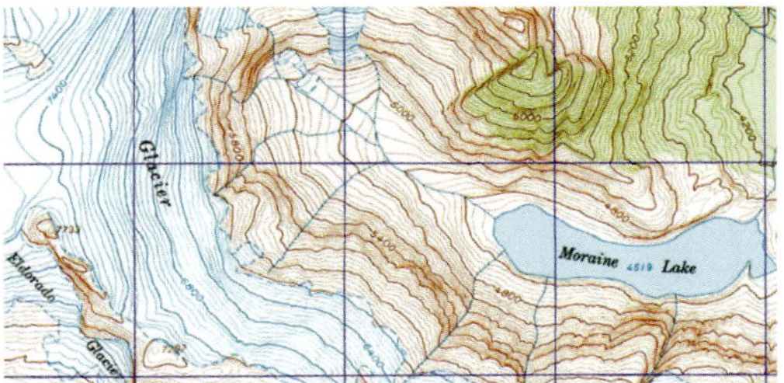

Figure 3-2. *Topographic maps use colors and symbols to illustrate terrain. On this particular map, here are what the various colors represent: white for glaciers or permanent snowfields, blue for water, brown for open ground, and green for terrain with trees and other vegetation.*

Colors

Topographical maps use colors to symbolize what the surface of the terrain might look like or be composed of (fig. 3-2):

- **blue:** lakes and rivers
- **green:** forested terrain, generally with larger trees
- **brown:** sparsely forested to nontreed terrain
- **white:** glaciers or permanent snowfields

Contour Lines

Contour lines on maps are drawn steadily at given elevations to illustrate the shape of the terrain. Contour lines drawn closer together represent steeper terrain—the land gains elevation more quickly over a horizontal distance. Contour lines that are farther apart represent lower-angle terrain—the elevation is changing more gradually over a horizontal distance.

Contour Intervals and Index Lines

Most topographic maps have darker contour lines at regular intervals to make it easier to count larger changes in elevation—this line is called an index line. The interval of specific contour and index lines depends on the region of the world and the map itself, and while there are common index-line distances, there is no universal standard. Fortunately, most maps label their index-line intervals or include them with the map scale, making it generally easy to figure out.

US Geological Survey (USGS) maps, which are among the most popular in the United States, have a contour line every 40 feet, with index lines every 200 feet. Canada and countries in Europe and South America use 10- to 20-meter contour lines, with index lines every 100 to 200 meters.

Map Scale

A map's scale is the ratio of a distance on the map to the corresponding distance in the real world. For example, 1:24,000 is a very common map scale: 1 inch on the map equals 24,000 inches in real life. It is important to note the scale not because you might be able to imagine what, say, 24,000 inches is in real life (it's 2,000 feet), but because you can compare it to other maps you might be referencing. All topographical maps will label their scale on the bottom of the page as a ratio, while most digital mapping platforms let you customize the map's scale.

Scale Bars, Distances, and Measuring with String

Most maps will also have a scale bar, which is a distance in miles and/or kilometers that relates to the map. This is helpful for estimating distances both visually and with a tool, such as a small-diameter string like the lanyard on your compass. You can hold the string at the desired distance on the scale bar and then move it around the map to approximate

PAPER MAPS SAVE THE DAY

BY IAN NICHOLSON

The Haute Route (pronounced "oat," with a silent *h*) is a classic, weeklong ski-mountaineering traverse that crosses dozens of glaciers through the heart of the Alps, from one epicenter in Chamonix and Mont Blanc to the other in Zermatt and the Matterhorn. It's a route I have guided more than twenty times, but despite its familiarity, I still bring paper maps. Occasionally, I have questioned this practice because the roughly 100-mile crossing requires eight full-sized maps.

While each day of this fabled traverse is amazing, the morning of the fifth is unquestionably the least fun, mainly due to one notorious nearly four-mile traverse along the southern edge of Lac des Dix between the Prafleuri hut and the Dix hut. This particular trip didn't stand out other than it was my first of the season. My co-guide, John Race, a veteran of even more Haute Route traverses, was in the front and led our group out of the hut, up and over the Col des Roux, and across the traverse, which involves a few unpleasant hours of gliding, poling, skating, and sidestepping, often switching rapidly between these techniques.

Our group finally reached the far side of the lake after a few hours, relieved to be done with this annoyingly physical section. There, on the climb up toward the Pas du Chat, which leads to mellower terrain on the way to Glacier de Cheilon and the Dix hut, the first thousand feet or so is steeper than 30 degrees—and all avalanche terrain. While I had never experienced it, we had heard about an interesting phenomenon that could make travel around the lake problematic: The Lac des Dix is a dammed lake, and as water is slowly let out in the winter, the surface ice settles, which creates a local (though artificially) shallow snowpack on the adjacent slopes. This, coupled with the lake acting as a cold sink and the high relative humidity, is the perfect recipe for persistent weak layers, like facets and surface hoar, that can cause avalanches.

We were the first group of the day across the lake and one of only a handful who had been on the Haute Route all year. After a break on the far side of the lake, we began to skin upward; after just a few hundred feet, however, I heard—and felt—the entire slope settle. John heard and felt it too, and we both were spooked. I'd been working at the Northwest Avalanche Center during recent winters and had spent a lot of time looking at and thinking about unstable snow. I told John, "If it didn't suck so much to go back the other way, never mind the fact that I have no idea where we'd actually go, there is no way I would continue farther up that slope." And just like that we turned around, reversing over what we had just come across.

All the other groups turned around, save for one who we later learned triggered the slope, suffering injuries, including a dislocated shoulder. After three more hours of horrible sidehill skinning, we arrived back at the Prafleuri. I looked at my phone to survey the terrain around us, but other than a section a mile or so down-valley, I didn't have any more maps downloaded and I wasn't getting a signal. As the groups piled in, we discovered no one knew where to go. Bobette, the owner and hutkeeper, told us about a tunnel under the hut that workers had used when they built the dam. We went down to check out the door, but it was locked (or frozen). Back inside, we broke out the maps.

Skiing the "couloir" created by the dam and the hillside on our escape from the Prafleuri hut to Pralong

We recognized that we could ski down the valley for a mile or two, skin over an unnamed pass, and then ski down a couloir made by a slope that had a concrete dam to a seemingly random point on a gated road near the Swiss town of Pralong. We calculated how long it would take and then used the Prafleuri hut's landline to call a taxi. We described to the dispatcher where we wanted to meet and that we'd be there in two hours, and the other groups followed suit.

We arrived fifteen minutes before the taxi, which drove us to Arolla, where we caught a lift to get back up to the Dix hut a completely different way.

KEY TAKEAWAYS: Paper maps can save your trip, since they help you deal with unexpected route changes. On extended trips on glaciers, you don't know what you might need to know—and you cannot count on having cell service. Always bring a paper map.

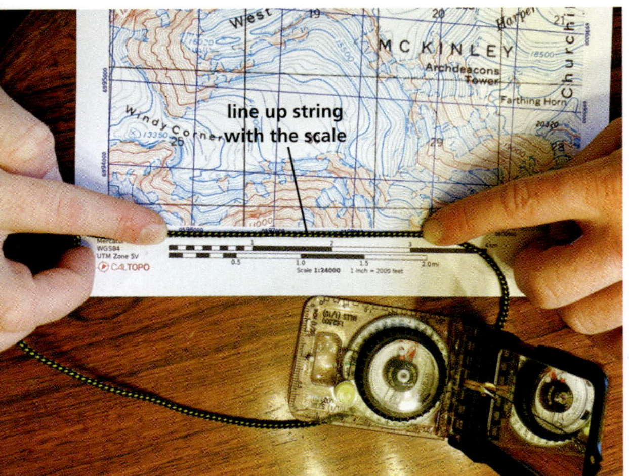

Figure 3-3. Use your compass lanyard to estimate distance. Simply hold up the string to the scale bar and measure away.

distance, which is helpful when the direction you wish to measure isn't straight (fig. 3-3).

> **Tip:** On trips above tree line, bring at least one paper map that shows the area of your goal climb and adjacent terrain. A print map weighs very little and offers an incredible amount of information. Plus, it never runs out of power or has a screen that can break.

Orienting Yourself

To orient yourself in the terrain, line up the map using your compass with north in the real world, or line up the map using visible landmarks like a mountain or mountain range. Doing so can make it much easier to interpret different terrain features.

CREATING A TOUR PLAN

While you can create a tour plan on a map while out in the field, a tour plan should begin at home: Create a line on a map of where you intend to go and then transfer that information to your phone or your GPS device, so that up in the mountains you can see where you are in relation to your goal, prelaying your route over the terrain with intention.

Free and paid web-based platforms like CalTopo.com, GaiaGPS.com, OnXmaps.com, Fatmap.com, and Avenza.com offer countless map layers and other features to help with planning. To place the line as accurately as possible, consult local guidebooks or other resources, which may have map overlays or photos with route overlays that you can transfer to your map. Read previous trip reports or search for other people's ground truth navigation files (see below) or common routes available on the web-based trip planner you are using.

> **Tip:** A **track** represents where someone has been (perhaps you on a past trip). It is created with ground-truth data collected by someone who visited that location. While a **route** is a line of travel estimated to be in roughly the correct place.

FILE TYPES

When you create a trip plan, you can often save it in different formats, which is important because not all apps, web-based platforms, or other navigation products use the same file types. Below are the three most common geospatial file types used by climbers, mountaineers, and other outdoor enthusiasts:

- **A .gpx file** is a ground truth navigation file that a traditional GPS, as well as most navigation apps, uses.
- **A .json file**, also represented by the extension **.geojson**, is another popular map-data

format used by some navigation apps and web-based navigation platforms.

- **A .kmz file** is the file type that Google Earth and similar products use.

SMARTPHONES FOR GPS DATA

Nearly any modern smartphone can be used as a GPS in the field, even without cell coverage, and can display your location on various maps or global imagery as long as you download these materials ahead of time. You should also overlay your tour plan so you can see where you are in relation to it.

TRACKING YOURSELF ON YOUR DEVICE

Get in the habit of tracking your trips (fig. 3-4). It can save you time in the field, especially on snow where the trail is not always obvious. Tracking your trip lets you see where you have been and how to get back there, which, while seemingly straightforward, retracing your steps can become extremely difficult in certain situations, like sudden poor weather and low visibility. Tracking also allows you to reference where you went if you ever return to the area and share helpful information with others.

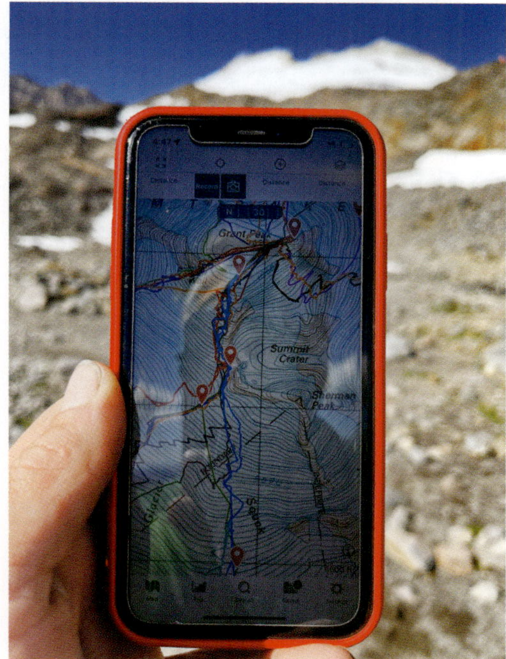

Figure 3-4. *Many apps help turn your smartphone into a fully functioning GPS device that can track your path or display a planned route.*

CREATING A TIME PLAN

Time plans complement tour plans nicely and can help you preassemble several helpful pieces of data. Generally, people build time plans point-to-point, placing points at key locations such as at a change in the terrain, travel, or where you start going uphill or downhill. To estimate how much time a given tour will take, you can calculate the total distance and elevation traveled. If you are just walking on trails or relatively gentle glaciers, start with 1,000 feet uphill per hour and 2 miles per hour will get you close. You can adjust that based on your group. For example, a faster group may hike 1,300 feet per hour, whereas a slower group may go 800 feet per hour. As part of your planning, be sure to share the final plan with the entire group (table 3-1).

The Munter method is the most precise and customizable method for calculating time, as it can be fine-tuned for more rugged travel or in slow-going terrain for superior accuracy (table 3-2). It is based on the metric system, but if you are handy with it, spreadsheet software can do the calculating for you. Be sure to share your trip plan with your party members so everyone knows what to expect (fig. 3-5).

TABLE 3-1. TOUR PLAN TEMPLATE									
Pineapple Basin									
Name	**GPS**	**UTM**	**Elev**	**Elev Change**	**Distance**	**Bearing**	**Munter Units**	**Time**	**Notes**
Parking Lot	P-Basin1	I0T 0618237E 5256189	3100ft	650ft/ 198m	1.71km/ 1.06 mi	290T	3.75	55 min	Follow Winter Trail
Source Lake	P-Basin2	10T 0616703ES256944	3750ft	655ft/ 200m	.4Skm/ 0.28mi	210T	2.5	40 min	Ascend uptrack right before Source lake
Entrance to Pineapple Basin	P-Basin3	I0T 0616535E 5256532	4400ft	853ft/ 260m	.8km/ .5 mi	165T	3.25	50 min	Ascend the basin, mindful of wind load
Top of Great Scott	P-Basin4	I0T 0616679E 5255768	5249ft	853ft/ 260m	.8km/ .5 mi	345T	3.25	15 min	Ski down the basin, mind the flats
Ski down to the Entrance	P-Basin5	I0T 0616535E 5256532	4400ft	650ft/ 200m	.56km / .35 mi	40T	2.5	10 min	Cut hard left out of the basin and across to get to no fog
Ski No Fog back to Source Lake	P-Basin6	10T 0616703ES256944	3750ft	650ft/ 198m	1.71km/ 1.06 mi	110T	3.75	20 min	Follow typical out track
Take return track back to parking lot		I0T 0618237E 5256189	3100ft						

REDUNDANCY IN YOUR TOOLS

The key to a safe, well-run outing is redundancy in your planning and mapping tools so that if one tool fails or goes missing, you have a backup.

SHARE YOUR TOUR PLAN

An easy way to create redundancy in your navigation tools is to share your trip plan with the other people on your trip and make sure they have downloaded the tour plan and corresponding maps prior to the outing. Have your party members download whatever navigation file(s) and the necessary software (i.e., navigation app) to their phone to provide a backup in case your phone dies, is broken, or becomes wet, lost, or otherwise unusable. This simple tactic should become a habit—any guide or avid climber can tell you that losing or having your primary phone get compromised happens just enough that it is well worth the effort.

TABLE 3-2. MUNTER METHOD FOR TOUR AND TIME PLANNING
Units
1 Munter unit for each 100 meters of elevation gain
1 Munter unit for each 1 kilometer of distance traveled
Imperial to Metric Conversions
1 foot x 0.305 = meters traveled
1 mile x 0.6 = kilometers traveled
Equation and Explanation
(Distance + Elevation) in Munter units / rate = Time in whole hours
Rates
Bushwhacking = 2
uphill travel on foot or skis = 4
flat on skis or downhill on foot = 6
downhill on skis = 10
Example: 1.5 km (1.5 Munter units) + 300 m of gain (3 Munter units) = 4.5 Munter units total Using the uphill rate (dividing by 4): 4.5 / 4 = 1.125 hours, or 1 hour, 7 minutes, 30 seconds

BATTERY BACKUPS

Bring an external power bank (sometimes called an auxiliary battery or charging brick) when using your phone as a navigation tool—using it to navigate, send texts on the edge of reception, and take photos or videos (accidentally or intentionally) can drain the battery more quickly than anticipated (fig. 3-6). The average smartphone takes between 3,500 and 5,000 milliampere-hours (mAh) to charge, depending on the model. It's critical to bring an auxiliary power source that can provide an appropriate amount of power (table 3-3).

Figure 3-5. *By sharing your trip plan with all party members, if one person's phone breaks, is lost, or runs out of power, you have a backup.* (Photo by Jared Drapala)

Figure 3-6. *On a stormy multiday trip, it's easy to run out of power. Bring an external power bank that lets you use your phone's GPS app so you won't run out of juice.*

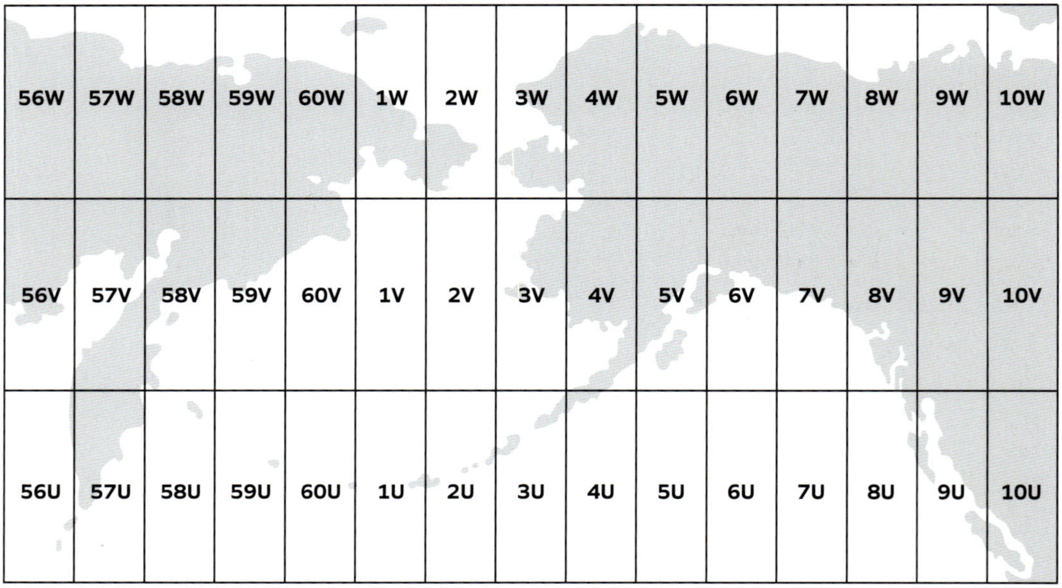

56W	57W	58W	59W	60W	1W	2W	3W	4W	5W	6W	7W	8W	9W	10W
56V	57V	58V	59V	60V	1V	2V	3V	4V	5V	6V	7V	8V	9V	10V
56U	57U	58U	59U	60U	1U	2U	3U	4U	5U	6U	7U	8U	9U	10U

***Figure 3-7.** A sample map showing the UTM zones for the Bering Sea area*

GPS FUNDAMENTALS

GPS is an acronym for "Global Positioning System," which works by triangulating your position using at least three of the thirty-one GPS satellites that orbit Earth. Your GPS receiver uses extremely accurate clocks to gauge the distance to the orbiting satellites by picking up the radio waves they emit.

UNDERSTANDING UTM UNITS

Universal Transverse Mercator (UTM) is a grid-based system that uses multiples of ten (fig. 3-7). The size of the zone varies based on its location on the planet, but each zone is further broken down into units of 1 square kilometer (1,000 square meters) and can be subsequently broken down into units as small as 1 square meter. UTM is the unit that most outdoor enthusiasts, climbers, and guides use.

TABLE 3-3. SMARTPHONE CHARGES BY POWER SOURCE

Source	Charges
3,000 mAh	0.75–1 smartphone charges
5,000 mAh	1–1.5 smartphone charges
10,000 mAh	2–3.5 smartphone charges
20,000 mAh	4–6 smartphone charges

Most GPS devices can also use latitude and longitude (lat/long) coordinates, but because it is easier to calculate distances and pull and apply locations on a map using UTM, it is ultimately more user-friendly. Comparing the two options is much like comparing the metric and imperial system: One system isn't necessarily more "accurate" than the other, but calculating

LIGHT IS RIGHT

BY GRAHAM ZIMMERMAN

As young climbers, Mark Allen and I woefully underestimated the nearly 5,000-foot southeast wall of Mount Bradley in Alaska one spring. We tackled an unclimbed route on its face, seeking hard mixed climbing—and we'd found it. Nearly every pitch was delicate and challenging—precisely what we sought—but the climb also took longer than we had anticipated. We had packed for a day and a half of climbing, but we found ourselves on the summit late on our third day, low on food after enduring an unplanned bivy.

Now up top, we faced a treacherous descent in worsening conditions. The two of us split a third of an energy bar, the last of our food, and then started to descend. We were navigating around avalanche-prone slopes just as a real Alaska storm blew in, when we were forced down the far side of the mountain into unfamiliar terrain.

We hurried down a glacier and bivied beneath a rock overhang at the base of one of Bradley's steep, glacially carved walls. The storm pinned us there all day. Twelve inches of snow and waist-deep drifts accumulated as we sat in our tent, hungry and exhausted, trying to stay dry. The one thing we did have was essential navigation equipment, including a compass, maps, and a GPS device.

On our map, we could see that we had approximately 7 kilometers of complex glacier terrain to cover, over 747 Pass and back into the Ruth Gorge to base camp. While we knew it would be challenging to cross that terrain in deep snow, we were at least able to plot our path to safety.

As we later struggled to push the trail forward through waist-deep snow, we traded leads repeatedly. We made slow progress to 747 Pass, between Mount Dickey and Mount Bradley, after being without food for nearly thirty hours. At the top of the pass, as the sun set, another storm blew in, reducing our visibility to the clouds of swirling snow immediately in front of us.

Mark pulled out our GPS device. It turned on, but its directions were incorrect. After failing to fix it, we used our map and compass in the dark to get a bearing on where we thought camp was.

As we slogged along, the final miles back to camp dragged on. Eventually, we came across a strange rib in the snow and followed it 100 meters to our camp. A fan had formed in our tent's wind shadow, creating the rib that had guided us back. By this time, ninety-nine hours had passed since we'd departed.

KEY TAKEAWAYS: Even when weight savings are paramount, navigational equipment is crucial. These tools allow you to consider your options in real time and navigate even with minimal visibility. You may even be able to go faster because you can keep moving.

Graham Zimmerman is a veteran of nearly three dozen expeditions, a climate advocate, a winner of the prestigious Piolet d'Or, a former president of the American Alpine Club, and author of *A Fine Line*. He lives with his wife, Shannon, and daughter, Sloane, in Bend, Oregon.

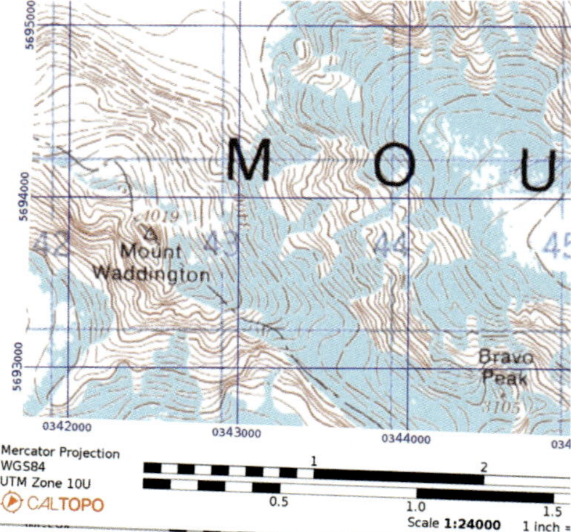

Figure 3-8. *On this map, the datum is WGS 84, and the map shows the easting and northing values are based on zone 10U as well as the difference between the darker (newer) WGS 84 lines and the lighter (older) NAD 27 lines.*

between units is generally much easier with systems based on multiples of ten.

FINDING THE GPS DATUM FOR A MAP

Every map that shows some sort of global positioning system, whether UTM or lat/long, will also list the datum used. On most maps, including USGS topographic maps, the datum is printed on the bottom-left side. Your first task is to make sure that the datum on the map matches the datum in your GPS device.

The data represented on a map begins with a series of surveys. When surveying large areas, surveyors need to chain together measurements based on "known points" and account for the curvature of the Earth. This process eventually produces a dataset of coordinates that covers the globe. Several of these global surveys have been carried out, each producing its own datum, and while these datums are close in their measurements, they can be different enough to throw off someone navigating in mountainous terrain.

For example, if your phone or GPS device is tuned to a different datum than your map and you know the coordinates of your destination (which you plugged in from either a paper map or your tour plan), you could be a few hundred feet off—which can be dangerous in a whiteout.

When tour planning digitally, you can set the datum to whatever you want; however, it may or may not line up with the map. Therefore, most mapping software platforms give you the option to overlay your own GPS lines, which you will possibly see in addition to older GPS grids. Most modern GPS software is automatically set for the datum WGS 84 (fig. 3-8), but it could be set for NAD 83; maps surveyed prior to 1983 are set for NAD 27. Each datum contains sixty zones, or sub-boxes. So it might not be a big difference between datums, but would be big enough to throw you off in the field.

USING GPS COORDINATES WITH A MAP

If you are planning your trip using map software at home, you can usually just click the location and your software will generate both the zone (sub-box of the datum) and the UTM or lat/long coordinates, which you can then transfer to your phone or GPS device. You can also do the same directly on most smartphones and GPS devices, where you can tap a chosen spot to generate the coordinates.

Plotting and pulling GPS coordinates from a map is a useful and easy skill to master. Keep in mind that because the world is round, while GPS coordinates are meant to be projected in

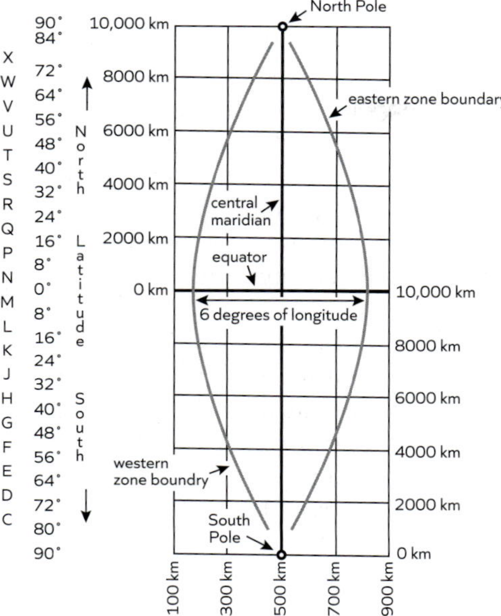

Figure 3-9. This graphic shows how the UTM zone grids overlap outside the curved boundaries of longitude, which enables measurements to be calculated in sets of ten. While there are, in theory, UTM coordinates outside these longitudinal boundaries, navigational applications won't let you access those coordinates, as they could be skewed by the curvature of Earth.

a two-dimensional plane, the zones are wider than the 6 degrees of longitude over which they're projected. Not only is there a wider strip of actual terrain closer to the equator and one that's narrower near the poles, but all the zones technically overlap on their boundaries (fig. 3-9).

The overlapping zones projected on the spherical Earth are not a problem because all UTM coordinates include a zone that indicates which strip of longitude (i.e., of land) is the middle of that zone (fig. 3-10). The UTM units themselves represent the number of meters

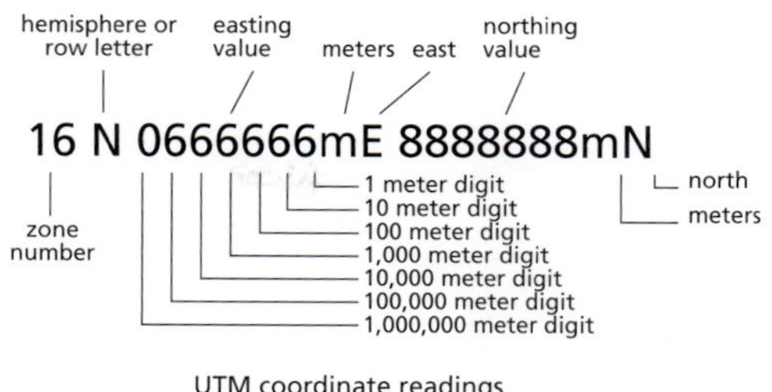

Figure 3-10. Breaking down how to read UTM coordinates, eastings, and northings.

from the boundary of that zone. All easting numbers are measured from left to right (west to east), while northing numbers are measured from the bottom up (south to north)—these are the numbers on the sides of the map that, respectively, count upward as you go east or north.

IDENTIFYING A UTM COORDINATE FROM A MAP

To identify a UTM coordinate using a map, it is helpful to have a map tool, something many compasses have—though a piece of paper or string will do in a pinch. First, figure out which 1,000-square-meter box the desired waypoint is in. Place the map-tool GPS reader on the GPS grid so that it lines up (fig. 3-11). Look at the sides of the map to figure out the final three digits of the easting and then the northing. Note that it is tough to get the final digit accurately, and most people just guestimate to the closest 10 meters.

If you don't have a map tool and your compass doesn't have one, just fold over the edge of your paper map and tear a new piece of paper off—or use some string. On this paper, draw the 1,000-square-meter grid size to exactly match that on the map by holding it up against the map as a template, or cut out a

Figure 3-11. Using a UTM grid reader helps you more accurately estimate UTM coordinates while pulling them manually.

Figure 3-12. If you don't have a UTM reader, you can create one with a piece of paper or even the corner of the map.

piece of paper the size of the UTM square on the map. Next, make nine evenly spaced hash marks on the paper—start with the middle one, then split the halves on either side, and so on (fig. 3-12). Most people find it easier to make the 5, then the 7 and the 3, then the 1 and the 9, and so forth. While this technically is not as accurate as a true map tool, it can get you pretty close in a pinch.

COMPASS NAVIGATION

While the GPS on your phone is easier to use and arguably a better individual tool than a compass because it can help you keep moving in complex terrain with limited visibility, on multiday climbs, a map and a compass will prove much more durable and fare better in poor weather, plus they can't run out of batteries—all for minimal weight. Remember, human beings have navigated extremely complex terrain for hundreds of years by map and compass alone!

UNDERSTANDING DECLINATION

A compass needle points toward magnetic north, which may or may not be in line with "true north," which is north on a map. To make matters trickier, magnetic north shifts around slightly and may be slightly farther east or west of true north for the given map you are in.

Declination measures the degrees of difference between true north and magnetic north (fig. 3-13). Many compasses let you preemptively adjust declination based on your location; however, if yours doesn't have that feature, you must add or subtract the degrees of difference between magnetic north and true north when moving bearings between your map and the field.

TAKING A BEARING IN THE FIELD

"Taking a bearing in the field" refers to using a compass to figure out which bearing

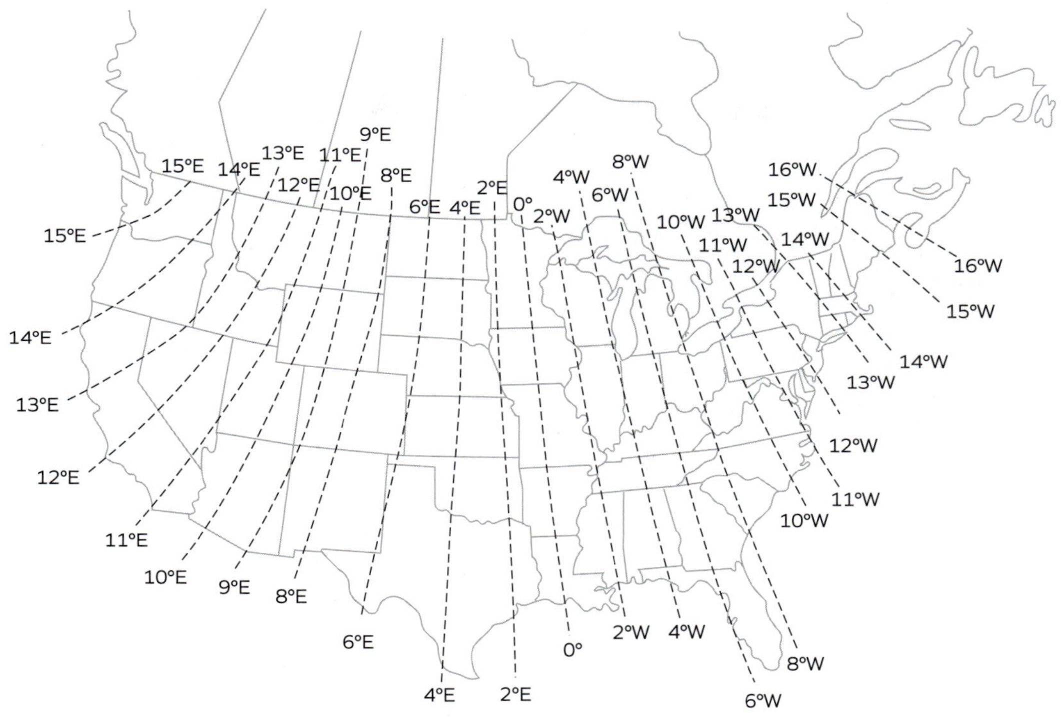

Figure 3-13. *Declination is the difference between magnetic north and true north depending on your location. This map shows approximate 2025 declination values for the contiguous United States.*

(direction) a given feature is from your current position. You can use this approach to identify features, help ascertain your current location, or travel to or from a given location (fig. 3-14):

1. Start by holding the compass flat. If it has a mirror, hold it at eye level; if it doesn't, hold it at chest level.
2. Point the compass toward the terrain feature or landmark you are taking a bearing on.
3. Rotate the bezel (a.k.a. the "azimuth ring," the circular housing that surrounds the needle) until the orienteering arrows ("the shed") surround the north-seeking end of the magnetic needle ("the red," almost always the red end, thus "get red in the shed").
4. Read the bearing at the index line, which is generally found at the very top or the very bottom of the bezel.

PLOTTING A BEARING

"Plotting a bearing" refers to the technique of taking a bearing ascertained from a known terrain feature and then applying it to the map. You can use this to determine your current location with either a second (and ideally a third) bearing (or a bearing and a

Figure 3-14. *Taking a bearing in the field is relatively easy. Simply point the compass at the landmark you wish to take a bearing from, hold it flat, and "put red in the shed"—orient the magnetic needle's red tip with your compass's main, orienting arrows. Here, Peter Broback is taking a bearing in Boston Basin in Washington's North Cascades.*

known elevation with the assistance of an altimeter):

1. Turn the azimuth ring so the desired bearing aligns with index line (fig. 3-15a).
2. Place the compass edge on the known feature on the map. If the compass has a mirror, open it to make this edge longer.
3. Pivot the compass until the meridian lines are straight up and down with the map (without turning the azimuth ring and ensuring that the desired bearing stays in the index line; fig. 3-15b).
4. Draw your bearing with a pencil along the edge of the compass that leads to the feature off which the bearing was taken (fig. 3-15c).

PULLING A BEARING FROM A MAP

Sometimes it can be useful to pull a bearing from a map; this allows you to travel to this location in the field. This can be difficult in terrain that isn't wide open, but on glaciers and other terrain above tree line, using this technique with your compass can save power on your phone or GPS device. To use this technique, you must know your current location. It does not work in very steep terrain. If you are at a pass, the edge of a lake, or another easily identifiable location, or you can plot your location using your UTM coordinates (or a single bearing and a known altitude, or multiple compass bearings), follow these steps to pull a bearing from a map:

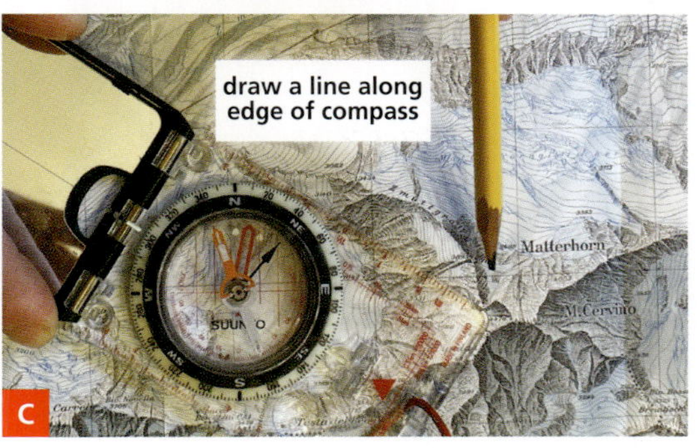

Figure 3-15. *Plotting a bearing:* **a**, *Turn the azimuth ring so that the bearing aligns with the index line—in this case 303 degrees.* **b**, *Place the edge of the compass on the point you took the bearing from—in this case, the 4,476-meter summit of the Matterhorn—and pivot off this point until the meridian lines line up with the lines on the map.* **c**, *Draw a line along the edge of the compass.*

1. Lay the edge of your compass so that it connects the two points you wish to travel between (fig. 3-16a).
2. Turn the bezel until north on the azimuth is in line with north on the map. Then use the index line to read the specific bearing you want to travel to (fig. 3-16b).

BEARING AND KNOWN ELEVATION

If you know your elevation because of a specific feature or you have an altimeter, you can locate yourself with just one bearing, as long as you have a rough idea of where you are (e.g., on the west side of the peak you are taking a bearing off of). Simply pull the bearing from the field and plot it on the map—your location will be where the plotted bearing intersects your elevation.

SATELLITE IMAGERY

Satellite imagery can be very helpful while touring, especially for the alpine climber and mountaineer traveling on glaciers or otherwise

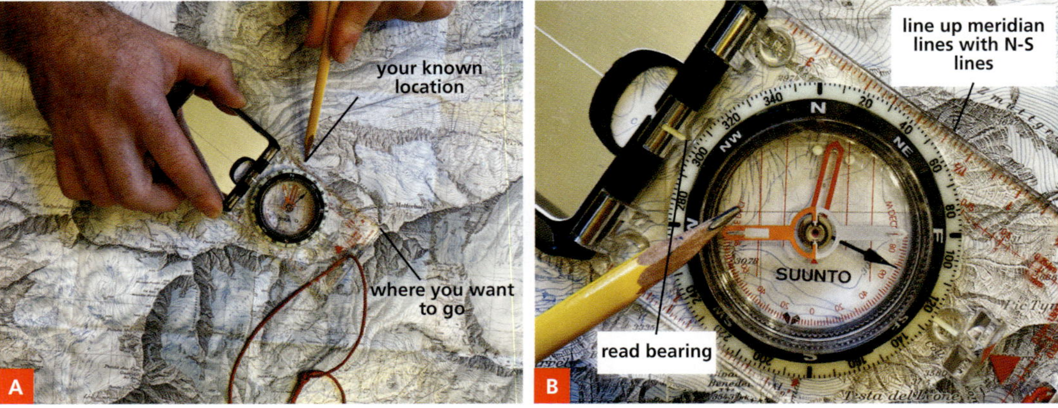

Figure 3-16. *To pull a bearing from a map:* **a,** *Lay the edge of the compass from the area you are in or intend to travel to the one you want to go to.* **b,** *Turn the bezel until the meridian lines line up with the north-south lines on the map. Then read the bearing on the appropriate index line.*

variable and rugged terrain. While crevasses will relocate as the glacier slowly moves, plotting your route to avoid heavily crevassed areas only helps set you up for success. Using satellite imagery can also help you identify features that don't show up as clearly (or at all) on a map (fig. 3-17), such as small cliff bands or specific open areas between trees.

For example, satellite imagery once saved my bacon in the Northern Picket Range of Washington, when a client injured his foot in a tumbling fall on talus and we needed to improvise to find the quickest way out. That day, as we bushwhacked desperately through slide alder, I remembered that I'd downloaded Google imagery onto my phone. Consulting that data helped me find talus and big-timbered terrain that would be quicker going, even though it also showed up as green on our topo map. We were able to save hours—and a lot of blood, sweat, and tears—on our way back to civilization!

Figure 3-17. *Satellite imagery can help you locate features that are hard to see on a map. This tour plan on the Coleman-Deming Route on Mount Baker avoids the largest crevasses.*

Opposite: *Mountains are an ever-changing and potentially dangerous environment. Alpine climbers and mountaineers rely on many specialized tools, including boots and crampons, to help navigate this terrain.*

CHAPTER 4

Tools of the Trade

When climbing mountains and moving across snow, ice, and glaciers, you should consider bringing several pieces of specialized equipment—ranging from critical to extraneous, depending on conditions—with you. In this chapter, the differences, advantages and disadvantages, circumstances, and ideal conditions for several commonly used pieces of equipment for general mountaineering ascents that involve glacier travel will be discussed.

ICE AXES

The ice axe is easily the most iconic and foundational tool for snow climbing and glacier travel (fig. 4-1). Also commonly known by its French name, *piolet*, the ice axe was used to climb many of the world's most classic mountain routes beginning over two centuries ago in its original form, the long-shafted alpenstock. While most climbers know that an ice axe is fundamental to snow climbing and glacier travel, some design characteristics make certain axes better for certain objectives or terrain. The main components are the head—composed of the pick and adze or hammer—the shaft, and the spike (fig. 4-2).

Figure 4-1. *Different ice axes are designed to excel at different things. The axe on the left is low weight, making it ideal for alpine rock climbing and ski mountaineering, or any other trip where weight savings are essential. The two models in the middle are the most technical, with a more aggressive pick, a stronger Type 2–rated shaft, removable pick and/or adze, and a built-in pommel. The far right is an all-around model designed for general mountaineering.*

THE HEAD

The head of the ice axe includes the pick, the adze or hammer, the material between those two, and often a hole called the "eye". Each component of the head can have different characteristics that affect performance and weight, making the axe more or less suited for different applications.

__Figure 4-2.__ The parts of an ice axe

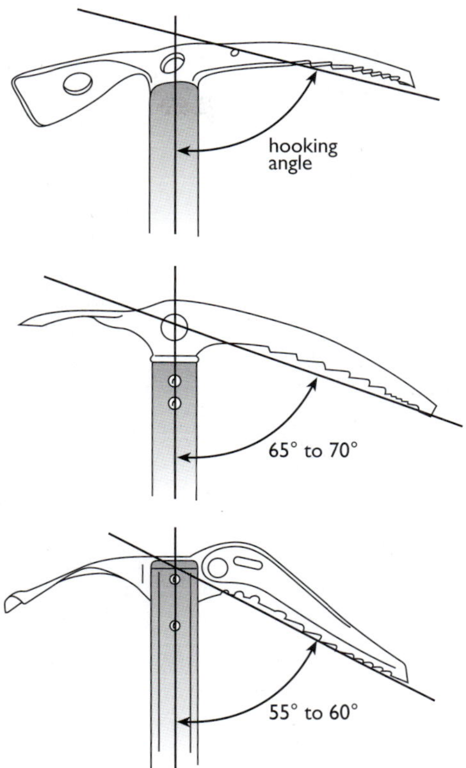

__Figure 4-3.__ Pick shapes of various ice axes

Pick Shapes

While some design aspects of the ice axe have changed, the three most classic pick shapes have remained basically the same for nearly fifty years. While you can dagger or self-arrest with any ice axe, pick shape is one of the biggest factors that dictate which terrain an axe is best suited for (fig. 4-3).

Positive curve: The positive curve C (a.k.a. "classic curve") is by far the most popular design; most modern general mountaineering axes use it. In this configuration, the pick makes a slight but continuous downward-arching curve, with the pick's end coming to a point below where the pick leaves the shaft. This design is popular because it strikes an excellent balance between usefulness in steep snow and for self-arresting. You can self-arrest nearly as well as with a neutrally curved model but climb steeper snow and ice far more efficiently and securely. The only downside is that when a positive-curve pick is swung into higher-angle and/or firmer ice, it doesn't clean nearly as easily as a reverse-curve design.

Reverse curve: A reverse-curve pick is best for climbing ice and steep snow where you will swing or drive the pick into firmer snow. Here, the pick trends down similarly to a positive-curve design (though more commonly at a steeper angle) before breaking to a less steep angle at roughly the halfway point. This

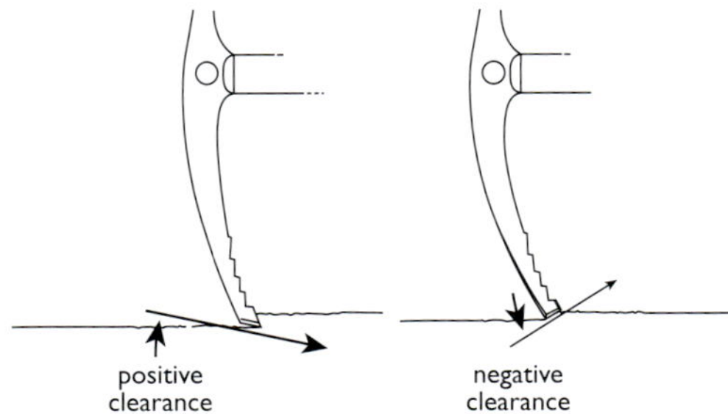

Figure 4-4. *Ice axe showing both positive clearance and negative clearance of pick.*

banana-like shape makes removing the pick far easier after it has been driven in because, when the shaft is rocked upward, the change in angle helps it release. The disadvantage is that reverse-curve picks are the least "smooth" while self-arresting, creating a "bumpy" feeling while stopping in firmer snow.

Neutral curve: A neutral curve is exactly what it sounds like: the pick comes out of the head very close to straight, with little to no droop. A neutral-curve pick is the best and smoothest for self-arrest but will be far less secure when swung into the ice. Despite this being the primary design for well over a century, very few models nowadays have a true neutral-curve pick, though some still get close.

Figure 4-5. *Rachel Spitzer on the steep North Face of the Tour Ronde, Mont Blanc Massif, where curved tools and crampons with supportive secondary points are best for the job.* (Photo by Jonathon Spitzer)

Pick Clearance

Pick clearance refers to the shape of the pick end that is designed to be inserted in the snow (fig. 4-4). It plays a large role in how easily an ice axe penetrates firm ice and, to a much lesser extent, how smoothly it performs when used to self-arrest (fig. 4-5).

Positive clearance: The pick's outermost tyne, tooth, or extension is on the bottom. This design is far better at penetrating firm snow and ice but isn't quite as smooth for self-arresting (though it certainly still works).

Negative clearance: The pick's outermost tyne is on the top. This design is not as good at penetrating firm snow and ice but self-arrests more smoothly.

Figure 4-6. *Earlier in the season, when the snow is softer, an adze tend to work better for digging and chopping.*

Figure 4-7. *Axes with hammers tend to be more useful when the snow is firmer. Lyra Pierotti is grateful to be wielding an ice axe with a hammer and not an adze while pounding a picket in dense late-season snow. In firmer conditions, you are more likely to have to pound pickets or even pitons, instead of building T-slot anchors.*

Hammers and Adzes

No particular head tool is better than another—they serve different purposes. An adze allows you to dig a T-trench, build a moat bollard, or chop a platform to stand or bivy on, while a hammer will be far better at pounding in cabled pickets or placing pitons.

For early season climbs, an adze is often the more useful tool (fig. 4-6). You will likely encounter softer snow, which the adze is superior at manipulating. You are also unlikely to be able to get enough strength and security from a vertically driven picket and are more likely to use the adze for other things like digging bollards, burying T-slots (also sometimes called a deadman), and so forth.

However, for late-season glacier climbs, a hammer can be beneficial because nearly all the pickets you place will be driven in vertically, and the odds of having to dig a T-trench-type anchor are low (fig. 4-7). It also gives you the option to pound in a piton to rappel over funky moats, recently exposed rock slabs, and other similar features, which are becoming more common as glaciers recede. If you had to choose one tool, an adze is more versatile, but a hammer isn't *much* less versatile.

THE SHAFT

It has become common for axe models to have a slight bend in the shaft. These bends are not nearly as aggressive as those in tools designed specifically for vertical ice climbing, but a slight bend can be advantageous over straight-shafted models, with a few exceptions.

A slight bend makes it easier to generate force to swing the axe into the snow on steep slopes. While low- and mid-daggering on more mid-angled routes (40–60 degrees), the user's hand is lifted slightly out of the snow, helping to keep the user warmer and drier. The bend also provides more leverage while

Figure 4-8. *Comparing bent-shaft (top) and straight-shaft (bottom) ice axes*

self-arresting. The only disadvantage of the bent-shaft model is that it's slightly heavier than a straight-shaft model of equal length, and it doesn't plunge-spike down quite as easily (fig. 4-8).

RATINGS AND TESTING

All axes certified by the UIAA (Union Internationale des Associations d'Alpinisme, or the International Climbing and Mountaineering Federation) have either a Type 1 or a Type 2 rating, depending on their performance in six tests that measure the strength of the shaft, pick, and the connection point between the two. The Type 1 ice rating is also known as a CEN-B, or basic, rating, while the Type 2 is also known as a CEN-T, or technical, rating.

Any model with either a Type 1 or a Type 2 rating is appropriate for use as an improvised anchor during crevasse rescue or to belay directly off on snow.

Ice-axe tests are designed to stress the axe beyond how it is typically used. For example, in one of the easiest-to-correlate tests, the axe is pulled perpendicularly from midshaft as if it were placed as a T-slot; a Type 1 axe must

Figure 4-9. *Using an appropriate-length ice axe will help you balance more effectively. Here, two climbers navigate steep terrain in Peru's Cordillera Blanca.* (Photo by Jonathon Spitzer)

withstand 2.5 kilonewtons of force, while a Type 2 must withstand 3.5 kilonewtons. The head-shaft interface when pulled perpendicularly—as if it were a vertically placed anchor—or while used in a standing ice-axe belay must withstand 2.5 kilonewtons for a Type 1 and 4 kilonewtons for a Type 2.

Choosing the best axe depends on what you intend to use it for. Do you need a Type 2 axe for general mountaineering? Certainly not. Can you still belay off your Type 1 axe in a T-slot or while clipped to the eye? Yes, but not for extreme loads. Do you need a Type 2 axe for harder or more involved alpine routes? Not necessarily, but it could be helpful. A Type 2 axe will be stronger, generally offer superior durability, and be more capable. For routes that require any sort of sustained, technical climbing where you expect to be pulling regularly on your tools and weighting only the pick, you should strongly consider a Type 2 model.

ICE-AXE SIZING

There are a lot of misconceptions about how long an ice axe to buy, and much will depend on your height. First, remember that the primary function of an ice axe is to assist with balance and security in steeper terrain, and second, to help you self-arrest if you slip. Gone are the days of endless, backbreaking step chopping, which required the longer ice axes and alpenstocks of yesteryear. Generally speaking, it is better to err on the shorter side, which lets an ice axe do its job more effectively (table 4-1). While a long ice axe may be more comfortable in less steep terrain where you can use it as a trekking pole, it is less effective in steeper, firmer terrain where you need the axe for security. Here, with your hand forced up into a less-than-ideal balance position near or above your shoulder, you won't be able to drive the spike deep into the snow. An ice axe that is too long also cannot aid with balance as effectively (fig. 4-9).

Figure 4-10. *Rebecca Schroeder attached her ice axe to her harness through the hole in the head to free her hands while climbing the Cosmique Arête above Chamonix, France.*

TABLE 4-1. SIZE GUIDELINES FOR CLASSIC ICE AXES

Height	Ice Axe Length
Under 5'6"	40–50 cm
5'6" to 5'8"	40–55 cm
5'9" to 6'0"	50–60 cm
6'1" to 6'4"	50–65 cm
Over 6'4"	50–70 cm

***Figure 4-11.** To stow your ice axe between your back and pack:* **a**, *With the pick slightly downward, tuck the spike through one of your shoulder straps.* **b**, *Tilt your head to the side and flip the head of the axe over your head.* **c**, *Cinch up your shoulder straps and sternum strap, making sure the pick points outward.*

***Figure 4-12.** Another great way to carry your axe for a brief time is to stick it spike-first between your back and your pack. Ensure that the pick faces outward and over your shoulder strap. If the axe is on the longer side, make sure that the spine sticks out the opposite side as the pick above your shoulder strap.*

Knowing how to stow your ice axe efficiently and securely is helpful. You may want to clip it to your harness to free up your hands (fig. 4-10) for a short stretch. To stow it longer, try situating it between your pack and back by putting it below your shoulder strap (fig. 4-11). Another option is to tuck it between your shoulder straps behind your back (fig. 4-12).

TREKKING POLES

Trekking poles have become nearly as common as an ice axe for mountaineers, and with good reason. On the trail, a pair of trekking poles can help provide stability, reduce overall fatigue, and decrease stress on your joints. On glaciers, you can use one pole in conjunction with an ice axe for the same benefits (fig. 4-13). Having a pole also lets you bring a shorter ice axe, because you can use the pole as your "cane" in less-steep terrain where the axe's spike

Figure 4-13. *Using a trekking pole with an ice axe on a glacier, as Tracey Bernstein does here on the Terror Glacier in the North Cascades, helps with balance on lower-angle terrain but also lets you use a shorter axe in steeper terrain.*

may not even touch the ground. Meanwhile, a shorter ice axe packs away more easily on the approach, is less obtrusive on technical rock climbs, and most importantly, is *much more* effective at increasing stability and security in steeper terrain, where you really need it. Trekking poles are also easy to tuck away in your pack straps for a brief stretch (fig. 4-14).

Trekking poles include wrist leashes, which help you avoid losing them, but they can be a hindrance at times. When traveling on a glacier with any sort of significant crevasse-fall hazard, consider not using your pole's wrist leashes. While the following may be sacrilegious to some people, should you need to self-arrest in a hurry, you can simply drop your pole and use both hands to self-arrest with your axe.

Figure 4-14. *To tuck your trekking pole away:* **a**, *Slide the basket side of your pole above the sternum strap until only about one foot is sticking out.* **b**, *Flip the handle over the top of your head and cinch down your sternum and shoulder straps to hold it in place.*

Figure 4-15. Steeper and/or firmer ice requires semirigid or fully rigid steel crampons, as worn here by Dave Burdick on the Triple Couloirs on Dragontail Peak, Washington.

Figure 4-16. John Willard uses semirigid crampons to ascend nearly 50-degree snow on Cutthroat Peak, Washington.

CRAMPONS

All crampons—metal spikes you affix to the bottom of your boots—increase your traction in the snow, but they come in different styles depending on their primary application. Their design focus revolves around the type of climbing they'll be used for and the material they are constructed with. Designs vary from fully rigid crampons strong enough for vertical ice (fig. 4-15) to flexible, superlight crampons barely suitable for firmer snow.

CRAMPON STYLE

Like ice axes, crampons come in many styles, designs, and materials, each offering different performance characteristics relative to their weight.

Fully rigid: Fully rigid crampons provide the most support for the user's feet and lower legs, making it easier to stand on the front points in firm ice. While this is a big advantage for waterfall ice, where maximum support is helpful, fully rigid crampons are generally heavier, less pleasant to walk long distances in, more prone to balling (filling with) snow, and don't work as well with softer boots.

Semirigid: Semirigid crampons are the most popular crampons for general mountaineering and glacier travel objectives (fig. 4-16). They usually still have an aluminum bar that connects the front and back of the

Figure 4-17. Rebecca Schroeder finds the strength and durability of her steel crampons to be well worth the weight while front pointing on thin granite edges on the crux pitch of the Cosmiques Arête on the Aiguille du Midi above Chamonix, France.

crampon, but it flexes slightly. These crampons are designed with a steel frame that lies flat; its lower profile makes it less prone to balling snow. While most people still consider semirigid crampons to be stiff, their little bit of flex increases comfort on long days compared with fully rigid crampons—they are comfortable enough for walking for long periods and for descending, but supportive enough for most steep-snow objectives, even when those objectives have a few sections of steeper ice.

Flexible: Flexible crampons use a very flexible metal or, more commonly, a piece of ultralight fabric like Dyneema that allows the crampons to be folded in half, making them more packable. While these are lighter, they perform very poorly on firm snow if your boots are not correspondingly stiff enough—these crampons rely entirely on the boots for rigidity.

There are many types of crampons with different designs and built with different materials. Choosing the right crampon for the application can be the difference between success and failure.

STEEL VS. ALUMINUM

Steel crampons bite into bare glacier ice and will unquestionably provide greater security in firmer conditions. If you are going to own only one pair of crampons for general mountaineering, choose steel (fig. 4-17). On the other hand, aluminum crampons are significantly lighter, but they won't bite into ice or very firm snow. Still, it's worth having an aluminum pair for their low weight on alpine rock routes that also have some snow and ice or for early season, when you're unlikely to find ultrafirm conditions.

TEN-POINT CRAMPONS

While ten-point crampons do not provide as much security as their twelve-point counterparts (fig. 4-18), there is an exception for folks with smaller feet. Crampons require a minimum amount of space between the points

HISTORY OF THE MODERN CRAMPON

Climbers have used various pointed pieces of metal strapped to or built into their footwear since at least the 1600s. Modern crampons didn't, however, become widely used until the early 1900s, when most mountaineers still wore hobnail boots. Hobnail boots are basically what they sound like: boots with a dozen or more short "nails" sticking out of the sole. Around 1910, an Englishman named Oscar Eckenstein designed the first "modern" crampon; it was removable and had ten downward-facing points. This crampon was produced commercially by the famed equipment manufacturer Henry Grivel in 1913 and quickly gained popularity because it could be strapped on as necessary and had superior traction compared with hobnailed models. This new design dramatically reduced the need for step cutting and thus allowed climbers to ascend more quickly and with shorter, lighter ice axes.

In 1929, Henry Grivel's son Laurent added two front points to the existing downward-only-pointing design, dramatically aiding climbers' ability to ascend steep snow and ice. Small improvements to their designs were made over the next decade. However, this new design was slow to catch on, until 1938 when, on the first ascent of the North Face of the Eiger, the Germans Anderl Heckmair and Ludwig Vörg used their front-pointed, twelve-point crampons to quickly catch up to and pass Heinrich Harrer and Fritz Kasparek of Austria, who were using more traditional models that required a flat-footing technique. The four men ended up teaming up to make the first ascent. As Harrer wrote in *The White Spider* about seeing the front-pointed models in action, "I looked back, down our endless ladder of steps. Up it, I saw the New Era coming at express speed; there were two men running—I mean running, not climbing—up" the Nordwand's steep Second Icefield.

to effectively "bite" into the snow rather than break up the snow surface. Points that are too close to each other around the arch of the boot (the rearmost point on the forefoot section and the frontmost point on the heel section) can cause a high-centering effect in firmer conditions, often the result of crampons that are too long relative to the boot. When the points are too close, generally on either side of the spreader bar near the arch of the boot, it causes them to cut into the snow less effectively compared to the rest of the points.

Ten-point crampons are shorter because they have only six points under the ball area of your foot rather than eight, allowing for a greater distance between the points in the forefoot and heel areas. This isn't a big deal for folks with larger feet but can be essential for those with smaller feet.

Figure 4-18. *If your feet are smaller (below US men's 6 or US women's 7, roughly an EU 38), 10-point crampons can be more secure, depending on your boot volume, because they are shorter. If the points on either side of the spreader bar are too close, they won't bite into the ice well.* (Photo by Jared Darapla)

HARNESSES

All climbing harnesses are Type-C sit harnesses, or harnesses that don't require an upper-body harness. Of course, any climbing-specific harness is suitable for glacier travel and crevasse rescue; lightweight rock climbing harnesses, particularly those used for sport climbing, can make great alpine harnesses, as they offer substantial comfort for their weight. But alpine harnesses certainly offer several advantages over more "traditional" rock climbing harnesses. First, they are lighter and more compact. And while they are less comfortable if you need to hang in them, you will survive any shorter-term use, such as a rappel or a semihanging belay. The discomfort that comes from the rare crevasse fall will be the least of your worries in that situation!

Alpine harnesses also have the huge advantage of being easier to put on over large boots, crampons, snowshoes, skis, or most other things you might have on your feet. They "clip around" the person rather than needing to be pulled up like pants.

PULLEYS

While pulleys are not required to perform crevasse rescue, they no doubt make it easier, especially if you are a smaller person traveling with a larger person or if you are carrying heavily laden packs (thus increasing the weight that must be hauled out). Even if you are technically proficient and are similar in weight to your ropemate, a pulley can still help (fig. 4-19).

ROPES

Many different types of ropes are suitable for glacier travel (fig. 4-20). Below is a breakdown of the key categories to help you pick the rope(s) that's best for your needs.

DYNAMIC ROPES

Dynamic ropes are ropes that stretch when weighted, to absorb some of the force generated by a climber's fall and reduce the energy the falling climber feels. This is contrary to semistatic or hyperstatic ropes, which stretch very little when weighted.

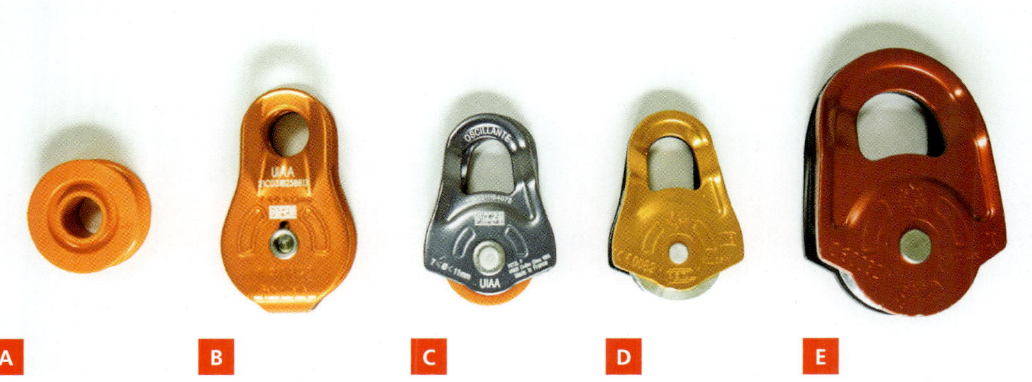

Figure 4-19. *Pulleys unquestionably make hauling easier. Consider them for trips where a climber may fall with a heavily laden pack. While all pulleys help, they are not all created equal. From left to right:* **a,** *a light plastic pulley;* **b,** *a fixed pulley that doesn't flip open;* **c,** *a light and efficient pulley;* **d,** *a prusik minding pulley;* **e,** *a large and ultra-efficient pulley.*

Figure 4-20. *Many types of ropes are suitable for glacier travel, but each has advantages and disadvantages.* (Photo by Graham Zimmerman)

Single Ropes

Single ropes are what most people use in rock climbing (fig. 4-21). They are strong and far more resistant to cutting, as well as mandatory if you are climbing any sort of steep, technical rock or ice pitches—both because of their durability and dynamic stretch. They are normally thicker (generally around 8.5–10 millimeters) than the rope types listed below, and stretch at close to 30 percent to reduce the fall force absorbed by the climber and any protective gear.

Half Ropes

Half ropes—meant to be alternately clipped in to each point of protection—are great for pure glacier climbs on which you don't intend to climb any steep rock. However, they are not as resistant to cutting as single ropes, which makes them best suited for modestly steep snow or ice (generally less than 50–60 degrees). In less steep terrain, the weight and force are distributed between your feet and the anchor system, but as the terrain steepens, all your weight and force will be on one rope, which will stretch more than its single-rope counterpart and thus be more susceptible to cutting.

Twin Ropes

Twin ropes are meant to be used together as well as clipped in to protection points in tandem. Manufacturers don't recommend using a single strand of twin-rated rope in a glacier environment, even with relatively low loads. Twin ropes are designed to have the most stretch, to help reduce the force exerted on a piece of protection, and to compensate for both ropes being clipped to a given piece of protection. They are thus often the thinnest and least durable and cut resistant of the three types of dynamic ropes.

STATIC ROPES

Static ropes come in two types—semistatic and hyperstatic—and are not meant for technical

Figure 4-21. *If you plan to climb vertical ice or cross any technical rock, as Jere Burrell is on the Lower Coleman Glacier on Washington's Mount Baker, reach for a single rope.* (Photo by Max Bond)

Figure 4-22. *A group walks across the Upper Curtis Glacier on Mount Shuksan. Semistatic and hyperstatic ropes are fine for general glacier travel, but do not use them for any climb where you need to lead belay.*

lead climbing, as they exert immense forces on the protection system and the climber in a fall (fig. 4-22).

Semistatic Ropes

Also known as low-elongation ropes or by the misleading moniker "static ropes," semistatic ropes generally stretch between 3 and 5 percent. They are unsuitable for lead belaying under almost any circumstances, but they can be used to belay a second climber on steep snow if you keep all slack out of the system. If there is a lot of slack (i.e., the belayer doesn't keep up as the second climber ascends) and the second climber falls, they can generate a tremendous amount of force that could compromise the anchor or cause injury. Fortunately, these ropes are perfectly suitable for glacier travel—the snow introduces enough dynamic properties into the system in a real-world crevasse fall that most climbers won't notice much of a difference between a dynamic and semistatic rope.

For glacier travel and crevasse rescue, an additional advantage of semistatic ropes is that they are generally more durable at similar diameters compared with dynamic ropes. They are also less expensive and are more efficient for hauling. Additionally, the fallen climber on a semistatic rope tends not to feel like they fell as far. However, even more so than with dynamic ropes, you must take care while traveling to avoid excess slack in the system, to prevent shock-loading, or suddenly exerting a high-force load on a climbing rope, piece of protection, or anchor system. Shock-loading is usually caused by a fall where the climber rapidly comes to a stop or or a fall is greater than the rope or length of material in the system. Consider using stopper knots to make it easier for the arresting group to catch the fall (see chapter 6).

Hyperstatic Ropes

Hyperstatic ropes are generally considered to be ropes that stretch less than 2 percent. Despite this ultralow elongation, many companies endorse their hyperstatic ropes for glacier travel, again because of the snow's ability to absorb force in a fall. Hyperstatic ropes often have the advantage of being even lighter weight than their dynamic or semistatic counterparts yet remain quite cut resistant. However, they are *not* for lead belaying because of the forces they will generate on the falling climber and protection (fig. 4-23).

COILING YOUR ROPE FOR TRANSPORT

Whenever you are not using the rope on the approach, you will need to carry it. While there are many ways to coil a rope to carry it, butterfly coils with a nail finish are preferred (fig. 4-24). This coil fits inside and outside of a backpack

Figure 4-23. *Some semistatic ropes, as well as some hyperstatic ropes, are suitable for glacier routes as long as it's unlikely that you will do any lead belaying. A group ascends the Disappointment Cleaver Route in late-season conditions on Mount Rainier.* (Photo by Bryce Hill)

Figure 4-24. *Butterfly coil with a nail finish:* **a**, *Butterfly coil nearly the entire length of your rope, folding it over on itself, rather than twisting it, with the coils hanging down from your neck to around waist length.* **b**, *Once you only have 3 to 4 feet of rope left, take the coils off of your shoulders and fold the short end over on itself to create a bight.* **c**, *Wrap the short end back around all of the coils traveling toward the bite you just made.* **d**, *Once only 4 to 6 inches of slack remain, poke the short end through the bight.* **e**, *Figure out which butterfly coil leads to the bight, then pull on it to cinch it.* **f**, *A finished butterfly coil with a nail finish ready for transport.*

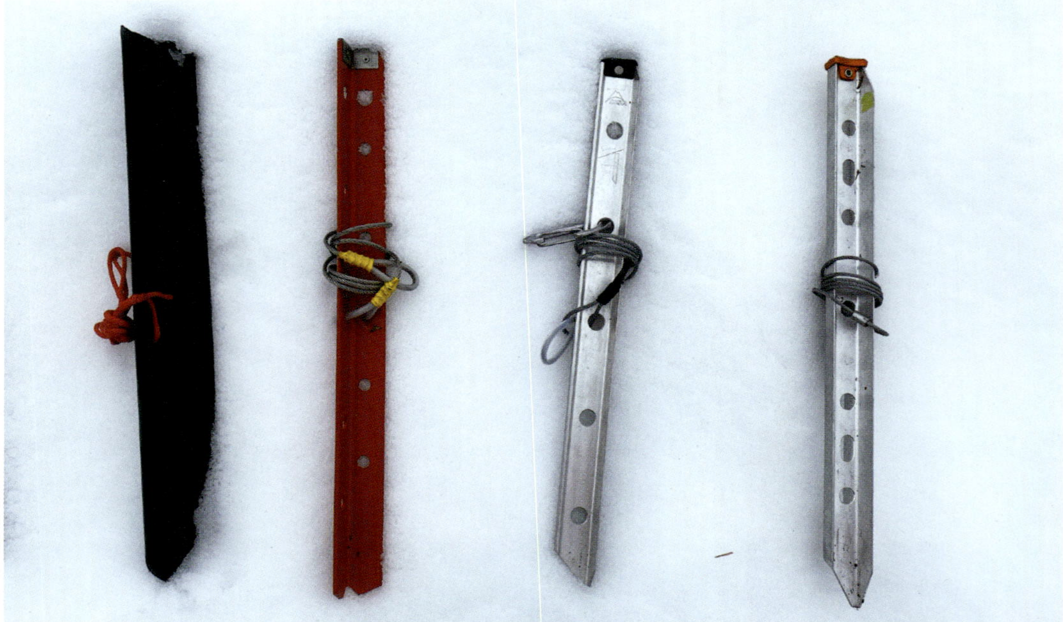

***Figure 4-25.** Four different snow pickets, from left to right: Smiley carbon fiber picket, Yates cabled picket, MSR Coyote cabled picket, and SMC cabled picket*

efficiently, but also, when you are ready to use it and lay it out flat, it tends to pay out the smoothest, letting you rig the rope easily.

TOOLS TO BUILD ANCHORS

Climbers use a variety of protection to build anchors, including snow pickets, ice screws, and V-threads. Used in a wide variety of ways, these tools all enable climbers to build anchors and points of protection in snow and ice. These anchors and protection points are critical for belaying, leading, rappelling, and performing crevasse rescue.

SNOW PICKETS

Snow pickets are a very effective tool for creating snow anchors to belay across crevasses, for protecting exposed sections of glacier and steep snow, and, of course, for crevasse rescue (fig. 4-25). While you can improvise a snow anchor with an ice axe and other items, nothing works as effectively as a picket for creating a quick, strong anchor. (See chapter 7 for more on anchors, including pickets.)

ICE SCREWS

Many climbers traveling on glaciers carry an ice screw—a ratcheting, hollow tube, generally between 15 and 22 centimeters long, with teeth on the bottom to bite into the ice—on their harness (fig. 4-26). The idea is that they can use the screw to build an anchor in bare glacier ice, drive it into a crevasse wall to help unweight the rope if they fall in, or build a

Figure 4-26. While ice screws may not be used a lot (much like snow pickets), it is generally a good idea for each climber on a rope team to have one. This climber has an ice screw clipped to his right leg loop, out of the way but secure.

V-thread anchor to rappel or belay. An ice screw is only as strong as the ice it is placed in. Evaluate ice carefully and be sure to clear off rotten ice so that the screw ends up secure in solid ice (fig. 4-27). Since glacial surface ice is generally not as strong as waterfall ice, most climbers err on the longer side (15 centimeters or longer), as longer screws are easier to use, stronger, and likely require fewer attempts to get solid V-threads depending on the user's skill level.

Once you have prepared the surface of the ice, position the ice screw perpendicular to the surface of the ice and then twist it to engage

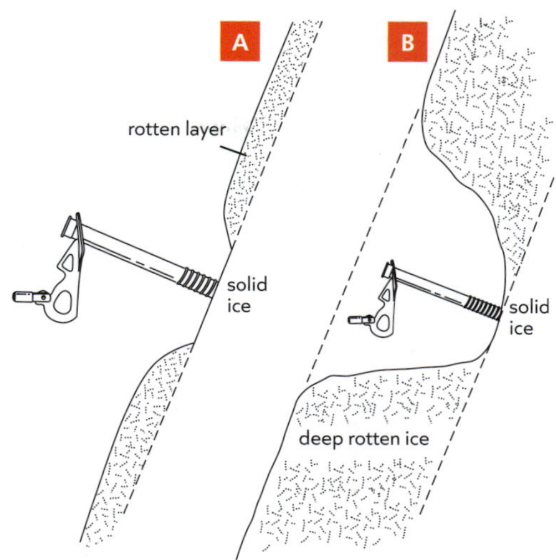

***Figure 4-27.** Ice-screw placements:* **a,** *with soft or rotten surface layers;* **b,** *in deep rotten ice.*

the threads (fig. 4-28). A screw not only lets you build an anchor when the snow is too firm for a picket, but if you fall into a crevasse, you can place the screw in the crevasse wall, clip yourself in to it, and unweight the rope. Shorter ice screws can be just as strong in reliable ice, but the surface ice of a glacier is typically aerated and of poorer quality, limiting the strength of shorter screws.

V-THREAD TOOLS

A V-thread, also known as an Abalakov—named after the Soviet climber Vitaly Abalakov—is a belay or rappel anchor created by threading a piece of cord or the rope itself (called a zero thread) into glacier ice. While it is possible to build a V-thread solely with a sling, it is certainly more difficult, and bringing a dedicated V-thread tool (fig. 4-29) is well worth its (low) weight on late-season

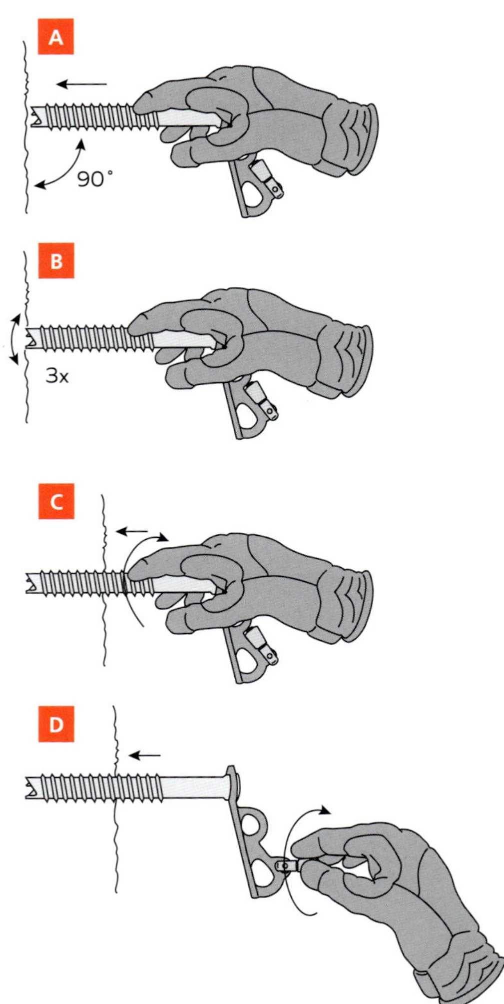

Figure 4-28. Placing an ice screw: **a**, *Press screw in perpendicular to surface.* **b**, *Twist in and out a few times to create a hole.* **c**, *Twist a few turns by hand until threads are engaged.* **d**, *Screw in with the crank until hanger is flush with the ice and facing down.*

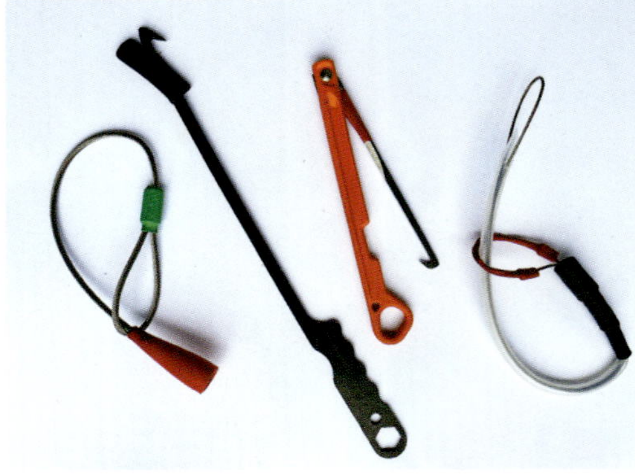

Figure 4-29. *Various types of V-thread tools*

Figure 4-30. *Peter Broback wearing gloves, sleeves, and a helmet while traveling across the Quien Sabe Glacier, Washington.*

THE PULLEY: HIGH EFFICIENCY, MINIMAL WEIGHT

BY SAM LUTHY

Park rangers on Mount Rainier get the opportunity to observe groups practicing crevasse rescue while on duty at the high camps of Camp Muir and Camp Schurman. On occasion, these same rangers are called to assist in the rescue of climbing parties from a crevasse. In our experience, we find that most parties on the mountain are successful in anchoring their rope to provide a fixed line for the member in the crevasse to climb out on if they can get through the lip.

The parties can build a hauling system; however, they often struggle because they don't know how to minimize friction and so can't actually haul their fallen partner upward. Many find that the mechanical-advantage system that they practiced on a slope with minimal rope drag fails to overcome ropes running over edges and through snow. For example, along with thoroughly prepping the edge or lip to minimize friction, a single high-efficiency pulley is very effective at improving the performance of a haul system, all with a minimal weight penalty. It's a tool that many climbers, particularly groups of only two or three, should bring for all glacier travel.

KEY TAKEAWAYS: It's essential to know how to increase the mechanical advantage of a system as well as techniques to reduce friction.

Sam Luthy is an AMGA ski guide and former climbing ranger on Mount Rainier.

glacial climbs where you might run into bare or very shallowly buried ice.

OTHER GEAR CONSIDERATIONS

Here are a few other, largely nontechnical items you'll likely want to pack, both for comfort and safety on a glacier. While none of these items are required, they are all a good idea and should be strongly considered (fig. 4-30).

GLOVES

Wear gloves any time you are ascending steep snow, as your ability to maintain your grip on your axe is compromised if your hands get cold—or worse, in a fall, you might sustain road rash on your bare hands as you slide down the slope. For more moderate glacier travel, wear gloves for the same reasons. If your partner falls into a crevasse, it's likely that, with bare hands, you could lose your grip on your ice axe, posing a risk to you, your partner, and even your entire rope team.

SLEEVES

Sleeves serve a similar but less critical role in protecting the climber while traveling on the glacier. Besides protecting your skin from the often-intense alpine sun, sleeves protect your arms from abrasions should you or a rope team member fall into a crevasse or on a steep slope and be dragged across the snow.

HELMETS

It is always hard to argue against wearing a helmet, as hitting your head is a possibility in an unexpected crevasse fall. However, looking at real-world data from Mount Rainier and Denali National Parks, while there are several instances in which climbers were hit by falling rocks in both parks, the number of people who have injured their heads in a crevasse fall is relatively low. That said, helmets are never a bad idea, and if you are carrying one with you, you might as well carry it on your head.

Opposite: *Danny Spreafico climbs the North Face of Mount Shuksan far above Price Lake in Washington's North Cascades*

CHAPTER 5

Moving on Snow and Ice

Figure 5-1. Leading up steep snow requires solid technique, as demonstrated by Jaques Sturm as he climbs through a bergschrund on Huantsan in Peru. Using techniques appropriate to the terrain angle will go a long way toward enhancing efficiency and security. (Photo by Joshua Jarrin)

Moving well is the foundation of speed, security, and efficiency in the alpine. While nearly anyone who can walk can make progress uphill on snow, being familiar with the fundamentals of movement will greatly increase your speed and efficiency in the mountains. On a long, tiring day, using solid footwork and ice-axe techniques will significantly conserve energy. The same thing can be said for security. Using appropriate crampons and ice-axe techniques on a steep or exposed section will decrease the likelihood of falling and thus decrease the entire team's risk of injury or mishap.

As you progress through this chapter and learn movement techniques, keep an open mind. All too often, climbers—even experienced ones—say, "Well, I've never done that technique. It must not be necessary." While most mountaineers will certainly use some techniques more than others, a lack of familiarity with a less-used technique is no reason not to attempt to become proficient at it or to learn the types of conditions or terrain where it works best. It may very well come in handy someday and even save your life.

FOOTWORK FUNDAMENTALS

Solid footwork on snow—using the right technique for the right terrain angle and

Figure 5-2. *If you don't have crampons on, kick across the surface of the snow, letting the lugs of your boots bite into the snow for better footing. You may need to kick a few times, as this climber is doing with his right foot.*

conditions—is the basis for all snow climbing, increasing speed, efficiency, and your margin of safety (fig. 5-1).

WALKING WITHOUT CRAMPONS

If conditions are relatively soft and you're walking in mountain boots without crampons, add a slight "kick" to every step (fig. 5-2). Even just the weight of your foot swinging downward and across the snow, rather than into it, greatly increases security compared to taking a simple step, as if walking down a trail. Most mountain boots are relatively stiff and have large lugs (treads); the subtle kick encourages the lugs to "slice" across the snow surface, providing better purchase.

WALKING WITH CRAMPONS

In softer snow, a light kick done similarly to walking on snow without crampons is

Figure 5-3. *Rolling your ankles outward (in this case, downhill) provides more security; all your crampon points will sink into the snow, compared with "edging," which in this example would engage the points only on the uphill side.*

generally sufficient for security and to help create a flat platform on which to stand. While counterintuitive, when walking in firmer snow, roll your ankles slightly outward and downward to help engage as many crampon points as possible (fig. 5-3). This is the opposite technique used in skiing where you attempt to "edge"—avoid that foot position due to the lack of point contact with the snow and the relatively low level of security it provides.

As the terrain gets steeper—up to about 40 degrees, depending on conditions—move the toes across the fall line even to the point where they are pointed downhill (fig. 5-4). This posture, despite forcing the upper body to face slightly downhill even while you're moving uphill, is less fatiguing in firmer conditions and allows you to get better purchase

Figure 5-4. As the slope steepens, get better purchase by pointing your feet slightly downhill. This engages the secondary points of the crampons, drastically increasing your security due to their angle.

as the secondary points of the crampons can also engage.

Regardless of which technique you use, it is nearly always most efficient to take small steps from an energy-conservation standpoint. While this is very evident for shorter folks following in the footsteps of taller people, even for a group of relatively uniform height, taking small steps will save energy over time. It's way more efficient to take a small step versus making a big, quad-crushing "high step," a difference that accumulates over the course of a day. Keep in mind that whoever is out front breaking trail should take smaller steps and trade out the role often. While this is slightly harder for the person in front, it is easier and more pleasant for the other people on your rope team, and with frequent switching, the whole group will reach the top less fatigued, helping conserve energy for the whole group (fig. 5-5).

Figure 5-5. If you are at the front of the group, set small, consistently spaced steps.

BASIC FOOTWORK TECHNIQUES

The following techniques can be used with or without crampons, as long as you make the key adjustments mentioned above, such as "slicing" your boot lugs into the snow with a light kick and rolling your ankles to engage more crampon points in firmer conditions. Additionally, each technique has a range that overlaps with the others, and each technique can be tempered to match slope steepness, how open or closed your feet are while using the duck walk, or how steep your crossover is on a diagonal ascent. An alpinist should be able to quickly move between techniques to best match the conditions and terrain.

PIED MARCHE

There isn't much in the way of technique when walking on terrain under 15 degrees, considered gentle walking, or *pied marche* (fig. 5-6). Simply walk the same as you would while hiking on the trail, other than maybe opening your hips a bit and being aware of your crampons in relation to your pant legs.

PIED EN CANARD

The duck-footed technique—also known as the "duck walk" or *pied en canard* (French for "foot like a duck")—is exactly as it sounds: walking with your feet slightly splayed outward, attempting to kick in a flat platform to support your heel for maximum efficiency. To start, face straight up the hill and splay your feet to the ten or eleven o'clock and one or two o'clock positions, crossing through each other as if you were ascending a staircase (fig. 5-7). As the snow gets steeper and/or firmer, slowly open your splay up so that it is comfortable and easy to walk with a flat foot. This technique is the most energy efficient and secure on slopes of around 15–40 degrees, depending on the snow-surface conditions.

Figure 5-6. Pied marche *doesn't require much in the way of specialized technique.*

PIED A PLAT

Once it gets too steep or too firm for duck-footed technique—between 30 and 55 degrees—consider a diagonal ascent (*pied à plat*; fig. 5-8). Like the duck walk's amount of "splay," the diagonal ascent works on a wide range of angles, depending on steepness. You can go straight up the hill, using a crossover technique, or you can take a gentler approach by moving forward and upward while zigzagging. As the snow gets steeper and/or firmer, roll your ankles to get as many crampon points into the snow as possible, letting your toes slowly swing downhill for steeper ascents, which, while less intuitive (as you are facing slightly downhill), is far more ergonomic and secure, while also being less fatiguing.

Figure 5-7. *The duck-footed technique, known as* pied en canard, *is the most energy efficient and secure on slopes of around 15–40 degrees, depending on the conditions of the snow at the surface.* (Photo by Dan Corn)

Figure 5-8. *Diagonal ascent (*pied a plat*):* **a,** *While it can be done at any angle, most people will start with their feet offset slightly.* **b,** *Cross the lower foot up and over your uphill leg, keeping your feet straddling the fall line for balance.* **c,** *Transfer your weight onto the newly uphill foot.* **d,** *Bring your newly downhill foot back to the uphill position and repeat the sequence, trending slightly forward with each step.*

TROISIÈME

The *troisième*, which means "three o'clock," as that is the position the climber's feet are in (twelve and three on a traditional clock face), is used on slopes of 35 to 70 degrees. For any dancers out there, *troisième* is third position in ballet. While *troisième* is commonly used by English-speaking climbers, it is also sometimes called "hybrid technique" because it is a combination of the diagonal-ascent and front-pointing techniques.

In this technique you point one foot forward to gain purchase and the other across the slope to help provide some sense of rest. One foot is across the fall line in a flat-footed position, with the other in a front-pointing position. To reduce fatigue on one leg, most

Figure 5-9. *In the hybrid technique, or* troisième, *you can trade off which foot is which as needed and as your legs and feet tire.*

Figure 5-10. *Front pointing is most effectively done with your heels dropping slightly below level. Do* not *stand on your toes with your heels elevated—it is an insecure and inefficient position.*

climbers will periodically switch off duties between each foot (fig. 5-9).

PIED TRAXION

Most commonly referred to as "front pointing," *pied traxion* is best for steeper, firmer snow on up to vertical ice, from 50 to 90 degrees. Front pointing involves standing on the front points of your crampons. To make front pointing more efficient, kick in relatively flat so that your front points, supported by your secondary points, take your weight. Avoid the temptation to stand on your toes, as this is not only more wasteful from an energy and efficiency-of-movement standpoint but also far less secure. Instead, a very slight drop in your heels lets your crampons bite in most efficiently (fig. 5-10).

Figure 5-11. *If you are sinking ankle deep or more in the snow, it's time to take your crampons off.*

CRAMPONS ON THE DESCENT IN SOFT CONDITIONS

Just because you're traveling on snow doesn't mean you have to wear crampons; in fact, once conditions are quite soft and the terrain relatively gentle, crampons present far more risk of hazard than help. If your crampons are consistently filling with snow or you're sinking ankle deep or farther, remove your crampons for more efficient travel (fig. 5-11). The risk comes when the crampons fill with soft, moist summer snow, which packs between the points until the teeth no longer bite, becoming "tippy feeling." This situation increases the likelihood you will fall, rip your pants, or—worse yet—puncture the opposing leg, which happens more frequently than you may suspect.

ICE-AXE TECHNIQUES

Ice-axe techniques entail everything from self-arrest and self-belay positions in glacier-travel mode to various ways to climb steep snow or vertical ice. This section also discusses how factors like terrain and conditions affect your choice of ice-axe technique.

SELF-BELAY VS. SELF-ARREST GRIP

It is essential to adapt and switch over to the ice-axe technique that best suits the conditions and terrain. There is intense debate about the pros and cons of the two ice-axe grips: self-belay (pick forward) and self-arrest (pick backward; fig. 5-12). While climbers on mellow glacier routes in Europe and South America almost exclusively use self-belay grips, the majority of climbers on moderate glacier routes in North America use the self-arrest grip. Each has its advantages, and both grips are useful, depending on the situation and terrain.

If there is any hazard of slipping and falling, use the self-belay grip, not only because it's easier to increase security with this grip by switching to a low dagger, but also because, for most slips, it is faster to self-arrest by driving the pick into the slope and not rolling into a full self-arrest position. For routes with essentially no slip-and-fall hazard but only the risk of hidden crevasse falls, use the self-arrest grip. Keep in mind that, while it isn't hard to self-arrest from a self-belay grip, it isn't as easy as with the self-arrest grip.

For steeper terrain (greater than 35–40 degrees), even proponents of self-arrest would agree that self-belay is far more appropriate. In this terrain, the goal is to keep from slipping down the mountain by low- and mid-daggering or by pushing the pick into the snow to stop a slip from becoming a fall,

Figure 5-12. *John Yarnall uses a self-arrest grip while climbing Mount Challenger in Washington's North Cascades.*

rather than attempting to self-arrest, during which the climber typically gains speed, potentially increasing the danger to themselves and their team, before they are able to roll into a self-arrest position.

Piolet Canne

The self-belay grip (*piolet canne*) is where the climber carries the axe from the head, with the pick pointing forward (fig. 5-13). This technique is standard for traveling on flat and gentle snow slopes where the ice axe is used primarily as a balance aid or walking stick. From this position, the climber can push down on the shaft more effectively because their palm is on the adze and can easily switch to mid-dagger should the terrain require it. Remember, it is still easy to self-arrest from the self-belay grip for general glacier travel, but it isn't as easy as with the self-belay grip.

Figure 5-13. *Self-belay grip (*piolet canne*) is best when you are ascending even moderately steep slopes because it offers increased security as you ascend. It can be used for gentle glacier travel, but climbers must be proficient with switching to a self-arrest grip as necessary, which requires practice.*

Self-Arrest Grip

The self-arrest grip is where the climber carries the axe from the head, with the pick pointing backward (fig. 5-14). There is no proper French name for this position since it is so seldom used. That said, it is the fastest position to self-arrest from and is thus preferred for gentle glacier climbs where the biggest hazard is an unforeseen fall into a hidden crevasse, a situation in which you'll need to self-arrest quickly to stop your teammate's plummet. On the flip side, the self-arrest grip is a poor and potentially dangerous position in steeper terrain, where the climber is primarily concerned with a slip-and-fall scenario, which they can quickly react to in the self-belay position.

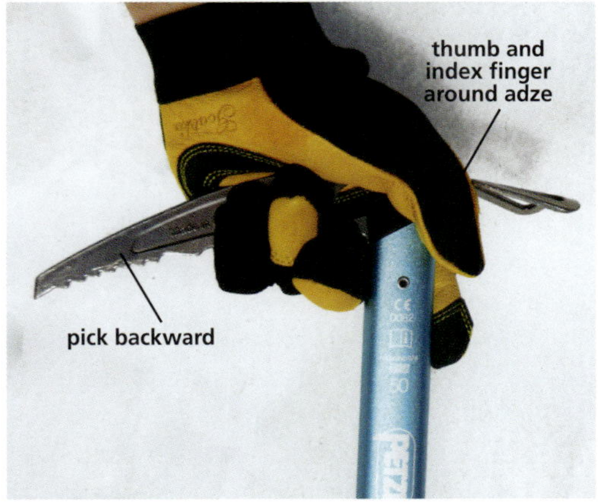

Figure 5-14. *The self-arrest grip is generally best for moderate glacier travel where the primary concern is a hidden crevasse fall. It is not as helpful as the self-belay grip in steeper terrain, which can reduce the likelihood of a small slip becoming an outright fall on steep terrain.*

At a minimum, self-arrest requires the sliding climber to rotate the axe from their side to their chest. In most circumstances, they'll need to roll off their buttocks to perform this maneuver, crucial seconds during which they will most certainly gain speed, putting themselves and their teammates at risk.

CHOPPING STEPS

This old-school technique has many new-school applications. Cutting steps was the primary way people climbed mountains for over a century before the advent of the modern crampon (or at least before crampons were improved). This is why many old ice axes are so long: Their main purpose was to cut steps, which needed to be done hundreds if not thousands of times on a given climb. Having a longer axe reduced the fatigue of this otherwise backbreaking effort.

Chopping steps is still a useful technique, as it can be an effective way to cross a short or firm section of moderately angled snow without having to stop to put on crampons (fig. 5-15). It can also be extremely effective for alpine rock routes where you know you need to cross a short section of snow but still want to pack light—without boots and/or crampons.

To chop steps:

1. From a diagonal-ascent position, hold the axe by its lower shaft and swing the adze into the surface of the snow. Aim to only graze and "shave down" the snow rather than remove most of it in one big hack.
2. Create two steps, with one lower and slightly behind the other.
3. Flip your ice axe into the self-belay or the low-dagger position.
4. Move both feet up into the new steps.
5. Repeat the process to create two more steps.

Figure 5-15. *Tagg Cole makes his way upward, two steps at a time. To efficiently chop steps, chop two steps, then move both your feet, stepping out of balance and then back into balance, then chop two more steps.*

Remember, aim to graze the surface, slicing just a bit at a time. While this approach seems slower than hacking deeply, it is just as fast (if not faster) and far more efficient because you'll often find you don't need to remove as much snow as you think to create a platform for your feet. Cutting two steps at a time allows you to use your axe in the dagger position to step up before flipping your axe into the self-belay or low-dagger position (see below).

Hand Positions for Climbing

Most terrain requires constant adaptation of techniques to maximize efficiency and security depending on how firm the snow surface is, the steepness, and the level of exposure.

***Figure 5-16.** Joshua Jarrin uses low dagger (*piolet panne*) technique in steep terrain near the summit of Cayambe in Ecuador. The axe shaft generally runs roughly parallel to the snow, with the pick driven in.* (Photo by Carla Perez)

***Figure 5-17.** Mid-dagger, or* piolet appui*, involves holding the shaft of the ice axe underneath the head and driving the pick into the snow, as Ian Nicholson does here on East Wilmans Spire, Washington.* (Photo by Dan Whitmore)

Thus it's no surprise there are various grip positions for climbing depending on the firmness of the snow and angle of the slope.

Piolet panne: The low dagger (fig. 5-16), or *piolet panne*, refers to ascending while holding the axe from the head or adze with the pick forward, and driving the pick into the snow with the shaft running roughly parallel to the snow's surface. This technique is good for moderately firm slopes from 35 to 55 degrees. While a little less secure than mid-dagger (below), it keeps you more upright and allows you to move more quickly—you can breathe better and take in more oxygen, as your torso is less "squished."

Piolet appui: Also called mid-dagger, for this grip the climber grabs the axe shaft just below its head and pushes the pick into the snow (figs. 5-17 and 5-18). The mid-dagger technique is a very fast, secure way to travel up or down slopes from 40 to 60 degrees. In lower-angle terrain, it makes breathing slightly more difficult than in a low-dagger position because you cannot stand upright, but it is more effective on firmer snow than other grips are.

Piolet poignard: Also called high dagger, this grip has fallen out of favor with the

Figure 5-18. Graham Zimmerman and author Ian Nicholson use piolet appui *technique to traverse below Riesenstein Spire in the Kichatnas in the Western Alaska Range.* (Photo by Ryan O'Connell)

advent of more aggressive picks and even general-purpose ice axes built with more curve, which make it easier to transition from mid-dagger to a full swing of the axe. While it is generally not used for sustained, steep slopes, the high dagger is still useful for neutrally curved picks (with no downturn whatsoever) or for short, steep steps where you are moving from steep to relatively flat and are essentially manteling, from a 40-to-60-degree slope into much lower-angle terrain. Mantling refers to reaching up and placing the axe above your head (most frequently the pick), and then working your feet up until they are nearly level with that placement.

To perform the *piolet poignard*, grab the head of the ice axe with most or all of your fingers wrapped around the pick, with the pick protruding near your pinkie, and then "stab" the pick into the snow (fig. 5-19). You can press the other hand into the snow for balance. Your feet will typically be in front-pointing or hybrid position, or maybe a very aggressive diagonal ascent with your toes pointed downward.

Piolet ancre: This high-dagger variation is also known as the *piolet ancre* (pronounced "onk"). Often, when people use the high-dagger technique, they use a mix of the traditional technique and this variation, which end up looking the same but have some subtle differences. To use this variation:

1. Place your feet generally in a *troisième* (hybrid technique) or, if needed, in a very aggressive diagonal ascent with your toes pointed downward. Swing the pick of the axe into the snow while hanging on to the shaft near the spike (fig. 5-20a).

Figure 5-19. *Grant Price demonstrates the high dagger, or* piolet poignard*, on Hell's Highway, Mount Shuksan, Washington.*

2. Use your free hand to grab the axe head (fig. 5-20b).
3. Maintain your grip on the shaft, and then move your feet upward (fig. 5-20c).

With modern tool design, climbers tend to use both *poignard* and *ancre* when navigating short but steep glacier features with traditional ice axes, such as when they climb into or out of a crevasse or moat, wind lip, or other wind feature in otherwise gentle terrain.

LEASHES IN GLACIATED TERRAIN

Leashes can be useful, but traditional wrist leashes have several drawbacks and are not an excuse to be more carefree with your axe. A common misconception is that you'll use your leash to keep your axe from getting away from you in the event of a fall. However, the reality is that you should *never* let go of your axe, and using a leash doesn't change that. If

Figure 5-20. *To use* piolet ancre*, follow these steps:* **a,** *While holding the lower portion of the shaft of your axe swing the pick of your ice axe into the snow.* **b,** *Use your free hand to grab the head of the ice axe.* **c,** *Move your feet up and stabilize yourself. Repeat.*

Figure 5-21. *While wrist leashes have declined in popularity for mountaineering routes in moderate latitudes, they still have a place in Arctic and Antarctic environments where big gloves or mittens and extreme cold make it more difficult to hang onto your axe—with the modification of an "umbilical cord" attaching the axe directly to the climbing harness. Here, the author uses a leash on the summit of Denali in –40°F.*

Figure 5-22. Piolet traxion, *or simply swinging your tool above your head, is the most effective and secure way to ascend sustained, firm slopes of around 60–90 degrees on compacted snow and ice. Here, Peter Webb swings into steep ice on the crux pitch of the North Ridge of Mount Baker in Washington's North Cascades.*

your partner falls down a steep slope or into a hidden crevasse, and you lose your axe and start careering down the slope too, your odds of recovering your axe are slim—even with the leash—while the odds of disaster for you and your rope team are high.

Another disadvantage is that climbers must switch the leash to their uphill wrist with each switchback, something every member of the rope team needs to do, resulting in a lot of waiting and wasted time. As a result, most climbers in more modest temperatures where they don't need huge gloves or mitts don't use leashes. Thick gloves and extremely warm mitts dramatically reduce your ability to both feel and maintain your grip on your axe, but even in areas where you need this level of hand protection, wrist leashes are rare.

During glacier travel in extremely cold temperatures, be it in the Alaska Range, the Antarctic, or the higher peaks of the Himalaya, you may use an "umbilical-cord" leash, which consists of a springy piece of webbing that attaches the axe directly to your climbing harness (fig. 5-21). This setup lets you change

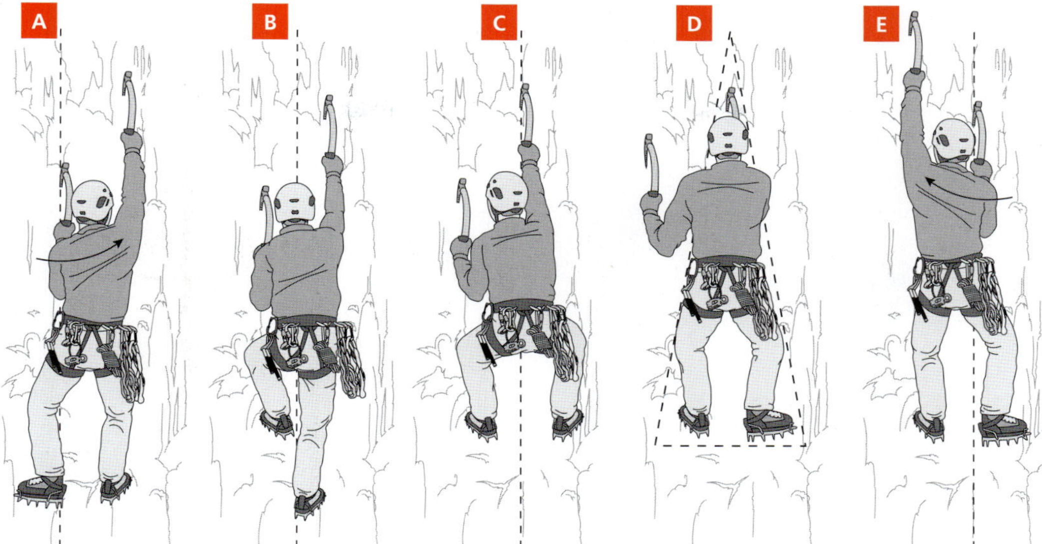

Figure 5-23. *The concept underlying the ice-climbing triangle is that it's most efficient to swing your tool beneath your shoulders, place it, move your feet up, and then swing past it with the other tool. The advanced progression shown here follows these steps:* **a**, *Swing one tool into the ice overhead.* **b**, *Move one foot up.* **c**, *Move other foot up so you are centered under the higher tool.* **d**, *Stand up "in the triangle."* **e**, *Remove the other tool and place it overhead with the other hand to begin the sequence again. Dashed lines indicate center of gravity. Arrows indicate direction that center of gravity shifts to be in line with upper tool.*

hands without having to switch the leash over to the uphill wrist.

TIP: In steeper, more exposed terrain, moving in balance is a very effective way to increase security. Focus on moving only one of your three points of contact at a time. This means very deliberately moving just your axe, and then one foot, and then your second foot, before you start the process again.

ICE CLIMBING

This book does not cover vertical ice climbing in depth, as there are several good resources that already do, including Will Gadd's *Ice & Mixed Climbing: Improve Technique, Safety, and Performance*. However, understanding a few basics about the concept can go a long way. *Piolet traxion*, or simply swinging your tool above your head (fig. 5-22), is the most secure and effective way to ascend steep, frozen waterfalls and sustained alpine ice and compacted snow from 60 to 90 degrees to overhanging.

THE ICE-CLIMBING TRIANGLE

In the ice-climbing triangle, your feet are slightly wider than shoulder width, while your tools are swung overhead and between your shoulders. The "triangle" is formed by your

THE POWER OF THE UPWARD-ANGLING KICK

It is a common yet subtle misconception that one key to ice-climbing footwork is to "drop your heels," a rule of thumb that fails to describe proper technique. First, ice climbers should avoid "climbing on their tiptoes," which creates far more strain on the calves and provides the least amount of security because front points tend to wobble.

Second, while dropping your heels once your front points are seated is better than climbing on your tiptoes, it is best to kick into the ice at a slightly upward angle, seating your front points just past the apex of your leg swing so your foot ascends slightly into the ice. Standing on the points as they were driven in not only provides the most efficient stance but also is generally the most stable and secure position.

two feet and one anchored ice tool. This technique not only helps you save energy but also facilitates a very well-balanced position and *far* more accuracy while swinging—it's quite difficult to be accurate and efficient with your placements when swinging outside the width of your shoulders.

USING THE TRIANGLE TO TRACK

"Tracking" refers to the act of repeatedly using the ice-climbing triangle to make upward progress. To track:

1. Swing a tool to a suitable location between your shoulders, with your arm fairly outstretched. Once you get a solid placement, immediately relax your grip, as the strength needed to "hang on" is much less than to swing (fig. 5-23a).
2. Paddle your feet upward until you are in a quasi-crouched position, with your knees bent close to 90 degrees. You will naturally "center" on your tool, which also creates the greatest balance (fig. 5-23b and c).
3. Visually scan for your next placement.
4. In one motion, stand upright and push down into your feet (fig. 5-23d).
5. Start back at step 1, swinging the next tool somewhere between your shoulders, with your arm fairly outstretched (fig. 5-23e). Repeat the other steps.

DESCENDING TECHNIQUES

It's just as important to be able to efficiently and securely descend snow slopes with a variety of surface conditions and slope angles as it is to ascend them. Similar to ascending, being proficient at multiple techniques and being able to select the right technique for the terrain and surface conditions will vastly increase speed and security.

PLUNGE-STEPPING

Plunge-stepping is the most common technique for softer snow on slope angles ranging from 10 to 40 degrees (fig. 5-24). It can be done with or without crampons, depending on the slope angle and snow firmness. While some people can occasionally get away with plunge-stepping down terrain even steeper than 40 degrees, most mountaineers will find it faster and more secure to face inward.

The key to plunge-stepping is to not swing the heel back into the snow but instead to plunge downward, compacting the snow under your heel and reinforcing your step. Many climbers swing their foot backward, essentially "cutting" themselves a foothold, but all the compaction happens behind the foot rather than under it, creating a downward-angled step you're much likelier to slip out of.

Figure 5-24. *Rebecca Schroeder plunge steps down Hidden Bowl after climbing Poster Peak near Washington Pass.*

However, if the snow is too firm to plunge-step, you will need to walk downhill in crampons, called *face-out cramponing*. Most people can face outward efficiently to 30 degrees and, with experience and solid cramponing skills, can even descend slopes up to the mid-40-degree range.

PIED EN CANARD

If the angle is under 15–20 degrees, most people can just walk normally; however, as the angle starts to steepen, you may want to employ the duck-footed technique (*pied en canard);* see the discussion on ascending in Basic Footwork Techniques, above). Splay your feet outward like a duck, lower your center of gravity, bend your knees, and feel your secondary crampon points engaging, as they are doing most of the work (fig. 5-25).

Figure 5-25. *Walking downhill using* pied en canard, *as Dale Remsberg does here, is an efficient and effective way to descend slopes from 0 to 35 degrees. Keep your ankles flexed so that all your downward-facing crampon points are engaged.*

CRAB-WALKING

Crab-walking is a good technique for lower- to mid-angled slopes that might be too steep for the duck-footed technique (greater than 35 degrees); however, unlike diagonal ascent, you do *not* cross your feet over each other, despite the similar stance (fig. 5-26). Instead, the downhill foot makes the initial progress and loses vertical distance when you step down, while the uphill foot then matches it as you bring your feet together. You can crab-walk in most of the lower-angle ice-axe positions.

PIOLET ANCRE AND RAMASSE

Before the advent of front points, *piolet ancre* ("pick in snow") and *piolet ramasse* ("spike in

Figure 5-26. *Depending on how firm the snow is, it can be easier and more secure to walk down like a crab, with your feet across the slope. Despite the foot position, you don't cross your feet over each other as you descend.*

Figure 5-27. Piolet ancre *and* ramasse *still have a useful place for descending longer, firmer slopes between 30-40 degrees where down climbing isn't as practical, is slower, or is unnecessarily tiring. Here, Chris Marshall places the pick in the ice and holds his ice axe in a cross-body position (*piolet ancre*) to descend such a slope.*

snow") were among the classic snow skills for descending. While they are no longer widely used, they do still have advantages in firmer conditions, in terrain that is "in between": for slopes generally in the 30-to-40-degree range, depending on surface conditions, that feel too insecure for face-out cramponing and too low angle for face-in downclimbing (see below).

It is rare that a climber exclusively uses only *ancre* or *ramasse*, and it is often best to switch between them depending on the slope. With either of these techniques, keep your center of gravity low and forward by bending your knees and keeping "your nose over your toes."

For *piolet ancre*, hold the axe across your body with one hand on the head in the pick-forward position and the other clasped near the spike (fig. 5-27). Drive the pick into the snow to aid balance and help keep your weight forward. While your inaugural steps may feel awkward, you will quickly see why this technique was so heavily used in the 1800s and early 1900s—it allows a competent climber to descend that in-between steepness quickly and securely.

Piolet ramasse is nearly identical to *piolet ancre*: Keep your knees bent, with a low center of gravity, and one hand on the axe head in the pick-forward position, with the other clasped near the spike. This time, however, drive the spike (not the pick) into the snow to aid balance and help keep your weight forward. Don't be afraid to switch back and forth between *ancre* and *ramasse*, depending on whatever feels more secure and comfortable.

FACE-IN DOWNCLIMBING

Face-in downclimbing can be a fast and secure way to descend slopes from around 40 to 60 degrees, depending on your skill level and the snow-surface conditions. While face-in downclimbing comes naturally to most people, and is more comfortable, there are a few things you can do to improve efficiency that can greatly increase your speed.

First, if the terrain feels remotely challenging for you, alternate between moving your axe and your two feet so that you always have "secure" contact with the snow—be deliberate about each movement (fig. 5-28) rather than just constantly moving until the terrain eases. Second, if you have two ice axes or tools in your hands, offset their placement so you don't waste time and energy placing them side by side. Third, if the snow is soft, drive your feet downward to compact it. Finally, in firmer conditions, identify the most secure and efficient technique—is the slope steep enough that you need to downclimb with your front points facing in, or need to use *troisieme* with one foot across the slope and one kicking straight in (fig. 5-29).

GLISSADING

Glissading—sliding down the snow, whether sitting, crouching, or standing—can be a very efficient and fun way to descend a mountain, but it does require caution. You'll want to first assess the terrain: does it end with a poor runout or are there other potential

Figure 5-28. *If the terrain you wish to descend is steep, exposed, or firm, strongly consider belaying each other. This practice is applicable for both the first climber down and the second. While the second climber might have little or no protection in taking a large lead, a fall while being belayed is nearly always significantly better than a fall while soloing without being attached to the mountain. Not only does belaying each person down drastically increase the safety of both party members, but it often takes a similar amount of time since you move a lot faster when you are on belay than when you are free soloing and risking a nasty fall.*

Figure 5-29. *When downclimbing, it can be a good idea, particularly if the slope is exposed, to slowly and carefully move only one point of contact at a time, as Sarah Janin does here on Mount Shuksan, Washington.*

hazards—crevasses, rocks, other climbers—you might hit if you lose control?

Sitting Glissade

To do a proper sitting glissade—probably the middling safest of the three glissade options, and perhaps the one most commonly used—sit on your butt with your body in an "L" position. Hold your axe in the self-arrest position, with the shaft across your body. To control speed, drag the spike and dig your heels in, keeping your legs on the wide side for stability; if you get out of control, you can always roll over and self-arrest (fig. 5-30). That said, your best defense is not to go too fast in the first place, consistently going slow rather than

Figure 5-30. *A sitting glissade, as Bryce Hill demonstrates, is not only efficient, it's also fun!*

trying to regain control by dumping a bunch of speed, which can be difficult in firmer snow or heavily traveled glissading chutes. Note that it's also hard to travel very far in a sitting glissade without getting wet—and if the conditions are firm, the friction can quickly wear a hole in the seat of your pants.

Crouching Glissade

The crouching glissade is the slowest and safest of the three techniques. From a standing position, simply lean back and use the spike of the axe as if it were a "rudder"—though it's more of a slow brake, as the axe doesn't really assist in turning.

To initiate speed, tip your feet downward; slow yourself by driving in your heels. Most people will find the crouching glissade takes more physical effort than the other two techniques but provides much greater control over speed, letting you slide with greater stability—and with less danger of ripping your pants. It's a good option for shorter, steeper, or firmer sections of terrain, where the sitting glissade feels too fast and standing too committing.

A FORESEEABLE SLIP-AND-FALL

BY EMILIE DRINKWATER

Being in an out-of-control plummet down a snow slope is a position you do not want to find yourself in—ever. Falling is my least favorite part of climbing. I like to think that my self-preservation instincts are responsible, but mostly I find falls terrifying. I can tolerate popping off a steep sport route or well-protected trad climb. On ice, snow, or a remote alpine climb, falling can easily result in injury or death.

Back to that out-of-control plummet. That day had started like any other—me trying to keep up with my strong, fast expert climber and guide friends on Mount Olympus, above Salt Lake City. We'd all done this route many times. Our plan was to solo it before the crowds arrived. The night before, I'd taken a hard look at my gear and decided to make everything lighter. I brought minimal water, no snacks, my lightest wind shell, an ultralight ski-mountaineering piolet, and I removed the antiballing plates from my crampons.

After a short approach on dry trail, we encountered a cold, shaded gully surrounded by rock walls, where we transitioned to crampons. Cramponing in the icy, firm snow was easy and fast. We reached the rock portion and transitioned into approach shoes. Off we went up 1,600 feet of low fifth-class climbing. After topping out, we made our way down the descent trail before rejoining the snow slope and switching back to crampons. The warming sun and increasing temperatures had softened the top four to five centimeters, making the surface greasy. The sticky snow immediately balled up in my crampons, and with every downward step, I had to whack my boots with my piolet. Soon I became lazy and embraced the ski-like feel of snowballs on my feet, allowing myself a bit of boot glissading. At one point, I found an antiballing plate, trash that I begrudgingly opted to carry out.

And then, just like that, I fell. Before I knew it, I was rocketing past my friends and toward the many dangers below: moats, undercut sidewalls, rocks and likely throngs of other climbers on their way up. *Self-arrest, roll over, stop yourself, you know how to do this!* But I couldn't and just kept sliding faster and faster. Out of the corner of my eye, I saw my last option before the slope rolled over and the moats gaped wide, and willed myself toward a muddy rock wall with outstretched legs, fully accepting that I would probably break both femurs.

Miraculously, I crumpled into rock wall and then jumped up and looked around, and called out, "I'm fine, I'm fine!" while laughing nervously. After brushing myself off, I realized that I was still clutching the antiballing plate. Interestingly, I have since learned of this clenched-hands phenomenon, in which the brain can't process what needs to be let go of during an unexpected and stressful situation. In the end, I walked away with only a gigantic bruise on my thigh, a small crampon puncture to my calf, and a newfound respect for snow slopes.

KEY TAKEAWAYS: Skilled footwork trumps self-arrest as a first line of defense. Practice with your crampons on different surfaces and in different scenarios. If there's any chance you could slip, note which hand is on your ice axe and visualize how you'd grab it with your free hand—and don't carry anything in your free hand! Lightweight gear is just that: ultralight, designed for light-duty use or as "just-in-case" tools.

Emilie Drinkwater is a world-renowned alpinist, IFMGA mountain guide, and AMGA national instructor team member based in Salt Lake City, Utah.

Figure 5-31. *Mike O'Connor performs a standing glissade.*

Standing Glissade

The standing glissade is also commonly referred to as "boot skiing." It's fast, you can more easily see where you are going, and it prevents the seat of your pants from becoming wet or damaged. To initiate, as with the crouching glissade, tip your toes downhill; to slow down, press your heels into the snow (fig. 5-31). You can even turn using snowplow-style turns, as if you were skiing. On slopes with little consequence, standing glissades work wonderfully; however, even the most skilled "boot skiers" still fall regularly and often unexpectedly, meaning this technique should not be used in consequential terrain where, for example, there is a poor runout, drop-offs, or collision hazards.

Figure 5-32. *All these techniques have a time and place to which they are well suited, and no single one is universally the best. A skilled climber is adaptable and adjusts their technique to best fit the terrain and the conditions they face. Here, Jim Mediatore prepared for steep snow but is ready to switch to self-arrest while crossing the Boston Glacier, Washington.*

SELF-ARREST

Self-arrest, the process of stopping yourself while sliding down snow, could be considered the "seatbelt" of the alpinist's tool kit (fig. 5-32). If one or more team members need to self-arrest, it is generally because mistakes were made. In other words, it's a safety measure of last resort, and your team should always take precautions to avoid it in the first place, such as belaying across a suspected snowbridge, making the entire group travel in low-dagger mode across moderately steep snow so that their picks are always in the snow except while moving them, and traveling in balance.

Switching Your Grip on an Ice Axe

You should now be familiar with two different ice-axe hand positions: self-arrest, in which you hold the pick backward, pointing toward your pinkie finger; and self-belay, in which you hold the pick forward, pointing toward your thumb. Regardless of which you use, to stop a slide, you need to end up in the self-arrest position. Fortunately, if you happen to be using a self-belay hand position, switching to self-arrest takes only a millisecond. It can feel a little strange the first couple times you do it, but it becomes second nature quite quickly and is part of the "standard" way to learn self-arrest (fig. 5-33).

Figure 5-33. *Self-arresting is the process of stopping yourself while sliding down snow.*

To switch grips:

1. As you're sliding, first gain control of both sharp ends of the axe; nearly always, you must use your hand to grab the shaft near the spike.
2. Rotate your wrist to ensure the pick points slightly away from your face, with your thumb on top, to reduce your chance of getting stabbed.
3. Using the hand that is on the lower part of the shaft, quickly release your grip on the head of the axe without losing contact, and then rotate the axe so the pick faces outward, with your hand in a position so that your thumb is closest to your body. The pick should end up near your pinkie and the adze near your thumb as the pick becomes embedded in the snow.

No matter what grip position you start in, if you fall, it is crucial that you have the skills to self-arrest as quickly as possible, while avoiding injury from the ice axe (fig. 5-34).

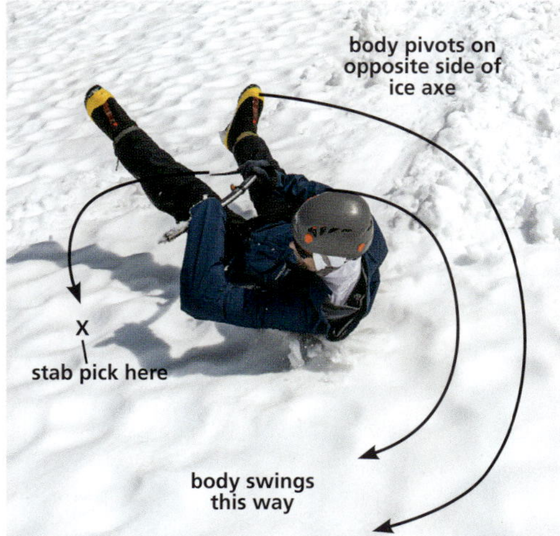

Figure 5-34. *Practice self-arresting until you are confident you can do it in any situation.* (Photo by Bryce Hill)

Figure 5-35. *Self-arrest technique when falling feetfirst on your back:* **a**, *falling;* **b**, *rolling toward the ice-axe head;* **c**, *rolling facedown onto your stomach to complete the self-arrest.*

Feetfirst on Your Back

While this isn't necessarily the most common way you'll fall, it is the foundational form of self-arrest off which the others build and must become instinctual (fig. 5-35):

1. From a sliding position on your back, bend your arm at the elbow so that your ice axe comes across your body. Grab and secure the shaft with your free hand, while your other hand holds the head in the self-arrest position.
2. Roll toward the pick side—rolling so that the pick has to cross your body can cause the spike to catch, making self-arrest more difficult in steeper terrain.
3. As the pick digs into the snow, lock the shaft against your body where it crosses your upper chest. This is the strongest position for holding the ice axe. Avoid letting the force extend your arms above your head, where you don't have as much holding power.
4. As the pick digs into the snow, kick in your feet (unless you have crampons on and conditions are firm; see The Dangers of Self-Arresting in Firm Snow, below). In softer conditions, most of your stopping power comes from your feet, not your ice axe, so kick your feet into the snow aggressively.
5. Tense your body so that no part of your stomach, waist, and thighs contacts the snow; this maximizes your holding power. Your body should be suspended on three points: your ice axe and your two feet.
6. Look down toward the axe spike not its head. In firmer snow conditions, the head will bounce as it embeds in the snow, almost like the needle in a sewing machine—you do not want to catch a rebounding adze in the face.

Headfirst on Your Back

The next self-arrest position to become proficient with is headfirst on your back. This technique is far more consequential than feetfirst, so select a practice zone with a safe, gentle runout. To perform this technique (fig. 5-36):

1. From a sliding position on your back, headfirst downhill, gain control of your sharp bits: Outstretch the hand holding the head of the ice axe at nearly full extension, and grab hold of the lower part of the shaft near the spike to ensure that your axe does not injure you.
2. Next, engage your core and do a slight "sit-up."
3. Once your torso is elevated in your sit-up, drive the pick down into the snow. This should cause your body to pivot around the axe, reorienting you into a face-down, head-uphill position.
4. As you slow, bring the head of the axe toward your shoulder, similar to the feetfirst self-arrest technique, and finish by looking down at the ice axe to protect your face from the adze. Keep your torso and thighs elevated, and use the pick and your feet as the primary contact points with the snow.

Headfirst on Your Stomach

Arresting a slide headfirst on your stomach (the "Pete Rose" arrest technique, for Rose's talent at sliding headfirst into bases during baseball games) isn't as technically complicated as headfirst on your back. Still, it can result in more injuries if performed incorrectly; therefore, it is strongly recommended

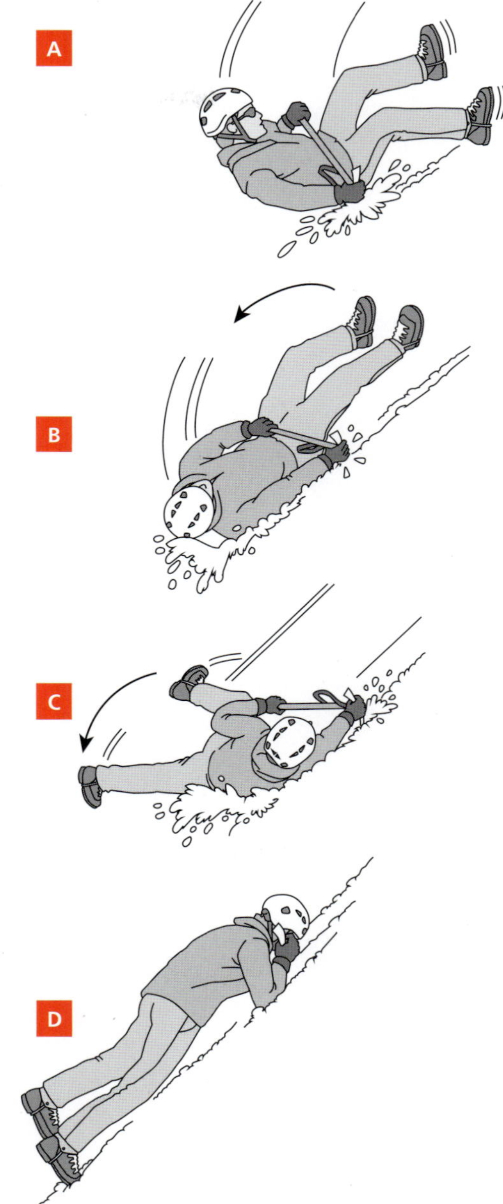

Figure 5-36. *Self-arrest technique when falling head downhill on your back:* **a,** *Plant the pick near your hip.* **b,** *Swing your legs downhill.* **c,** *Twist and roll your chest onto the shaft.* **d,** *Swing your legs downhill and press your chest and shoulder onto the ice-axe shaft while slightly lifting the spike end.*

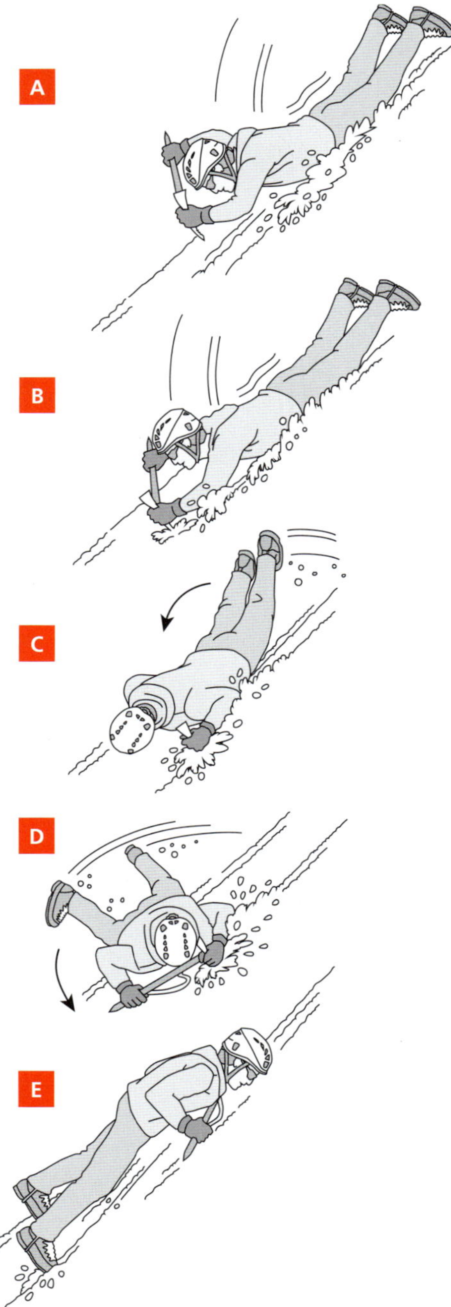

that you become proficient with the previous two self-arrest techniques before attempting this (fig. 5-37):

1. Start by sliding downhill on your stomach, headfirst.
2. Gain control of your sharp bits: Outstretch the arm holding the head of the ice axe, and pivot the lower end of the axe off the snow to grab the lower shaft with your other hand, protecting yourself from the spike.
3. Stab the pick into the snow with your outstretched arm. This will cause your body to pivot around the axe into the more desired head-uphill, face-down position. If you stab the ice axe into the snow with the axe-holding arm bent instead of outstretched, you run the risk of your face, stomach, or other body parts sliding right over the axe, which can result in injuries.
4. As you slow, bring the head of the axe toward your shoulder as with the previous self-arrest techniques and finish by looking down at the ice axe to protect your face from the adze. Keep your torso and thighs elevated, and use the pick and your feet as the primary contact points with the snow.

Self-Arresting Without an Ice Axe

It is essential you know how to self-arrest without an ice axe; there's a very real chance you may one day fall and drop your axe—or perhaps you have underestimated the terrain

Figure 5-37. *Self-arrest technique when falling head downhill, facefirst:* **a,** *Reach downhill and to the same side as the ice axe's head.* **b,** *Plant pick into snow.* **c,** *Pivot body around pick.* **d,** *Swing legs downhill.* **e,** *Press chest and shoulder onto the ice-axe shaft, while slightly lifting the spike end, to complete the self-arrest.*

THE DANGERS OF SELF-ARRESTING IN FIRM SNOW

Attempting to self-arrest in very firm conditions can be less successful than in softer snow, so you should take pains to first reduce the likelihood of falling by using the appropriate snow-travel techniques and positions, and/or by using running belays or more traditional belays to protect the party.

Additionally, be wary of your crampons when trying to self-arrest in firm snow—you risk catching the points unexpectedly, creating a very real chance of a serious ankle injury or being "tossed" into an even less desirable position.

The solution on firm snow is to wait until you've righted yourself into a head-uphill, face and stomach-down position and have slowed significantly, which greatly reduces the likelihood of unexpectedly catching a crampon and injuring yourself and/or making the fall worse. This technique should be used with caution, because in softer conditions the pick of your ice axe will not be enough to slow you or your group down in the event of a fall where you don't also have the braking action of your feet.

and left the axe on your pack—but still need to self-arrest.

The goal is to kick your feet in and end up with your hands overlapping, palms down, with your arms making an upside-down U shape. As you would with an ice axe, the most effective position is having your hands around chin level, and it remains imperative that you get your stomach and thighs off the snow. If sliding upside-down and headfirst, you will still need to actively do a sit-up to allow your legs to turn around and reorient yourself with your head uphill, but this takes significantly more core strength than it would with an ice axe.

No Ice Axe? Try a Rock!

If for some reason you don't have an ice axe, look for a rock to take its place. For example, if you need to reach an alpine rock climb that is still guarded by snow or cross a short stretch of steeper snow on your way to a glacier, a nice, pointy rock can work well, at least for relatively short sections (fig. 5-38). An "ice axe"-shaped rock can be tough to come by, so instead look for a triangle-shaped rock, grasp one of the flat edges in your palm, and drive

Figure 5-38. *Using a rock to traverse a steep slope on the west side of the Twin Sisters Range* (Photo by Aaron Hartz)

the point into the snow. This shape is also nice for digging out steps if you don't have crampons.

It is important to choose the right technique at the right time. Most people can walk confidently on snow, but during long days or on steep and/or exposed slopes, don't underestimate how efficient it can be to use the technique best suited for the terrain and conditions. Being familiar with a wide variety of techniques and being able to apply them correctly will minimize your risk and allow you to move efficiently in the mountains.

Opposite: *Mike Pond leaps over a crevasse on the Inspiration Glacier in Washington's North Cascades National Park.*

CHAPTER 6

Rigging the Rope and Travel Techniques

Knowing the highly technical skills of crevasse rescue and improvised ascension is as important as learning the "basics"—knowing how to rig the rope for glacier travel, adjust it based on the number of climbers and the terrain, and move across the glacier as a group. Mastering these foundational skills sets you and your group up for success by helping you avoid crevasses, minimize the distance someone could drop should they fall in, and set up to catch any fall successfully.

RIGGING THE ROPE

The set distance between climbers on the rope depends on the number of people on the rope team rather than other factors such as rope length (assuming that it's sufficient for the number of travelers) or the region in which you are traveling. A common misconception is that the distance between team members should be twice as far as the widest covered crevasse—one with a snowbridge across it (fig. 6-1). While that sounds like a good rule of thumb, climbers are often wildly inaccurate when trying to gauge this distance—or most others in the mountains, for that matter. It is better to rig the rope so that the odds of a climber dragging another member into the crevasse are extremely low to nonexistent. What follows are some tried-and-true methods to set you and your group up for success.

SPACING AND THE RULE OF 10

The rule of 10 provides a good framework to figure out how far away travelers should be from each other, depending on the number of climbers on the rope. In this formula, you subtract the number of climbers from 10 to find the number of arm spans (roughly 5 feet) on the rope you should be traveling apart. For example, two climbers should be traveling roughly eight arm spans (or approximately 40 feet) apart because 10 – 2 = 8. Three climbers should be seven arm spans, or 35 feet, apart (10 – 3 = 7), and so on. Margins are slimmer with only two climbers than with three.

TABLE 6-1. THE RULE OF 10

Climbers	Arm Spans Apart
2	8 (approx. 40 ft.)
3	7 (approx. 35 ft.)
4	6 (approx. 30 ft.)
5	5 (approx. 25 ft.)

Note: Add two more arm spans to accommodate for knots with 2–3 climbers and one extra arm span with 4–5 climbers.

Figure 6-1. *You never quite know what lurks below: Jake Skeen on an exciting snowbridge on the Quien Sabe Glacier, North Cascades, Washington.*

The rule of 10 assumes that each length of rope is measured roughly fist to fist across, with your arms fully extended in a T, usually equating to roughly 5 feet, as stated above. Taller climbers should not extend their arms all the way, while shorter climbers might add a little extra length (fig. 6-2). Do these "pulls" fist to fist rather than fingertips to fingertips, which is generally closer to a person's height. The goal is to get "close" to 5 feet per pull, ultimately achieving the values in table 6-1, rather than being exact (fig. 6-3).

KNOTS IN THE ROPE

Tying knots between the climbers—commonly called stopper knots though also occasionally referred to as brake knots—is a well-studied and effective tactic for assisting the arresting climber(s) in catching a crevasse fall, as they jam into the lip of the crevasse (fig. 6-4). L'ENSA (École Nationale de Ski et d'Alpinisme, or the French National Ski and Mountaineering School) has extensively studied knots in a variety of conditions and situations. They found that stopper-knot efficacy varies with

YOU RARELY SEE THE CREVASSES YOU FALL IN

BY KYLE HORNER

In early August 2022, I spent five days in the Colonial Glacier Basin in North Cascades National Park, Washington, with two guests, Dan and Joe, for an intermediate alpine-mountaineering course. The first day was a classic Cascades approach involving 5,000 feet of vertical gain with overnight packs to reach camp at the lake at the toe of the Colonial Glacier.

The next morning, we got right into crevasse rescue instruction. We started at the toe of the glacier on what I assumed was seasonal snow left over from the previous winter. In the second half of the day, armed with new knowledge of snow anchors and mechanical advantage, we went up the glacier toward the only visible crevasse. Up close, we discovered it was about 15 feet deep, did not have overhanging snow, and had less-than-vertical walls—perfect for a few rounds of realistic crevasse-rescue practice.

The third day we woke up early, crossed the Colonial Glacier, roped up, and then continued over to the Neve Glacier and up Snowfield Peak. A number of other parties were on the route as well, many of which chose not to rope up on the Colonial Glacier. It was a great day.

On our last day of climbing, the three of us climbed Colonial Peak. We roped up for the snow on the ascent using standard spacing for glacier travel. After summiting and then descending, we faced just a few hundred feet of low-angle snow before we would reach the terminal moraine, where we'd take our crampons off and walk back to camp. Given that we had explored the glacier thoroughly over the last few days while roped, and given that the glacier seemed quite benign, my team unroped for this last section. We could hear water running underneath the snow, but it seemed well covered, and we only had to cross where we imagined the flow was one time.

Not ten feet from what appeared to be solid ground where the snow met the moraine, I heard a yell from behind me. I turned to look and saw that where there had been two people, now there was only one: Dan

Just because you can't see crevasses doesn't mean they aren't there. The arrow indicates the seemingly benign spot where this particular incident happened. (Photo by Kyle Horner)

had had a trapdoor-style fall in which the snow gave way below his feet. Before he even knew what had happened, he'd fallen into a hidden crevasse beneath the seasonal winter snowpack.

I quickly got the rope out and attached myself and Joe in glacier-travel mode in case I fell in while attempting a rescue. At this point, Dan also hollered up that he was all right.

After I probed around the lip of the hole with my ice axe and cleared away overhanging snow, I was able to look inside. Dan was about 10 feet down, up to his knees in snow on a sloping ledge. The crack continued down under the glacier, however, and the clear sound of running water echoed from the bottom. We then got to work: we padded the lip of the crevasse with an ice axe, Joe built a snow anchor and dropped down a loop of rope to Dan, and then we pulled Dan out with a 2:1 edge haul (see Chapter 9, Mechanical Advantage).

Dan turned out to be uninjured and in surprisingly good spirits, so we quickly made our way back to camp and cooked our last dinner before our hike out the following morning. Events like this one are what I call "free lessons," and I am grateful it was only a close call.

Looking down into the crevasse where Dan fell, as we pulled him out (Photo by Kyle Horner)

KEY TAKEAWAYS: Every glacier has the potential for hidden crevasses and caverns beneath its seasonal blanket of snow, and an unroped fall into even a small crevasse can have deadly consequences. The surface of the snow might not give you any clues to crevasses or caverns hollowed out by water, as water running under the snow is a mechanism to create dangerous hidden caverns—if you hear running water, avoid walking over that area!

Kyle Horner is an AMGA and IFMGA mountain guide who pursues experiences in the mountains despite the risks, not because of them. Being able to facilitate experiences for people to explore the natural world at its wildest so that they return to their everyday lives with a fresh perspective and having learned vital lessons is what motivates Kyle to get out of the tent at 3 a.m.

Figure 6-2. *While the length of people's arms vary, using arm spans to estimate the distance between people on the rope is a quick and efficient way to find the desired spacing. One arm span for the average adult is roughly 5 to 6 feet.*

Figure 6-3. *Determine the distance between climbers based on the number of climbers on the rope. Here, Caroline George, Ben Croft, and Adam George cross below the Glacier du Géant in the Mont Blanc massif, France, with around 40 feet, about 8 arm spans, between them.* (Photo by Jon Griffith)

the conditions of the snow on the surface, but that knots always helped. Knots proved most effective in warmer, softer conditions, which are most commonly associated with "trapdoor" crevasse falls (see the "You Rarely See the Crevasses You Fall In" sidebar).

The primary downside of stopper knots is that it's significantly more difficult to perform a direct-line haul and they complicate self-rescue for the fallen climber (fig. 6-5). Despite these slight disadvantages, the enormous benefits of stopper knots and their ability to assist or completely catch a fall make them worth it. In one look at several real-world crevasse falls compiled from Denali and Mount Rainier, assessments indicated

Figure 6-4. *While they are not a sure bet, stopper knots significantly increases a rope team's odds of arresting a crevasse fall. Tie stopper knots roughly 3 meters (9–10 feet) from each person on a rope team and then in 2-meter (6–7 feet) intervals beyond that.*

Figure 6-5. *In the warmer, softer conditions in which climbers are most likely to trapdoor into a hidden crevasse, stopper knots help the climbers on the surface catch the fall.* (Photo by Bryce Hill)

that less than 20 percent of people could self-rescue if they fell into a hidden crevasse (i.e., they fell through a trapdoor and then were able to ascend the rope), with the rest needing to be hauled out by their partners or other parties still on the surface. Based on this assessment, stopper knots were not an obstacle to rescue more than 80 percent of the time.

WHERE TO TIE STOPPER KNOTS

The L'ENSA studies on the effectiveness of knots and their placement determined that the first knot should be 3 meters (approximately 9 feet) from the climber, with two or more knots tied 2 meters (approximately 6 feet) from each other after that (fig. 6-6). When knots were tied closer than 3 meters, they caught less frequently because they would often slip past the lip of the crevasse before the rope came taut—this rope tension being what causes the knots to auger in.

Knots in the middle of the rope can also be effective, but the L'ENSA studies found that if those first three knots didn't catch, there was some other mitigating factor, like the shape of the lip or the snow surface being extremely firm or extremely soft; in cases like these, more knots were rarely the solution. Also, having eight to ten knots in your rope makes it "feel" heavy, and they tend to hang up regularly, which is annoying and encourages more slack in the system, increasing both the fall length and force generated.

Keep in mind that, depending on a person's height, each knot takes around half an arm's length of rope to tie. Since most folks will tie around four to six knots between two members of a rope team, two to three additional arm spans of rope may be required to create enough slack for knots while still maintaining an appropriate distance between climbers.

TYPES OF STOPPER KNOTS

As with studying how widely to space the knots, a tremendous amount of effort has also gone into studying different knots and their effectiveness in varying snow conditions.

The alpine butterfly is the stopper knot most climbers use in glacier travel (fig. 6-7). It strikes a nice balance of stopping power versus ease of tying and the amount of rope required. The alpine butterfly offers reliable stopping power but is less annoying while you walk if the glacial surface is textured. On the warmest

KNOTS IN THE ROPE: NO REASON NOT TO

BY JOSHUA JARRIN

In July 2022, I guided longtime clients Geoff and Doug on the standard route of Pollux in the Alps. We started in Zermatt, Switzerland, taking the first lift to Klein Matterhorn, where we met two friends: Carla Perez, an aspiring guide from Ecuador, and Charlotte Solans, a French recreational alpinist with the same objective.

We traversed the glacier as two rope teams, staying relatively close to each other, and reached the summit in clear skies with stunning views of the Monte Rosa massif and surrounding peaks. By the time we started to descend, the sun had significantly softened the snow, and Carla suggested joining rope teams for the return. I hesitated—more people on a rope often slows the pace, but it also increases holding power in the event of a fall—but ultimately, I agreed. We extended our rope team with Carla's second rope, maintained 30 to 35 feet of spacing, and added knots between each climber. In such warm conditions, any of us could break through a hidden crevasse.

Near the final plateau back to the lift station, Geoff, third in line, suddenly fell through a trapdoor into a hidden crevasse. As the lead climber, the only indication I had was the team stopping. Used to brief pauses, I initially called out, "Come on, guys, we're going to miss the lift!" But then I turned and found Geoff hanging, neck-deep in a crevasse. The knot closest to him had caught, preventing a deeper fall. Thanks to our setup, it took only a little effort to pull him back up.

Minutes later, just a short distance farther, Charlotte also fell—this time disappearing. Carla took the brunt of the pull, but the knots helped absorb the force, making it easier to hold. After another quick rescue, we continued, reaching the lift just in time. Looking back, joining teams and tying knots between climbers was key—without these adjustments, our day could have ended very differently.

KEY TAKEAWAYS: While they are not a guarantee, adding knots in the rope can significantly reduce the length and impact of a fall. Consider tying knots between all rope team members—not just for the lead climber. In our case, both climbers who fell were toward the back. Though they may slow the overall pace, larger rope teams provide better protection in a fall. Adapt to conditions and do what's best for the group.

Joshua Jarrin is the former technical director of the Ecuadorian Mountain Guides Association and an IFMGA guide. Jarrin has established new routes and climbed around the world.

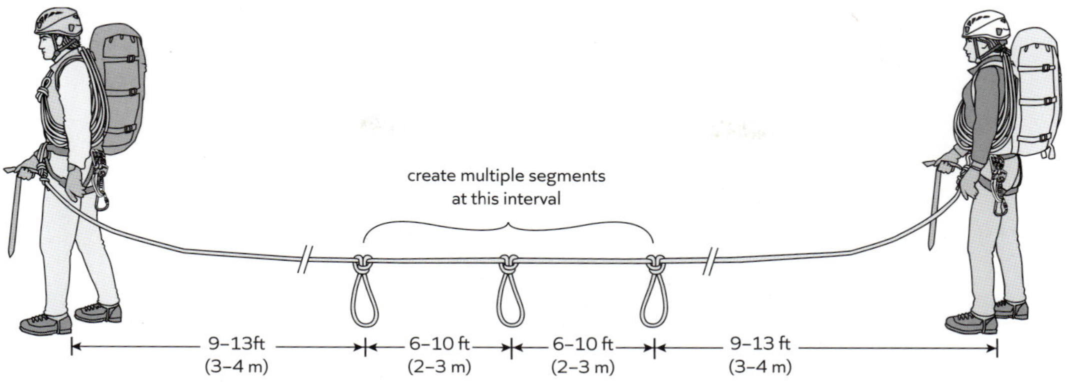

Figure 6-6. *The distance between climbers should be 25 to 45 feet (8 to 15 meters), depending on the number of climbers on the rope team.*

Figure 6-7. *An alpine butterfly is the most common stopper knot for glacier travel.*

days of early summer, alpine butterfly knots are not as effective as L'ENSA knots (below) in very moist and/or wet snow, but they perform similarly in firmer snow-surface conditions.

The L'ENSA knot (a.k.a. brake knot or monkey's fist; fig. 6-8) is basically a figure-eight on a bight passed back around on itself, forming a bulkier version of the alpine butterfly.

In tests in softer snow (i.e., a moist to wet snow surface, which is the most common for "trapdooring" into hidden crevasses), bulkier equaled better, while in firmer snow, brake knots proved as effective as butterfly knots but with the disadvantage of requiring more rope to tie.

Strongly consider stopper knots on hot days in the spring up until the early summer to midsummer, when many snowbridges are still covered with snow. Later in the summer, once most snowbridges have fallen and you are wearing crampons on the glacier most of the day, it's usually better to go with the alpine butterfly. In winter snow or very soft, moist, isothermic snow, the L'ENSA is ideal.

CONNECTING TO THE ROPE

As you'll recall from chapter 2, the figure-eight on a bight and the alpine butterfly are the most common knots climbers use to connect to the rope, but a simple overhand on a bight is also acceptable (fig. 6-9). Choosing among

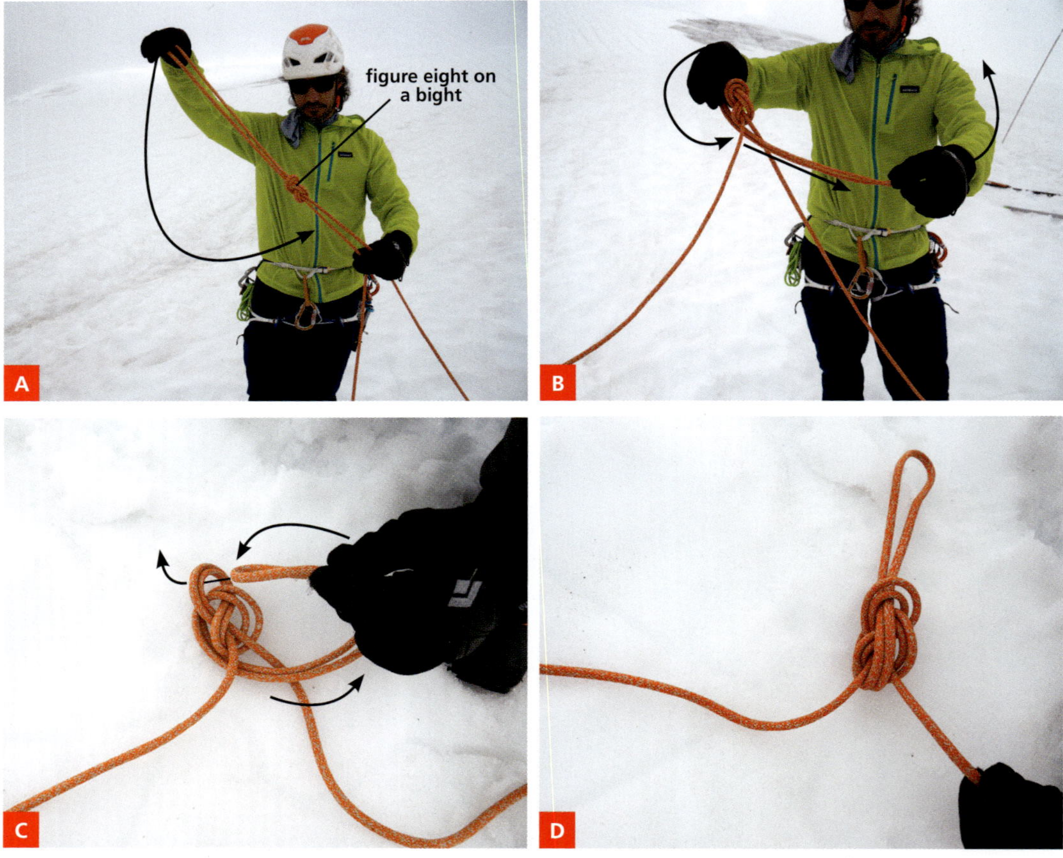

Figure 6-8. *To tie a brake knot, or L'ENSA knot:* **a,** *Start with a figure-eight on a bight with a very long loop, 1.5 to 2 feet.* **b,** *Pass the long loop underneath the upside down V created by the two long ends of rope at the bottom of the knot.* **c,** *After passing it underneath the knot rethread the loop through the top hole in the original figure-eight knot.* **d,** *The finished L'ENSA knot, or brake knot.*

these three is mostly a matter of comfort and familiarity to ensure that whatever knot you use is tied correctly. The knot should be as short as possible—without too long of a loop—to be comfortable while walking while still being roomy enough to clip in a few carabiners. If the knot is too long, it could get tangled up with your knees and increase your likelihood of tripping.

While it might seem like a good idea to girth-hitch the rope to your belay loop or your hard points instead of clipping in to a knot on the rope with a locking carabiner, this isn't the case. If the girth hitch becomes loaded, it traps you in the system. Being stuck when the rope system is weighted, with limited, potentially complex systems required to escape, can create several significant problems, particularly if you end up being the rescuer. While clipping in with carabiners might seem to add one more point of possible failure, the truth is that a locking carabiner plus a nonlocking carabiner provides more than enough security, to the point where they are the clear choice over girth-hitching any day.

To attach the knot to your harness, it is best practice to use one locking carabiner and one nonlocking carabiner, opposite and opposed (fig. 6-10a). This practice is beneficial because, as you are potentially on the glacier for hours at a time, it is easy for that locking carabiner to come undone slowly; the second, nonlocking carabiner guards against catastrophic failure.

You could also consider a single triple-action carabiner, either clipped directly in to the harness's belay loop or to the hard points on some of the newer ultralightweight

Figure 6-9. *The author with a mountaineer's coil clipped into a triple-action locking carabiner with an overhand on a bight* (Photo by Sharon Birchfield)

Figure 6-10. *Three acceptable ways of clipping the knot to your harness:* **a**, *one locking carabiner and one nonlocking carabiner, opposite and opposed;* **b**, *a single triple-action locking carabiner;* **c**, *a triple-action carabiner with a captive eye.*

BE RESCUE READY

Carry your gear ready to perform crevasse rescue rather than self-rescue. The reasons are twofold: First, it is estimated that self-rescue is only a viable option in less than 20 percent of real-world crevasse falls. Second, the effectiveness of stopper knots in assisting the team in catching the fall is undisputed, even if they make self-rescue more difficult. Thus any rope team traveling on a glacier should be ready to quickly set up a hauling system on the surface rather than expect the fallen person to self-extract.

Carry the gear you will need for crevasse rescue easily accessible; on your harness, your pack's waist-belt or the bottom of your shoulder straps attached to your backpack. Set yourself up for success; because the most likely scenario you will face is having to haul someone out of a crevasse versus having them self-rescue, avoid traveling with two prusiks on the rope. Since most climbers use knots in the rope, it is far more efficient to haul on a different strand instead of the one they fell in on. In more complex glacier travel a personal prusik can be useful for adjusting space between climbers, but having to remove it and switch it to a new strand adds yet another step for most crevasse rescue scenarios you may encounter.

harnesses, if there isn't a belay loop. Regardless, follow the manufacturer's recommendation for your particular harness.

STOWING THE EXTRA ROPE

Except for the biggest teams, the front and back climbers will need to stow extra rope, carrying it with them to build a crevasse-rescue system. Each of the following techniques offers particular benefits and potential pitfalls, depending on the climbers and the situation. No one technique is best.

MOUNTAINEER'S COIL

The mountaineer's coil is a classic and effective way to carry coils (fig. 6-11). These coils are very durable, meaning it is easy to drop them, adjust layers, take a break, and put them right back on again. They also don't require the climber to have a backpack on or space in their backpack, making them great for light summit pushes. The main disadvantage is they take a little more care to set up and break down than other methods.

CARRYING YOUR ROPE

Besides wearing a mountaineer's coil, climbers traveling on glaciers use a variety of methods to carry the extra rope on either end of the rope team that enables the rope team to set up a rescue You can tie the remaining rope into a butterfly coil, stuff the rope into a dedicated stuff sack in your pack, finish the butterfly coil with a gasket finish, or tie it off in a kiwi coil.

BUTTERFLY COILS IN YOUR BACKPACK

Butterfly coils with a nail finish can be carried inside a backpack, but since the coils are not as compact as a gasket finish, they are less preferred for this technique (fig. 6-12). What they are best for is carrying on the outside of a backpack because of their ability to lay flat.

Using a gasket finish on a butterfly coil is the most compact and offers the advantage of being packed in your backpack like any other item (fig. 6-13). You can take out a rope coiled this way while searching for items and pack it away without the coil coming undone. A rope coiled this way is quite compact and stable.

Figure 6-11. *To tie a mountaineer's coil, follow these steps:* **a**, *Start from where you intend to clip into the rope and work outward (versus toward the middle) of the rope. Hold your hand at waist level and take coils in around your neck with the opposite hand until you have a few feet remaining.* **b**, *Take the coils off your shoulder and create a bight with the rope that leads from your harness clip in to the coils.* **c**, *Take the short end of the rope and wrap it around all of the coils in the direction of the bight you just made.* **d**, *When you get down to the last 6 to 8 inches of rope, poke the end through the bight, and pull all of the coils away from you to cinch up the bight because it connects to the clip-in point on your harness.* **e**, *Slack between the coil and tie-in knot ensures that you will be able to access the coils should you need them, even if your tie-in point becomes loaded.*

Figure 6-12. *To make a butterfly coil:* **a**, *Coil the rope over your neck in arm lengths.* **b**, *When you have a few feet of rope left, pick it off your neck, pass it over your head, and hold it one hand.* **c**, *Wrap the end snugly around the coils below your hand.* **d**, *Pass a bight from the end through the coils.* **e**, *Wrap the bight across the top. f, Pull the long end to cinch it tight.*

Figure 6-13. *To create a gasket finish on a butterfly coil:* **a,** *Create a bight on the rope closest to your tie-in knot.* **b,** *Wrap the open end around the coils, and poke it through the bight.* **c,** *Pull your clip-in strand to cinch the end.* **d,** *Put the rope in or attach it to your pack.*

Figure 6-14. *To stack the rope into a stuff sack in your pack:* **a**, *It's a good idea to tie a barrel knot into the end of the rope, and then stack all of the rope that is not in use.* **b**, *Put it in your backpack.*

STACK ROPE IN THE BACKPACK

Stuff the rope into a stuff sack that lives in your backpack (fig. 6-14). This method makes it easier to carry but also lets you search around in your pack without tangling the rope. It is also easily accessible if you need more rope for transitioning to longer snow pitches or onto rock.

Some people prefer to have the rope "stuffed," or stacked, in the backpack if there's space, as it's quick and comfortable (fig. 6-15). This method can be quite effective if you are carrying less than 10 to 15 meters of rope and is most useful for times when you are crossing a glacier to access a rock route, climbing a long and steep snow pitch, or making a rappel—essentially any scenario in which you'll need quick access to the full length of the rope.

This method has some disadvantages, however. First, it generally makes it difficult to access other items in your pack. Second, if you dig around too much, the rope can become so disorganized that you'll wish you'd just coiled it.

While it's a little goofy looking it is unbelievably faster and easier to stack ropes into a backpack or a stuff sack with the rope clipped above while you pull it down. If you don't have a friend near, you can take this boating technique and clip a carabiner to your helmet to redirect the rope so you can pull it downwards into the pack (fig. 6-16).

KIWI COIL

The Kiwi coil is like a mountaineer's coil, except you start from the end of the rope rather than the inside, moving out with your

Figure 6-15. *A straightforward approach is to simply stack the rope directly into your pack.*

Figure 6-16. *Clipping a carabiner to the chin strap of your helmet allows you to pull rope downward, letting you restack rope unbelievably fast.*

coils. It is primarily, but not exclusively, used by guides so they can adjust the length of their rope as they encounter different types of terrain, and it more easily facilitates switching into both pitching and short-roping. The advantage of the Kiwi coil is that you can easily adjust the length of rope out and quickly tie back in (fig. 6-17).

However, these are the "least durable" coils, meaning adjusting layers, removing your backpack, or otherwise removing them tends to loosen part of the coil. These coils also require that you tie and clip an additional knot to your harness so that you don't become trapped in the coils and can escape them if necessary. Similar to the mountaineer's coil, the Kiwi coil is slightly slower to rig and requires care to break down—the coils need to be "untied" one at a time.

UNDOING MOUNTAINEER'S AND KIWI COILS

Both the mountaineer's coil and the Kiwi coil are extremely functional ways to carry rope; however, when uncoiling the rope, make sure you do so one strand of the coil at a time (fig. 6-18). In other words, resist the urge to drop the rope on the ground and haphazardly pull on strands. Because every coil contains a half twist, pulling will create a "rat's nest" that takes ages to undo. So while it might seem

Figure 6-17. *To tie a Kiwi coil:* **a,** *Tie into the end of the rope and work inward. Hold one hand at waist level and coil the rope with the other end. Coil until you reach the desired distance on the rope.* **b,** *Slide your shoulder out so that coils hang on your neck like a lei. Even the coil lengths by chopping your forearm into them. Then put the coils back on your shoulder.* **c,** *Take the long end of the rope and pass a bight through your belay loop.* **d,** *Continue by passing this bight from the outside in and around all of the shoulder coils you have made.* **e,** *Then take this bight and tie an overhand around the long end of the rope.* **f,** *It is critical to then tie an overhand knot and clip it to your belay loop so that if the rope becomes loaded, such as in a crevasse fall, you can still access the rope in your coils.*

Figure 6-18. *Undoing one strand of a coil at a time*

slow, with a little practice you can break down even a large mountaineer's or Kiwi coil in thirty to forty seconds, all while minimizing twists and kinks.

Note: It is *critical* to tie an additional knot (an overhand on a bight is fine) between your tied-off coils and the long rope leading to the next climber. That way, if your tied-off coils get loaded by a fallen climber who cannot unweight the rope, you are still able to escape them, without involved technical maneuvering.

GENERAL TRAVEL PRINCIPLES

With preparation and planning, teams can minimize their risk while traveling across glaciers in all sorts of mountainous terrain (fig. 6-19). Glacier travel is based on two key principles: First, you should proactively routefind to avoid as much of the most hazardous terrain as possible (including crevasses and possible overhead hazards). Second, you should travel oriented such that you minimize the size of an unexpected fall. This is related to how the group orients itself as it crosses crevasses in moderate terrain, but it could also involve the use of specific techniques and equipment like belays, anchors, and various pieces of snow protection on particularly tricky, exposed, firm, or steep sections of the glacier.

PARTY SIZE

There is no perfect group size, but there are certainly some things to consider when divvying up rope teams. For example, a group of two must be extremely well versed in glacier travel, because if one person falls in, there is only one other rescuer to catch the fall, build an anchor, potentially rappel to the fallen person, and haul them out. For two-person teams, each person should carry their own equipment to build a snow anchor, ample rope to perform any number of rescues, and additional tools like a mechanical ratchet (e.g., Petzl Micro Traxion or Edelrid Spoc) and possibly a pulley.

Groups of three or four will provide more resources as well as more catching and holding power than a group of two (fig. 6-20). However, a bigger rope team isn't always better: teams of five are tricky, as a rope team of five can start to struggle with pacing as the terrain inevitably changes, creating a "Slinky" effect in which one person is in mellower terrain going faster, forcing someone else in steeper terrain to go uncomfortably fast.

These inevitable changes in terrain and speed mean that each member must "feel" the rest of the group through the rope and take care to minimize slack between rope team

Figure 6-19. *A group in glacier-travel mode on the Khumbu Glacier below Mount Everest, Nepal* (Photo by Jacob Schmitz)

Figure 6-20. *Smaller teams of two to three climbers can be more nimble on a glacier, but party members need to be skilled and well-prepared because they have fewer resources and less pulling and holding power than larger groups.*

members, even if they have to walk unnaturally slower or faster (fig. 6-21). Each group must self-assess to see if at least two members have the skill to guarantee a self-arrest should one person on the rope team fall in. Because of these concerns, parties of six should definitely break into two rope teams of three people.

MOVING TOGETHER

The adage "A smile, not a mile" rings quite true for managing slack while moving across a glacier. The rope should hang off your harness, making a "smile"—not a big, sagging U—between you and the next climber. A good guideline is that the rope should touch down just in front of you, within a range of 2 to 4 feet, though of course it's inevitable that this number will shift as the rope team experiences changes in slope angle, or the team turns or is forced to navigate around specific features.

Basically, you do not want so much slack that you need to flick the rope out of the way constantly, increasing your chances of stepping on the rope and how far a team member would drop into a hidden crevasse.

TRAVERSES

While maintaining appropriate rope tension is great, it won't really help if the group is

MAINTAINING SPACE

BY IAN NICHOLSON

I led my seventh trip on Denali during a particularly stormy season. However, my group was strong and managing well, pushing upward despite it snowing every day of our excursion. On the sixth day, when we hoped to move from the 11,000-foot camp to the 14,000-foot camp, it was no different: zero visibility and light snow. We slowly packed up our camp, having cached a load near the landmark of Windy Corner the previous day, then started up Motorcycle Hill. We neared the top, a typical spot for a first break. I could barely see 20 feet in front of me. Then, something moving caught my eye. It looked like someone had left a duffle bag behind, which I thought was strange. Suddenly the duffle moved—it was a person!

"Hey, do you need help?" I shouted. They were in a self-arrest position just a few feet from an abyssal hole in the glacier. Scratch marks led from where I stood to where they'd almost been pulled into the maw.

I approached, where I learned this climber and his partner—in the crevasse—were members of an elite Air Force Special Forces group called the PJs, based in Fairbanks. They'd been last in line on their team after caching a load near Windy Corner, when apparently they'd started chatting around 10 or so feet apart with a 45-foot U of slack between them. Luckily, the uphill person fell in (rather than the downhill person), but the force was enough to pull his climbing partner almost to the crevasse lip.

The PJs are trained in rescue techniques and physically very strong, things I knew firsthand from having trained with them. However, the climber who had arrested the fall could not get his picket into the icy snow and had been holding this self-arrest position for the last twenty minutes.

"I got you," I said.

My three ropemates, waiting below, could not see what was going on and had started to wonder about the standstill. I sat next to the PJ, ditched my coils, and dropped a loop down to the other PJ in the crevasse, who I could see was attempting to ascend the rope deep within the glacier. I told him to clip the bight and then I braced my feet toward the crevasse.

"Everybody walk downhill!" I shouted to my group.

"Why?!" they responded.

"We are saving someone!"

In thirty seconds, the fallen PJ was back up top, and not much worse for wear either, aside from being a little banged up with a few cuts on his face.

My fellow guides Zack Keskinen and Josh Garner rolled up beside me to see what was up. The PJs thanked us profusely; the following day, when they arrived at the 14,000-foot camp, they held a special ceremony during which they presented our group with their team's coin. And at the end of their trip, they also made sure to talk to climbing ranger Dan Corn; later, each of us was presented with the Denali Pro Pin for going above and beyond to help other teams in need.

KEY TAKEAWAYS: Maintain spacing on a glacier. Avoid the temptation to walk with too much slack in the rope, even close to camp—you never know where hidden danger lurks. Make sure that more than one member of each rope team knows how to perform crevasse rescue.

POKING HOLES IN HEURISTICS

BY LYRA PIEROTTI

In late April, my team landed on the Southeast Fork of the Kahiltna Glacier in the Alaska Range and set up base camp. For a few days, we would teach our guests crevasse rescue and glacier-travel skills before heading out to climb Point Ferene. This crossing required navigating the notorious Ferene shear zone, where at least two of my colleagues had taken 60-foot falls into crevasses in recent years. They both emerged relatively unharmed—and very grateful for the days they had spent drilling rescue skills with their clients.

Compared to their conditions on similar trips, the crevasses were more exposed given that year's lower snow coverage, and the cold, faceted snow made it challenging to build snow anchors. But we got through all our prerequisite training, and after a few days, we were ready to climb Point Ferene.

Following the track from the previous year's climb, I quickly spotted open crevasses that blocked passage. Spying another line, I steered our teams slightly east to link up with what looked to be smooth snow and assembled my 3-meter probe. Probing would give me a solid heads-up if there were crevasses unsafe to cross on foot. This zone is highly textured because of its flow dynamics as a shear zone, so it is hard to tell which slump indicated a crevasse and which is just a wind lip. Not long after I had started, my probe accelerated quickly, and I stumbled forward. I had found the void of a crevasse. After probing more, the area felt large enough to fall into. We reversed and tried a new angle.

We did this for at least an hour, finally emerging on the other side, then found what looked like a suitable place to build our camp—large, flat, and smooth. I started probing the area systematically. At one corner, I found another smaller void. I took out my shovel and dug, my rope taut to my team, then knelt down and looked into the crack. The snow extended down for a couple feet and then cut back under me at an angle. I asked my team to start backing up, then crept backward on all fours from the edge of this glacial trapdoor.

After we reversed our tracks through the shear zone, we set up camp in the middle of the glorious Kahiltna Glacier to choose another objective.

To climb complex routes, you can streamline your decision-making by relating it to something you already know—like another high-alpine glacier in a neighboring valley, or the same glacier but on your trip last year. These mental shortcuts, or heuristics, explain in part why experienced climbers are often more efficient than beginners at navigating complex, challenging routes—they take certain shortcuts rooted in their extensive experience. But these heuristics can become traps: When a climber fails to recognize that a pattern has changed or doesn't fit at all, they may miss critical warning signs, which can have serious consequences.

Using your tools is the best way to avoid heuristic traps. The mountains are always changing; you must check your assumptions and be willing to view old routes as new.

KEY TAKEAWAYS: Heuristics are useful for navigating complex environments repeatedly without becoming overwhelmed. However, you must become skilled enough to know when these shortcuts lead to traps, so you can avoid them.

Lyra Pierotti is an IFMGA mountain guide and personal trainer based in Leavenworth, Washington.

traversing horizontally in steeper terrain, above a crevasse or other hazard where self-arresting does nothing to limit the immense and sudden force of a fall. While there is no perfect matrix, if the likelihood of a fall relative to its consequences becomes too great, either put in a few pieces of snow protection and perform a running belay or consider traditionally belaying this section (fig. 6-22).

You may think these measures would take too much time, but for just one or two short sections, it doesn't really slow you down, since the time you'd lose having to creep along

Figure 6-21. *Having more people on a rope team and in a group can mean greater holding power in the event of a crevasse fall, but everyone must also be more diligent about managing the slack in the system. Here, a larger group travels with excellent tension and spacing between climbers on Mount Baker, Washington.* (Photo by Bryce Hill)

Figure 6-22. Sarah Janin descends a steep, exposed section of glacier after belaying her rope team down. The team anchored themselves and then belayed her down as they navigated the Upper Curtis Glacier, Mount Shuksan, Washington.

together, taking extra care to prevent a fall, is likely greater. Practice protecting these types of sections so that you can move through them efficiently and know that you can execute them when your team wants them. Don't hesitate to ask for a belay if you feel it's merited, even if no one else is speaking up.

TEAM TECHNIQUES AND MANEUVERS

As a rope team moves on a glacier, they often need to adjust the orientation of their rope to minimize the risk of a pendulum fall or an unnecessarily long fall in the event of a snow bridge failing or a member of the group falling in a hidden portion of a visible crevasse. One or more members of the rope team will most likely need to adjust their position so that the group crosses the crevasse or snow bridge as perpendicularly as possible, but a team may need to deploy a number of techniques, depending on the terrain.

Figure 6-23. Don't assume a snow bridge is solid—to get a good idea, probe it with your ice axe, your trekking pole (without the basket), or a true probe.

PROBING

Simple stabbing of any suspect feature or snowbridge with an ice axe or a trekking pole (with the basket removed) has saved countless people from tumbling into the abyss. What are you feeling for? A marked decrease in resistance (fig. 6-23). If your probing tool is short and you feel a notable decrease in resistance (particularly if you can push to the point of no further resistance, and the pole just falls into

Figure 6-24. *As the leader of the rope team, don't be afraid to alert the other climbers that you are crossing a suspect section of glacier and to increase tension in the rope, possibly until it lifts off the ground. These climbers are probing near Ingraham Flats on Washington's Mount Rainier.* (Photo by Jonathon Spitzer)

Figure 6-25. *It is important for the person in front to steer the rope team in relation to the hazard. Ian Nicholson leads the way through a very tricky section of the Tiedeman Glacier in British Columbia's Waddington Range.* (Photo by Ryan O'Connell)

space), then don't cross there. An ice axe can work as a probe, but because it's pretty short, it's only good for identifying thin bridges, not thicker ones. Remember, if the snow is soft enough, a bridge can be 2 to 3 feet thick and still give way.

Because they are a tool that most people traveling on glaciers already carry, trekking poles without a snow basket can work remarkably well (fig. 6-24). If you drive an average-length pole down three-fourths of its length and meet progressively more resistant snow, you're likely going to be okay.

However, if you plan an extended trip earlier in the year when the snowpack is thicker on the glacier's surface, a true avalanche probe is certainly the best tool. Not only does it let you probe deeper, but it lets you probe farther out in front of you.

BEING A LEADER

Certainly, decisions about when and where to climb should be discussed as a group, and countless studies have shown better decisions are made in higher-risk environments when more voices contribute. However, when it comes to maneuvering the group, having only one person issue direct, clear commands about where and how to cross various crevasses or potentially hazardous pieces of terrain is invaluable. It is important that the person in front keeps track of what is going on, identifies potentially tricky sections, and directs the group through any key maneuvers (fig. 6-25).

Again, this person shouldn't dictate major decisions, but instead help "steer the ship" through smaller features to coordinate pivots, instruct the group to walk in echelon, or ask that the group increase rope tension while getting a closer look at a snowbridge or similar feature. It is helpful if the leader is in the front, but it's hardly required; with just a little more communication about what rope team members see, the leader can almost as easily run the show from the middle or back.

INVESTIGATE BEFORE COMMITTING

It's a good idea to at least get an idea of what a snowbridge looks like, even if it takes a few extra steps. This precaution becomes more important when you are on routes without a trail in the snow or it's warm outside. If you cannot get a good view by adjusting your approach, ask your fellow climbers for tension. In response, they should get ready to self-arrest and walk such that the rope is tight enough to be lifted completely off the ground.

END-RUNNING

One of the most common techniques used in glacier travel is end-running. End-running sounds just like what it is—traversing along the edge of a crevasse before finding a suitable place to cross (fig. 6-26). While assessing the "end" of the crevasse, ask yourself: can you see the whole crevasse close up where the walls pinch back together (the ideal conditions), or does the crevasse just continue under another snowbridge? Sometimes, you have to go quite a long way to get around a crevasse (fig. 6-27).

Obviously, if there is a well-worn path in the glacier, then follow it when doing an end run. However, when the whole team is roped

Figure 6-26. Here, a group ends-runs a crevasse: **a**, *Swing to cross a crevasse as perpendicularly as possible, with the middle climber probing the nearer crevasse for a possible end run, to stay inline while crossing the first crevasse.* **b**, *With tension, the group then moves together over the next crevasse.*

Figure 6-27. *Sometimes the crevasses are just deep and wide enough that you must go to the end of them to cross. Exercise caution while traveling parallel to a crevasse.*

together while end-running a crevasse, look for a path that allows the rope to run as perpendicular to the crevasse as possible. If the climber falls in and the rope is parallel, they will "swing in," increasing the odds of injury as well as the force that their teammates must catch. A parallel position also leaves the rope team in a riskier position closer to the edge of the crevasse.

Keep in mind that, while it can be intimidating, stepping *over* a narrow crevasse where you can see two vertical sidewalls (even if there's a dark abyss between them) is actually safer than circling around the "end" where you can't tell if the crevasse pinches down or is just covered by a snow bridge (fig. 6-28).

Figure 6-28. *It can be less risky to step over a crevasse you can see with vertical sidewalls because it is a known quantity rather than end-running a crevasse that clearly keeps going and just has a snowbridge on top.*

STAYING PERPENDICULAR

As stated elsewhere, a team should aim to cross every crevasse perpendicularly. Whenever a team needs to end-run, to approach a crevasse that is running at a different angle, or to move through several crevasses in close proximity, they all must adjust where they are

Figure 6-29. *In a perfect world, your rope team will cross crevasses as close to perpendicular as possible, as Dave Collingwood and Dan Whitmore are doing here on the Inspiration Glacier in Washington's North Cascades.*

walking to cross all crevasse(s) as close to a right angle as possible (fig. 6 -29).

For example, it is common for a team to walk perpendicular to crevasses until the first climber gets to a crevasse that needs to be end-run, when they walk parallel to it. At this point, the second climber should walk either in line with the first (which is called "in echelon"; see below) or at a minimum diagonally directly to where the first person crosses the crevasse. The second climber should not follow in the first's footsteps because this puts unnecessary slack in the system and exposes the first climber to a larger fall.

Figure 6-30. *Walking in echelon is a common technique that mountaineers rely on.*

WALKING IN ECHELON

Walking in echelon is a common technique that should be in most mountaineers' quivers. It simply refers to walking "in line"—that is, single file. In glacier travel, this comes with the caveat that none of the members should follow in the leader's exact footsteps. This formation is commonly used to protect a leader who is end-running a crevasse or while traversing a hillside horizontally (rather than inline, following the leader's footsteps) to help protect against crevasses that run parallel to the group's direction of travel (fig. 6-30). Note that *echelon* is a French term for the rungs of a ladder, which is how each climber appears as they make their way across a glacier. Sometimes, it is helpful to navigate crevasses using a hybrid of techniques (fig. 6-31).

PIVOTING

Alpinists who intend to travel in groups should also know how to pivot as a unit. Pivoting refers

Figure 6-31. *Dave Collingwood and Dan Whitmore use a hybrid of techniques on the Challenger Glacier in Washington's North Cascades.*

to the entire team "pivoting" around a point, used most frequently when the lead climber wants the group to pivot around a crevasse that is running at an unexpected angle, to facilitate the team crossing the crevasse at 90 degrees. However, the rope team could pivot around any member—the lead, middle, or last climber—depending on the direction of travel.

JUMPING

While it might sound extreme, jumping over a crevasse (assuming it isn't too big) is often a very practical approach in situations where it might be less hazardous than performing an end run (fig. 6-32). However, jumping must be a well-coordinated effort between the person jumping and the rest of the team: the jumper needs enough slack—ideally not too much—to completely make it across the crevasse.

While giving too much slack is certainly not ideal, it is *far* better than not giving enough, which runs the risk of having the rope become taut on the jumper before they clear the crevasse, potentially causing a hazardous fall with a lot of energy. During a jump, the rest of the rope team members should be proactively in self-arrest position, axes up and ready to catch a fall. If the jump is being belayed (see chapter 8), then the team should give appropriate slack.

DESCENDING

While walking downhill, it is very important to adhere to the mantra of "A smile, not a mile." This not only safeguards against a crevasse fall but also prevents downhill team members from tripping on the rope due to the uphill member of the rope team introducing too

Figure 6-32. *When the crevasse width is reasonable and the team can coordinate effectively, jumping over the crevasse can be a viable way to cross a crevasse that is too big to step over.*

Figure 6-33. *The uphill climber must pay attention to the slack in the rope so that it does not trip the downhill climbers. Here, John, Michael, and Luke Yarnall descend with good tension on the Formidable Glacier on the Ptarmigan Traverse, Washington.*

Figure 6-34. *As a general guideline, it is best to maintain spacing and stay spread out even while taking a break on a glacier. Avoid introducing too much slack, even while standing or sitting still.* (Photo by Bryce Hill)

much slack into the system. Ideally, downhill climbers should walk such that the rope stays a few feet above their heels (fig. 6-33). When descending keep in mind that while the person leading the descent sets the pace, the uphill person oversees making sure there's not too much slack in the rope.

TAKING BREAKS AND SETTING UP CAMP

When taking a break or pitching camp on a glacier, you'll apply many of the same techniques used to investigate crevasses or suspect features. Begin by marking a perimeter with ski poles or wands, and then probe *everything* inside that perimeter—not just the perimeter itself—sinking a probe every 3 feet or so in any place that people will wander without a rope. While it's time-consuming, taking these few extra minutes is worthwhile to ensure the entire group isn't about to relax and untie from the rope above a hidden crevasse.

It can be tempting to bunch up during a break on a glacier, but it is best practice to spread out. If you have multiple groups, you can no doubt pull alongside one another, but tragic accidents have occurred over the years when groups clustered above unknown hidden crevasses. As a rule, keep your spacing consistent, whether traveling or resting (fig. 6-34).

Figure 6-35. *Peter Webb travels about 45 feet from the author on the gentle final slopes en route to the summit of Peak 12,200 (a.k.a. Lisa Peak) in the Alaska Range.*

SPACING IN THE POLAR REGIONS

In the Arctic and Antarctic regions, where the mountains see extended periods of extreme cold, consider spreading out even farther than you would in the midlatitude ranges. Snowbridges often weaken more quickly and facet out (a metamorphic process that occurs when the snow becomes less cohesive), which means that a very large bridge that would normally break up slowly in places like the Alps, Ecuadorian Andes, or the North Cascades will fail catastrophically in places like the Alaska Range, Saint Elias Range, or Antarctica. Particularly with smaller groups (two to three people), adding two to three extra arm lengths (an extra 10 to 15 feet) of rope creates a greater margin for error (fig. 6-35).

Opposite: *Bryce Hill pounds a vertical picket during some live-load crevasse-rescue practice.*

CHAPTER 7

Snow and Ice Anchors

It's essential that you're able to create strong snow anchors in a wide range of conditions, both for standard glacier travel and as part of the technical hauling systems used for crevasse rescue. This chapter covers critical considerations for snow anchors, the most common tools and techniques to construct them and maximize their strength—including building combination anchors—and the limitations of each given technique.

SNOW ANCHORS

When building a snow anchor, your goal should be to quickly produce an anchor that will not fail under the expected loads. Catastrophic failures do happen, but they are infrequent in the real world. While it's difficult to accurately assess anchor strength out in the field, numerous tests on snow anchors in real-world applications have proven just how many people are using snow anchors very close to their failure limit without even realizing it. To set yourself up for success, you must thoroughly work-harden the snow, angle back any vertically driven pickets, and double up pieces of snow protection whenever there is a sliver of uncertainty.

STRENGTH

The old adage "A snow anchor is only as strong as the snow it's put in" couldn't be truer. You may know about the "average" strength of a snow anchor in "good" snow as measured in tests, but without good, strong, dense snow, you won't be able to place an anchor in the real world that even approaches these test results (see table 7-1). Even more

TABLE 7-1. STRENGTH REQUIREMENTS FOR SNOW ANCHORS

Purpose	Force
Crevasse rescue	2 kN
Belaying a second climber	1 kN
Catching a fall while belaying a climber crossing a crevasse	1–4 kN
Catching a sliding climber falling onto a piece of protection (the force on the piece)	1–4 kN
Catching a lead climber taking a steep, sliding, factor 2 fall directly onto the anchor	3–6 kN

TABLE 7-2. ANCHOR STRENGTHS IN DENSE 1F TO PENCIL-HARD SNOW

Anchor	Strength
Top-clip picket	1–3 kN
Picket in a T-slot	3–7 kN
Mid-clip picket	3–7 kN
Ice screw in glacier ice	7–8 kN
Ice axe in a T-slot	3–6 kN

so than with rock protection, "good snow" or "strong snow" are subjective labels and take experience to assess. As a guideline, if the snow is softer than stiff 1F on the resilience scale (a strength of around 200 kilograms per cubic meter), then you must dig down farther and/or work-harden the snow (fig. 7-1). Additionally, if your foot penetrates more than 10 to 15 centimeters, expect to dig deeper and/or work-harden the snow.

Figure 7-1. *Andrew Megas-Russell digs a deep T-slot early in the season. An anchor is only as strong as the snow you are building it in. In softer snow, you often have to dig quite deep to reach dense snow.*

WORK-HARDENING

It is untrue that snow should not be disturbed prior to placing your snow anchor. Studies done by L'ENSA, an extensive study done in New Zealand by Don Bogie from the Department of Conservation and in California by Art Fortini from the Sierra Madre Search and Rescue Team, and systematic tests done by Mount Rainier National Park climbing rangers have shown that, in nearly all cases, work-hardening—or compacting the snow, whether by stomping on it or compacting it manually—before constructing the anchor makes it stronger, sometimes by as much as 50 to 100 percent (fig. 7-2). For comparison, think about a snowball: What makes it better—lifting loose snow up off the ground, trying to disturb it as little as possible before throwing it, or mashing and compressing it first? The answer is certainly compressing it; the same holds true for snow anchors.

Table 7-2 lists average anchor strength based on four studies done in dense 1F to pencil-hard snow. As is expected, in harder snow, strengths were higher, and in less dense snow, strengths were inherently weaker.

STRENGTH OVER TIME

While you can work-harden snow to make anchors stronger, under normal summer conditions (i.e., warmer temperatures), anchors will decrease in strength over time. Luckily, this weakening generally takes longer than it takes you to perform crevasse rescue or belay a partner across an exposed section of glacier or up a steep pitch of snow. However, you must also factor in both the sun's heating effect on the snow surface and the

Figure 7-2. Backfilling can increase your anchor strength slightly by ensuring that the buried object is pressing against an even surface area, and it will keep the area from melting out as quickly. However, tests have shown you don't get as much of a strength boost as you'd think from backfilling alone—you also need to work-harden the area.

Tip: To help keep your anchor from melting out and losing integrity, bury it in the snow and periodically check it, adding snow as necessary, especially if it's either particularly warm and/or sunny, or you intend to use the anchor for an extended period.

force of the anchored object itself, both of which break down the bonds between the snow grains, weakening the integrity of the anchor. This same deterioration in the snow can even occur on overcast days with warmer temperatures, though at a slower rate than it does in direct sunlight.

CABLED PICKET

Cabled pickets, also known as mid-clip pickets or Kiwi pickets (as New Zealand was the first place that saw their widespread use), have become the new standard for snow anchors because of their strength and ease of placement. They are best placed around 20–30 degrees past perpendicular to the slope angle, away from the direction of loading (see Snow-Picket Placement Angles, below).

To bury a cabled picket:

1. Tilt the picket to approximately 20 to 30 degrees past perpendicular to the slope angle.
2. Hammer the picket until it's completely buried (fig. 7-3a). Ideally, you should encounter progressively stronger snow (and greater resistance) along the way.
3. Once the picket is fully buried, tension the cable with your ice axe, pulling on it or clipping it in to your harness and setting it with your body (fig. 7-3b). When tensioning the piece, ensure that the top of the picket doesn't pop up, which would signify the cable isn't cutting into the snow as effectively as it needs to.

The picket should feel like it is being driven into progressively more resistant snow, with no hollow areas. While there is no precise minimum number of hits, vertically driven pickets—even cabled ones—that take fewer than ten hits should generally be suspect (fig. 7-4). In good snow conditions, which is frequently 1F to pencil-hard midsummer snow, at least two different studies have found mid-clipped pickets to provide around 3–7 kilonewtons of strength, which should be sufficient for the majority of crevasse-rescue

Figure 7-3. *Jake Skeen buries a cabled picket just past 25 degrees perpendicular to the snow surface:* **a**, *First, he hammers it until it is buried.* **b**, *Then he tensions the cable in the direction of the anticipated load. That setup ensures that the cable cuts through the snow and the picket does not pull up out of the snow when the cable is tensioned.*

situations and is similar in strength to a traditional picket in a T-slot or T-trench position.

Keep in mind that if you pull the cable in the direction of pull and the picket pops up, it means the cable hasn't sunk all the way down to the appropriate level. In this case, pull the cable a few more times in the intended direction of load, or even scribe it a little: *Scribing* means using your axe's pick (rather than the adze) to create a narrow channel for either T-slot anchors or the cable of a vertically driven cabled picket, to allow it to stay in place when loaded.

SNOW-PICKET PLACEMENT ANGLES

In several studies, L'ENSA found that placing a vertical snow anchor, such as a picket, at a 25-degree angle leaning away from the direction of pull makes the anchor approximately 40 percent stronger than one placed at a 90-degree angle to the snow surface. They also found a significant decrease in strength below 20 degrees and therefore recommend that most climbers aim to place vertically driven snow pickets 20–30 degrees beyond perpendicular (fig. 7-5).

Figure 7-4. *If you need to pound in a picket but don't have a hammer, don't use your adze; it will destroy it. Instead, flip your axe upside down and strike the picket with the middle of the axe head.*

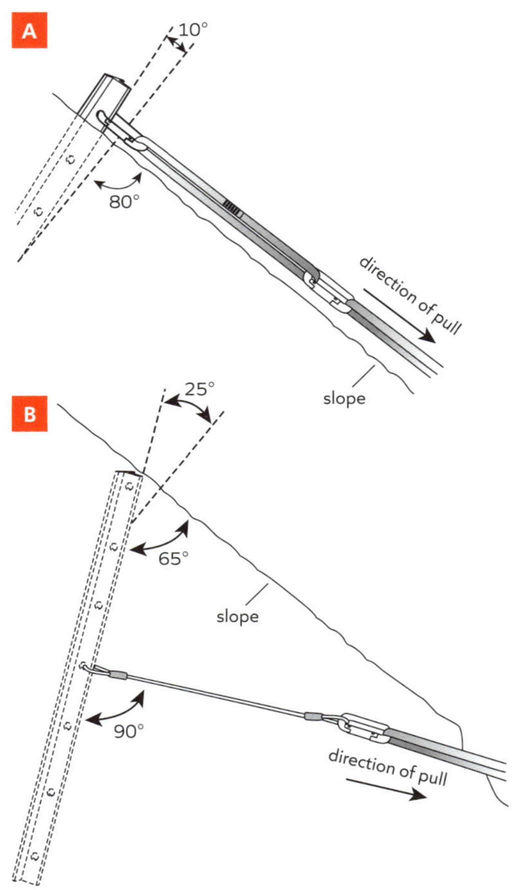

Figure 7-5. *Follow these general guidelines for placing pickets:* **a**, *in very firm snow, place a top-clip picket at 10 degrees offset from an imaginary projection perpendicular to the snow slope, then clip the carabiner and runner at surface.* **b**, *Place a mid-clip picket 25 degrees offset, and drive it below the snow surface so that the cable pulls on the picket at a 90-degree angle.*

TRADITIONAL PICKET IN A T-SLOT

With a traditional, noncabled picket, the most frequently used anchor—due to the strength this configuration provides—is a T-slot, also known as a T-trench. Here, you bury the picket in a horizontal position, with the long end opposing the load and a sling attached to the picket in the middle extending toward the load (figs. 7-6 and 7-7). For this anchor, you must ensure the trench made for the sling is deep enough so that the sling won't pull the picket up and out. In good summer snow, this configuration offers around 3–4 kilonewtons of strength, which is similar to a cabled picket in the same snow conditions. If the upper portion of the snow is extremely soft, T-slot anchors have the advantage because they are deeper in the snow, where the snow is stronger—during much of the climbing season on glacier, the deeper you go, the denser the snow.

To boost the strength of your T-slot and reduce the chances of it being pulled up and out of the long hole, undercut the edge of the T-slot in the direction of the load (fig. 7-8).

Figure 7-6. *Jeff Ward places a midslung picket in a T-trench.*

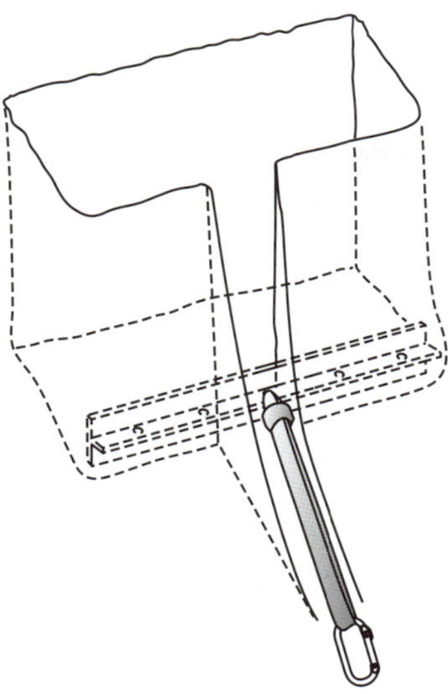

Figure 7-7. *Make sure the walls that support the picket are vertical or ideally slightly overhanging, to ensure that the picket won't be pulled out. Also, make sure that the T, or the trench that goes toward the load, is deep enough.*

Simply drag your adze on the wall you intend to load, creating a small overhang on that side. Backfilling snow onto the anchor once it has been placed can increase its strength; the process of work-hardening gives the anchor a continuous surface to press against. However, since removing a significant amount of snow from the picket's front side will reduce its strength, it is always best to backfill from the picket's nonloading side.

CARRYING YOUR PICKET

For most glacier climbs, consider carrying the picket on the outside of your pack under the compression strap, with a carabiner clipping it to your pack as backup (fig. 7-9). While using a backup carabiner means it will take a few

Figure 7-8. *Jeff Ward ensures that the trench leading toward the load is deep enough and undercut along the edge of the T-slot that is parallel to the load, which reduces the chance that the picket will be pulled up and out of the hole.*

extra seconds to remove the picket, it is well worth the effort to ensure that you don't lose the picket unexpectedly, like in a crevasse fall. For climbs on which you regularly need to access your snow pickets, a good tactic is to clip the second-highest hole (or third highest depending on the model) to the lower part of your pack's shoulder strap. This not only helps it ride higher and more out of the way than if you clipped it to a gear loop on your harness but also keeps it readily available for placement.

VERTICALLY DRIVEN PICKET

A traditional top-clipped vertically driven picket should only be used in very firm, hard snow—pencil hard or harder—as it is significantly weaker than the two previously mentioned anchors. In good conditions, a vertically driven picket has a strength of only 1–2 kilonewtons, though it is frequently weaker. It is also easier to misjudge the strength

Figure 7-9. Instead of using the uppermost hole, clip a picket a hole or two from the top. Attach it to the lower portion of your shoulder strap rather than your harness so that it hangs higher and out of the way.

of a vertically driven picket compared to a T-trenched one. Finally, a vertically driven picket can shift or tilt, far less than a T-trenched one before failing.

While there are no guidelines on the exact hits-to-strength ratio, as covered earlier, it should take at least ten hits before the picket is driven into consistently more resistant snow. If it "falls into" weaker snow at any time, the placement is likely extremely weak, even if it was difficult to break through a refrozen surface crust, as any layers of less dense snow equate to a weaker anchor.

When it comes to relative strength of anchors, studies have found that in 1-finger-stiff snow, a traditional top-clipped vertically driven picket held less than 2 kilonewtons, whereas a cabled picket or a traditional picket in a T-slot or T-trench position could hold between 6 and 7 kilonewtons, and an ice axe in a T-slot held from 4 to 5 kilonewtons. All of these placements could be made stronger by work-hardening the snow, with the degree of strengthening depending on how much effort was put into compacting the snow as well as how conducive the snow was to compacting. For example, moist early to midsummer snow is far more conducive to compressing and gaining strength than colder, late-winter or early-spring snow. In many cases, when dealing with moist early- to-midsummer snow, extensive work-hardening might double the strength of many placements.

ICE AXE

An ice axe is well designed to hold a load when it's T-trenched (i.e., used as a T-slot anchor) for belaying or as a snow anchor during crevasse rescue. If you're using a sling, it's best to clove-hitch it around the shaft rather than use a girth hitch, because the point from which the hitch pulls can apply a twisting force to the ice axe, and the clove hitch applies less torque (fig. 7-10).

However, unlike a snow picket, you don't want to place the sling in the true middle of the axe; instead, you want it to pull from the balance point. The axe's head, pick, and adze offer additional surface area and holding power, and pulling from the balance point allows the axe to load more evenly; if you were to place the clove hitch at the middle of the ice axe's shaft, the entire shaft could easily pivot forward from the pick, potentially allowing the sling to slide off the spike side

Figure 7-10. *A clove hitch is less likely to put torque on an ice-axe anchor compared to a girth hitch and thus is the preferred technique. This matters some with a more rounded-shafted ice axe, but it could have a much bigger impact on squarer anchors like skis or similarly shaped items.*

Figure 7-11. *If you are using an ice axe as a T-slot in a T-trench anchor, place the anchor material as the balance point rather than the middle of the shaft. Find the balance point by holding your ice axe (pick down) up in the air and balancing it on your index finger.*

of the ice axe (fig. 7-11). Lastly, it is almost always better to place the axe in a pick-down position, as it can easily be "pushed" into denser, and thus stronger, snow.

ICE ANCHORS

In areas where the snow has melted or been blown off the glacier, you may encounter bare glacier ice, which requires different tools to build anchors than seasonal snow does. Glacier ice is much denser than seasonal snow—and pounding a picket into it is likely an impossibility.

ICE SCREWS

For navigating late-season conditions, an exposed section of glacier, or the inside of a crevasse, an ice screw is likely the only piece of protection that works. As such, it's essential to carry an ice screw for glacier climbing after midseason. While there isn't much difference in the strength of 13-centimeter- versus 17-centimeter-long screws when used in waterfall ice, in glacier ice where the outermost layer tends to be rotten from warmer temperatures, there will be. For most glacier climbs, then, favor screws from 16 to 22 centimeters.

Figure 7-12. To place an ice screw: **a,** *Use the head of the ice axe to clear away the rotten, weaker snow.* **b,** *Drive the teeth in for a few rotations until the screw bites. Then drive the screw in until the head is flush with the surface.*

To place an ice screw:

1. As with placing a screw in waterfall ice, clear away the outermost, weaker layer of surface ice to get to the higher-quality ice, which provides greater holding power (fig. 7-12a).
2. Apply consistent pressure to the top of the screw as you twist it with your wrist, driving the teeth into the ice (fig. 7-12b).
3. A turn or two after the screw can stand on its own, use the knob to "drive" it home.
4. Drive the ice screw all the way to the head and tuck the knob back in to minimize it catching on anything.

Cleaning Ice Screws

"Cleaning" ice screws refers to the process of removing them from the ice, cleaning the ice out of the core, and racking them on your harness. Cleaning the ice from the core is essential because, if left inside, it can freeze and render the ice screw useless until it has thawed. To clean the core, simply tap the screw's hanger—not the shaft, which will damage the screw—on your ice axe upside down until the ice falls out. If you have only one ice screw, drive your axe pick firmly into the snow and clip the spike to create a viable anchor for lighter-duty applications (fig. 7-13).

OTHER ANCHOR OPTIONS

As discussed earlier in this chapter, many snow anchors are likely strong enough for the tasks at hand, but in many situations, climbers are unknowingly operating very close to the failure limits of their snow anchors because they are unable to assess their margins. This is especially true for "improvised snow anchors." Take extra care to assess (and work-harden) the snow and the possible loads that could be experienced, and when needed, stop and consider other options that may be better.

Figure 7-13. *You must clean the core of the ice screw after removing it. If the ice freezes inside the ice screw, it will render the screw useless. Tap the head, not the shaft nor threads, of the ice screw on the axe.*

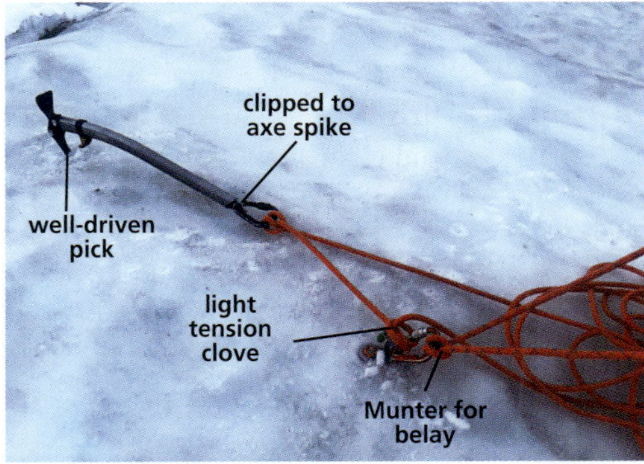

Figure 7-14. *Ice screw anchor backed up with an ice axe.*

SNOW FLUKES

Snow flukes work very well in certain types of snow and thus don't totally deserve the saying "It's a fluke when they work." They're great in soft, moist 1F to softer pencil-hard snow, where they are often quite strong (holding 3–7 kilonewtons) and offer the unique characteristic of "diving down" as they get loaded, assuming the load is below (downhill of) their placement. They are a viable option in early to midsummer snow as well as during the "peak" trapdoor season.

The unfortunate truth is they are difficult to place in firmer snow, where they often barely bite—even with repeated pounding that would seat a vertically driven picket. Also, with repeated pounding, they can often break up the snow surface in firm conditions, reducing their potential holding power. The fact that their range is less than that of snow pickets makes them less popular.

COMBINATION ANCHORS

While a one-piece anchor can be "strong enough," always consider linking an additional piece of snow protection. First, anytime you use a single T-slot or cabled picket, you have *zero* margin for error should it fail. Second, it's extremely difficult to get an accurate gauge of the quality of the snow or the anchor's placement.

Fortunately, there are several quick and easy ways to "chain together" snow anchors (fig. 7-14). And unlike in rock climbing, where you might place three cams and then equalize them, most people performing crevasse rescue are likely to place one piece of snow protection to take the weight of the hanging climber before reinforcing it with a second anchor in a different location. The nice thing about in-condition snow is that you can build an anchor basically anywhere.

Saxon's Cross

In good snow conditions, the Saxon's cross (fig. 7-15), also known as the iron cross, is one of the more popular crevasse-rescue anchors

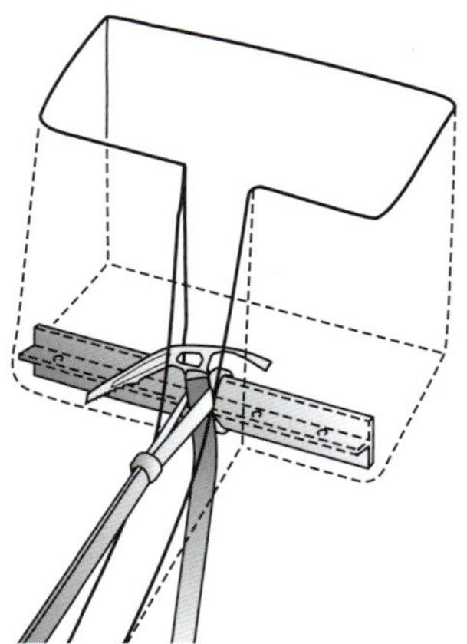

Figure 7-15. *The Saxon's cross is strong and quick to construct, making it a great option for crevasse rescue.*

for its speed of placement and simplicity, especially as it lets the initial anchor hold the load, allowing the rescuer holding the fall to transfer the load and then subsequently reinforce it. The Saxon's cross also takes advantage of gear that climbers will already be carrying.

To build a Saxon's cross:

1. Build a traditional anchor with a picket and sling.
2. Drive the ice axe in vertically right next to the sling extending toward the load. While you can drive the axe "inside" the sling, this is not necessary, as it doesn't increase effective strength but does increase the risk of damaging the sling if you stomp on your ice axe. You can place the pick over the picket (away from the crevasse) to help "pin" the picket in place (fig. 7-16).

What makes the Saxon's cross such an effective anchor is the ice axe, which uses its vertical holding power to reinforce the picket's most vulnerable spot—the middle. When a picket is pulled until failure in the T-slot or

Figure 7-16. *To build a Saxon's cross, put a picket in a T-slot and then drive a picket vertically to reinforce it.*

T-trench position, it erodes and fails from the middle, its weakest spot as it's the only part of the picket not directly supported by the snow.

Vectoring

The next simplest way to combine anchors is to vector them into position. Vectoring is not perfect, but if the pieces are equalized, it provides a redundant piece of protection if one piece should fail, with minimal extension that can subject the remaining pieces to a large amount of force.

To vector an anchor:

1. Pull the weighted rope sideways (perpendicular from the anchor and the hanging climber). Approximate how far you can pull the rope horizontally—it's generally farther than you think.

ANCHOR DISTANCES AND ANGLES

When it comes to the distance between anchors, there is no hard-and-fast rule because the stiffness of the snow plays such a large role in how far the "stress bubble" extends beyond a given anchor. However, a good guideline is to place pieces of snow protection no closer than they are long, with double or triple that distance being ideal.

Meanwhile, for angle, always place pieces fairly in line with the load, reducing the angle in the anchor used to equalize them—this will generally put less load on them than two pieces placed far apart.

The weight distribution of a load is never truly shared equally between two pieces of protection, because that would require the material equalizing them to be in the same plane. However, generally, the lower the angle, the better (see figure). At 60 degrees, the pieces take roughly 58 percent of the weight each; at 90 degrees, each piece takes 71 percent; and at 120 degrees, each piece feels 100 percent.

Reducing the angle between pieces in an anchor decreases the amount of force applied to each piece even though the actual load doesn't change. Since snow anchors are often operating with such slim margins (compared to rock anchors), try to reduce the angle as much as possible. This means that when "doubling up," place the snow anchors front-to-back (using at least the length of the protection being buried as the horizontal distance between the two) rather than side-by-side.

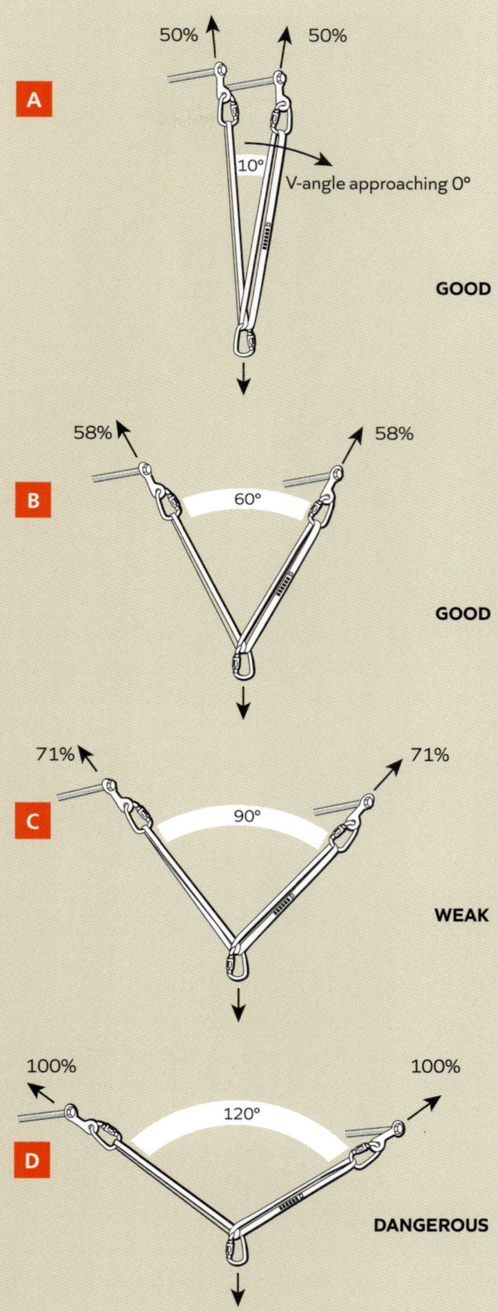

The individual pieces that make up snow anchors are generally not as strong as those in rock anchors, so the angle between them needs to be kept to a minimum. The way a load is distributed depends on the angle: ***a****, approaching zero degrees, each anchor point receives half the load;* ***b****, an angle of 60 degrees or less is ideal;* ***c****, beyond 60 degrees, the load on each point increases;* ***d****, at an angle of 120 degrees, the load on each point is 100 percent.*

Figure 7-17. *To vector an anchor:* **a**, *After placing a second piece of protection at a suitable distance (based on a rough estimate with the piece upside-down and the sling fully extended), pull tension sideways on it.* **b**, *Clip the carabiner to the original anchor.*

2. Measure out your second anchor and its sling material to a point roughly 20–30 degrees from the first anchor piece, and then place this second piece such that the material just barely reaches the point you were able to "vector," or pull the rope to (fig. 7-17a).
3. Clip this second piece to your original anchor strand (fig. 7-17b). Ideally, once it's clipped, the anchor legs will form a narrow V and the two pieces will share the load.

This configuration results in the second anchor piece pulling some tension, thus sharing the load. This second anchor piece should also have its own material, creating redundancy and reducing or eliminating the potential for suddenly loading the anchor with a large force.

Mule Hitch

Pulling tension and using a mule hitch, also known as a trucker's hitch, is a great way to share the load between two pieces of snow protection—after one piece has been placed. Also, because each piece has its own "leg," this anchor provides great redundancy and minimal extension and only requires a piece of material barely longer than the distance between the two pieces of protection.

To create this anchor:

1. After accounting for angles and proximity to the first piece of snow protection, place a second anchor (fig. 7-18a).
2. Attach a long piece of material to this second anchor.
3. Run the carabiner to where the first anchor is holding the load.

***Figure 7-18.** To pull tension using a mule hitch:* **a,** *Attach a long piece of material to the second anchor (often the one not yet holding any weight).* **b,** *Thread this anchor material through part of the first anchor and pull tension.* **c,** *Mule hitch the material to share the load and create redundancy if the first anchor point were to fail.*

4. Either clip in a new carabiner or use the existing carabiner and run the material through this.
5. Pull tension until the pieces are roughly "equalized." In general, look for a slight V to form, assuming both pieces in the anchor are of equal strength (fig. 7-18b).
6. Once the desired tension is achieved, tie the material off on the carabiner using a mule hitch and back it up with an overhand on a bight (see chapter 2) to prevent it from coming accidentally united (fig. 7-18c).

Block-and-Tackle

The block-and-tackle is another way to tension a second anchor to share the load and create redundancy. It's basically a mini-haul system: You will haul on the block-and-tackle until the anchor piece you're pulling on in opposition to the fallen climber takes an appropriate amount of weight.

To build a block-and-tackle:

1. Place a new anchor piece an appropriate distance for the situation and at the length of cord you are working with: that is, ideally, once tensioned the angles of the two strands should be under 20 degrees, but they can extend to 45 degrees if needed.
2. Attach a long piece of cord (a cordelette works great, though you can use a double-length sling in a pinch) to the new anchor (fig. 7-19a).

Figure 7-19. *To build a block-and-tackle:* **a**, *Start by tying a knot or clipping the end of a long piece of material to one of anchor points.* **b**, *Pull the material down and clip the material through a carabiner on the lower anchor point.* **c**, *Continue to clip the material in a circular fashion, in the same orientation to minimize twists, which increase friction.* **d**, *Once you have clipped enough times to create sufficient mechanical advantage, generally two to three circles, pull up on the strand until the weight distribution between the anchor points is roughly equalized.* **e**, *Tie a mule hitch around all of the strands to create mechanical advantage and keep tension on both anchor points.* **f**, *Tie a overhand knot to ensure the mule does not accidentally untie.*

3. Clip in a circular fashion between the anchor and the new carabiner on the rope (fig. 7-19c).
4. Pull or haul until the new anchor has taken roughly half (or an otherwise appropriate amount) of the load (fig. 7-19d).
5. Tie off the material you just clipped in a circular fashion with a mule hitch around all the strands in the block-and tackle; finish with an overhand on a bight as a backup (fig. 7-19e–f).

Tip: Don't place the anchor too far away from either the position where you are holding the fall after self-arresting or the location of the second anchor from the first. Many people make the error of building the anchor too far away, which takes longer to construct and introduces the risk of it ending up out of reach should the rescuer lose any ground.

Pre-equalized Anchor

While performing crevasse rescue, a traditional, pre-equalized anchor can be harder to set up solo because it involves equalizing parts of the anchor before any individual leg is loaded. While it is harder to use for solo crevasse rescue, it has countless other applications, such as for building belays on steep snow, for crossing suspect snowbridges, and for crevasse rescue with more than one rescuer.

1. Place two pieces of solid snow protection relatively in-line to reduce the angle within the anchor, and thus the load borne by each piece. As a guideline, the pieces should be no closer than they are long. For example, if the ice axes and/or snow picket being buried are 2 feet (60 centimeters) long, then they should be no closer to each other than 2 feet (60 centimeters).

Figure 7-20. *To set up a pre-equalized anchor, clip both anchor points with a sling or similar material. Pull the material into a V in the direction of the anticipated load, and tie an overhand knot.*

2. Clip a cordelette or other long piece of material to each piece of protection.
3. Pull the cord tight in the direction you expect the load to come from.
4. Tie an overhand on a bight (fig. 7-20).
5. Belay from or clip into this master point. Again, you can use the shelf, but if you do, always clip something—most commonly a carabiner—in to the master point.

PICKET FENCE

Much like Saxon's cross, the picket fence technique is another way to easily combine anchor pieces to increase the strength. Unlike a pre-equalized anchor, picket fence

Figure 7-21. *To use the picket fence technique:* **a,** *Place one anchor (in this case a vertically driven red Yates cabled picket) and clip a large or mid-sized locker at its furthest extension.* **b,** *Drive an ice axe (also tilted back) into the center of the carabiner so that it is pressed against the further-from-the-load side of the locking carabiner. Use this second point as a power carabiner to work off of.*

can be done subsequently to reinforce an anchor, even if part of it is already loaded. Also commonly referred to as anchoring inline, the picket fence technique is generally better for firmer snow conditions where a vertically driven ice axe will add a little strength to your anchor. While it is quicker to set up, this technique is generally weaker than the Saxon's cross in the same snow conditions because of the way Saxon's cross reinforces the weakest point of a picket. In strong, stiff snow conditions, the picket fence can offer plenty of strength for a wide range of applications. To create it, drive one picket down vertically and clip a carabiner to its extension (fig. 7-21a). Then drive an ice axe into that extension point under tension (fig. 7-21b).

Opposite: *Louie Allen in a couloir on the West Ridge of Forbidden Peak in Washington's North Cascades*

CHAPTER 8

Belaying on Snow and Glaciers

There are countless reasons to belay on snow: maybe you need to cross a suspect snowbridge. These include snowbridges that are less than 3 feet (1 meter) thick over a crevasse, bergschrund, or moat (fig. 8-1). Warm, soft snow conditions can warrant a belay for even thicker bridges, depending on the snow.

Also consider a belay when ascending or descending steep slopes or sagging glacial snow where a belay would be more efficient than simply moving together roped. While it might seem slower at first, for truly firm, steep terrain, you can move much more quickly—and with lower risk—than when roped up as a group, when one slip could imperil the entire team.

Suitable for belaying on steep snow, each of the techniques in this chapter has its pros and cons for different conditions and situations. The key becomes learning when and how to quickly implement a belay for tricky snow and glacial features, something that comes with experience (fig. 8-2).

Approach strange glacial features like moats, wind lips, and unusual bulges or depressions with caution. Don't be afraid to probe them to see how thick they are. Many people are afraid they won't know what to "feel" for, but it's not complicated: What you

Figure 8-1. *Some terrain may be too dangerous to solo or move together on while roped, like the terrain Sam Hennessey finds while crossing a bergschrund to access the east face of Mount Dickey in the Alaska Range.* (Photo by Rob Smith)

Figure 8-2. *When you are able to quickly set up a belay, you will be more likely to use it when you need it. Here, Jackson Marvel descends a very steep and exposed section of Jannu after making the first alpine-style ascent of the North Face.* (Photo by Alan Rousseau)

Figure 8-3. *A steep slope isn't the only terrain that requires a belay. Here, Andrew Krause belays Sharon Birchfield over a massive overhanging lip, McAllister Glacier, North Cascades, Washington.*

want to feel is progressively more resistant snow that gets "stronger" with depth. What you don't want to feel is airy snow or snow that gets less resistant or dense with depth. If you encounter an inch or two of less dense snow that quickly regains its prior, consistent stiffness, that's fine, but any significant decrease in density overall likely signals a problem. Consider belaying across such features (fig. 8-3).

Climbers are often willing to belay each other up steep slopes, but all too often on the way down, they rely on a "long rope and hope" mentality and travel spread out as if in anticipation of a hidden crevasse. Consider both climbers on the way down (with the second climber getting a reverse lead belay) down or across steep slopes, over precarious snow bridges, or above exposure (fig. 8-4).

BELAY STANCES

Many belays can be performed by incorporating a climber's body into the system as part of the anchor. This quick solution typically provides more security than moving together in self-arresting position or using a running belay.

SEATED

This basic technique is easy and fast but requires very malleable, dense snow, often found in summer (figs. 8-5 and 8-6). The key is to kick very good "buckets" with your feet to

Figure 8-4. Belaying partners on steep features is often safer than simply spreading out on a rope. Note the belayer's well-braced feet. (Photo by Jessica Eaton)

create something to push against in the event you need to hold a fall. While this belay is not very strong under even the best of circumstances, it can be useful for belaying a second climber up things like a steep section of snow or as they climb out of a less-than-vertical crevasse, situations in which you can keep the rope tight and slack out of the system, reducing the forces generated.

Tip: It can be hard to flip the rope over your backpack to get it down to your hips for belaying. Instead, try stepping over the rope and pulling it up to waist level or, better yet, turn into the rope (i.e., turn from the load side toward the brake side) while holding the rope at waist level.

SEATED WITH A BACKUP

A seated stance with a backup is nearly as quick to rig as a seated stance without one,

Figure 8-5. Jesse Selwyn hip belays Mike O'Connor down a steep slope over an unnamed col to access the Southern Pickets in Washington's North Cascades. Note how Selwyn's feet are secured in snow buckets.

with the added advantage of greater holding power as long as the anchor is reasonably solid (fig. 8-7). The buckets you kick should still be solid so the belayer has something to push against when belaying. However, keep the material connecting the belayer's harness to the anchor taut, with very little slack, as this allows the belayer to adjust the amount of load they absorb versus what the anchor takes.

RUNNING BELAYS AND THEIR LIMITATIONS

Running belays are belays in which a group stays in a spread-out, glacier-travel

Figure 8-6. *Sitting hip belay:* **a,** *Tom Vogl in a seated belay position in the snow. His heels are dug in to be secure, and he has created a small depression in the snow to help resist force. From this position, he can take in or pay out slack, depending on which direction the climber is moving.* **b,** *Tom Vogl demonstrates the brake position with his braking arm across his torso.*

Figure 8-7. *Setting up a backup anchor:* **a,** *To get a good, snug setup, set the backup piece first, and then create the seated stance.* **b,** *Move into position so that the material connecting your harness to the anchor is tight.*

TURN YOUR POLE INTO A PROBE

Most climbers use an ice axe that is 40–70 centimeters long, which makes a poor tool for probing to assess the thickness and strength of a snowbridge. While a trekking pole with a snow basket is a poor tool as well, as the basket is designed to provide resistance and support even in soft snow, if you know how to remove your pole's basket, you can turn it into a more effective probe. Use a pole without a basket to assess glacial snowbridges, to inspect moats as you access or leave the glacier, and to set up camp.

Play around at home—with practice, it's quick and easy to remove the basket on most poles. The key is to not lose the basket while you probe!

Figure 8-8. *Running belays involve the first person on the rope team placing protection and clipping the rope into it and the last person cleaning (removing) it or leaving it in place for the team's return.*

configuration, clipping in to protection that they place (fig. 8-8). In rare circumstances the group may use preexisting protection, such as on well-established routes like the West Buttress of Denali. Running belays are a form of simul-climbing, where if one climber were to fall, the group can reduce the odds of being plucked off the mountain by way of their collective holding power, as augmented by the protection.

In most cases, the leader of the rope team places or clips the running protection, and

Figure 8-9. *A few climbs will have in situ protection, such as the West Buttress of Denali, whose Autobahn stretch from the 17,200-foot camp to Denali Pass usually has nearly one hundred pickets placed by the National Park Service, as it has been the site of several accidents.* (Photo by Jonathon Spitzer)

the last rope team member removes it. It can be a very effective tool for routes that involve "in-between" terrain—too steep for just walking but not steep or exposed enough to require pitching it out—or for shorter sections of steeper terrain where the chances of a fall are extremely unlikely (fig. 8-9).

There are three significant challenges with running belays. The first is "pushing" terrain where you really should start pitching it out. If terrain is too steep and consequential enough, the climbers must exercise extreme caution not to pull each other off, which causes them to move more slowly but without the benefit of a typical belay.

The second danger is in not taking the time to put in enough placements relative to the terrain or not having enough available gear—for long stretches, you need a lot of protection—which can leave the group exposed. For instance, on a long traverse, the group might have only two pickets, and it could be cumbersome and dangerous to pass these back to the lead climber, especially when they may not be anchored in the snow.

The final danger comes from the leader feeling rushed by the climbers behind them and therefore not taking the time to make the placements strong enough to catch a fall. Unlike rock climbing, where a climber can quickly place a cam or a nut in a crack, with snow the leader may need extra time to shape and work-harden an anchor.

In short, if you plan to use running protection, bring enough snow pickets or other pieces of protection to protect the terrain adequately *and* take the time to properly place them.

HIP BELAY WITH A BACKUP

When you are belaying with a hip belay and a backed-up stance, you can increase the belay's strength significantly by keeping the load side

A BELAY FOR THE AGES

BY IAN NICHOLSON

One of the most legendary snow-belaying stories of all time is Pete Schoening's catch with a variation of a boot-axe belay on K2 in 1953, which saved his life and that of his teammates in very steep terrain. Although told many times over, this story's lessons remain as timeless now as they were seven decades ago.

On the expedition, the group set out from their camp at 7,700 meters to attempt the summit. Schoening, Charles Houston, Robert Bates, George Bell, Robert Craig, Art Gilkey, Dee Molenaar, and Tony Streather got tantalizingly close to the top but were forced to turn around due to poor weather. The storm then trapped the group at their high camp just below 8,000 meters.

After being stuck at the high camp for ten days, the group had all but run out of food and fuel, and the storm had damaged or destroyed most of their tents. During this time, Gilkey developed painful blood clots, which limited his mobility and, if they reached his lungs, could kill him. The group was forced to descend despite no break in the weather. Pummeled by the raging storm, the climbers wrapped Gilkey in a sleeping bag and began their retreat.

After spending most of the day working their way down, the group had descended roughly 1,000 feet to a point where the clouds broke and they could see their way across the final steep, icy traverse to their next camp. Craig went first, to unbury the camp from the snow.

As Bell began crossing the slope, he slipped and immediately started rocketing down the face; Bell then pulled his ropemate, Streather, off his feet. Their rope caught the other team, which consisted of Schoening, who was belaying Houston, Bates, and Molenaar as they managed Gilkey, who was tied in a makeshift hypothermia wrap in a sleeping bag and deconstructed tent. As Bell and Streather's rope came taut on the larger group, it yanked the climbers off their feet. Both groups began sliding uncontrollably down the icy slope below, plummeting toward the abyss.

As the five climbers and a tethered Gilkey careered down the icy slope, Schoening had only seconds to act before their weight hit him with the force of a semitruck driving at highway speed. He slammed his ice axe into the snow behind a boulder and braced with his hip belay. The rope came taut, squeezing Schoening with incredible force. Schoening recalled watching their state-of-the-art nylon rope (a relatively new piece of gear for the time) shrink to half its original diameter as his teammates' weight loaded it. Somehow, he had miraculously caught the fall and brought all the climbers to a stop. "The belay" would be considered one of the greatest saves in mountaineering history. The event wasn't without tragedy, though: while Schoening had caught the team, Gilkey disappeared in the fall, somehow coming out of the tent and sleeping bag the group had been transporting him in.

KEY TAKEAWAYS: Choose your climbing partners wisely, and make sure your team is skilled and prepared for the unexpected.

Figure 8-10. Quing Xin Cheang belays Sam Marjerison through a tricky section of glacier. It is often easier to place the backup piece first (in this case, an ice screw), and then slide into position so that your connection to this piece is taut.

of the rope (the strand going up or down to the climber) on the same side as the material connecting you to the anchor (fig. 8-10). As the climber's body weights the belayer, it will cause the belayer to rotate toward the climber. Having the load strand on the same side as the anchor tether minimizes this rotation. However, if the load is great enough and the anchor tether is on the opposite side (the brake side), the belayer can be twisted out of position (fig. 8-11).

THE MUNTER VS. THE HIP BELAY

The Munter hitch, like the hip belay, is a quick belay that climbers frequently employ on glaciers or steep snow (fig. 8-12) as it also takes little to no gear, but it has a few key advantages and disadvantages compared with the hip belay, so consider these when making your selection.

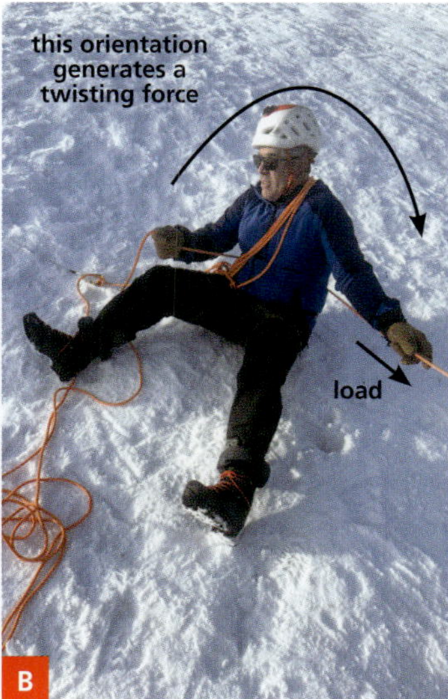

Figure 8-11. *For a sitting hip belay, the load strand should be on the same side that the belayer is clipped in on. If they are on opposite sides* (**a**)*, then if the load is great enough, the belayer could be spun out of position* (**b–c**.)

Figure 8-12. *A Munter hitch, used here on a section of bare glacier ice, is better than a hip belay when you anticipate the loads will be higher.*

To begin with, if the loads are greater or will be on the belayer for an extended period, the Munter is stronger and less painful for the belayer. The Munter is better for belaying in steeper or firmer conditions—any situation where all the climber's weight could end up on the belayer.

Meanwhile, the hip belay is slightly faster and you can take in or give slack even quicker, making it a superior option for belaying someone up steep snow where they might be climbing quickly and where, if they were to fall, some of their weight would still be borne by their feet even if they're "hanging" on the rope.

For very steep terrain, such as climbing out of a snow moat or perhaps a steep wind lip,

Figure 8-13. *Climbing a 60-degree wind lip near East Klawatti Col in Washington.*

Fiure 8-14. *Aiden Whitelaw sits down on a rock ledge with a strong leg brace against the snow in an overhanging moat to lower his partner down a steep slope.*

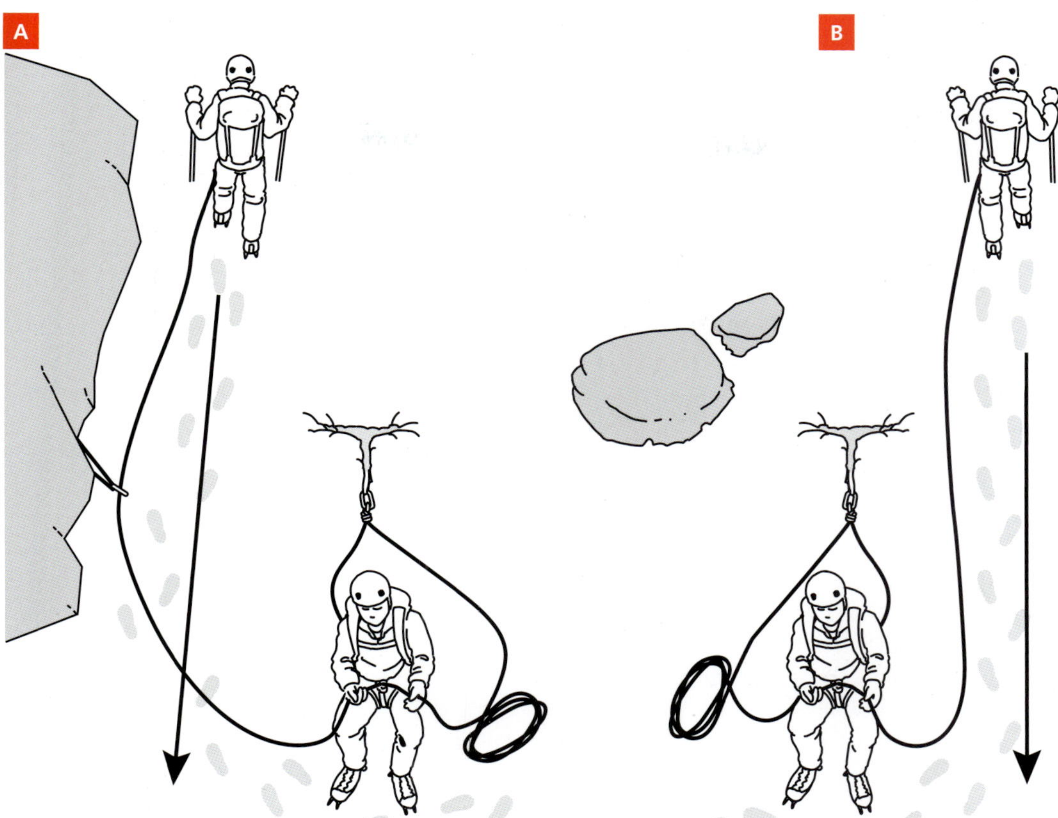

Figure 8-15. *When belaying a leader in a seated stance, the belayer should face downhill until the leader gets in protection, ready to catch a downward-pulling fall as the leader slides past the belay:* **a**, *belaying a leader continuing up on belayer's right;* **b**, *belaying a leader continuing on belayer's left. Note the belayer's setup in each scenario.*

it's best practice to belay a leader (figs. 8-13 and 8-14). Depending on the circumstances, a Munter or hip belay can be easy to deploy briefly to get through such features.

SEATED WHILE BELAYING A LEADER

For sustained snow climbing (35–50 degrees), using a hip belay to belay the leader from a seated stance can be a viable option, as climbers tend to move faster in terrain at this angle. Plus, it can be hard to keep up with a Munter or a traditional belay device.

When you are belaying a leader from a seated stance, first strongly consider a backup, since the odds of needing to hold a greater load are higher compared to just belaying a follower. Also, have the belayer face downhill until the leader places a piece or two of quality protection (fig. 8-15), at which point the belayer can then rotate 180 degrees and

WHEN TURNING AROUND IS NOT AN OPTION

BY PAUL KOUBEK

In 2007, I was working with Madhu Chikkaraju and Frank Preston, leading a student group in Patagonia. We had taken a boat out of Caleta Tortel, Chile, and then had our supplies horse-packed by a Don Julio Vasquez to the toe of the Steffen Glacier. Our goal was to cross the Northern Patagonian Icefield and hopefully summit a few peaks along the way.

Around twenty-five days into our expedition, deep in the Patagonian wilderness, our group set up to cross the unnamed saddle between Cerro Arco and Cerro Arenales. A complex crevasse field stood in our way. The Chilean military maps I had studied carefully before the expedition declared this area of the Campo de Hielo Norte to be an "SVE" or *sin visión estereóscopico*—in other words, a blank spot on the map. During my hours on Google Earth before the expedition, I could see only a blur, and the maps that I had commissioned from Aoneker GIS Solutions of Bariloche, Argentina, were also not helpful.

So we would have to solve this problem on the ground.

We pitched our camp for the night and left the students and any unnecessary gear—we wanted to be nimble. Frank, Madhu, and I spent a solid half day exploring all available options, but every possible sneak-through proved impassible. We had initially deemed one potential option impassable, but it was the best thing we could find. Madhu and I positioned ourselves carefully in our most athletic stance, braced on our knees, ready to self-arrest, while Frank tiptoed across. After he made it across, he looked back and exclaimed, "I feel sick to my stomach."

Thinking on my feet, I had Frank build a deep, redundant anchor on his side of the snowbridge, while Madhu and I built a redundant anchor in the maritime, early summer, firm, glacial corn snow on our side. Frank then untied and prusiked back across the line. The three of us left the rope and soloed unroped across the glacier back to camp, where we ate, drank, and explained the plan.

Early the next morning, we crossed the snowbridge. You might notice in the photo that the person crossing the snowbridge is clipped in to the rope system that we created *and* being belayed by their rope team. My concern was that, if the bridge broke, the person might get caught in the blocks of ice and snow of the failed bridge—an unacceptable risk.

I have employed this technique exactly once in my thirty-year glacier-guiding career—unusual times call for unusual measures. In most other situations—say, guiding the Upper Ingraham on Mount Rainier or the Stöckji on the way to Zermatt from Chamonix—I would have simply turned tail. However, in this situation, turning tail would have meant multiple days of hard glacier travel without food. Would we have made it across the snowbridge without the added redundant safety system? In hindsight, probably. But the bridge was of questionable strength, and my job as a guide is to bring everyone home uninjured. We had the tools (and, frankly, the time) to construct the added safety system.

Belaying across an incredibly delicate snowbridge near Campo de Hielo Norte (Northern Patagonian Icefield), on approximately day twenty-four of a thirty-five-day crossing (Photo by Paul Koubek)

KEY TAKEAWAYS: Approach thin bridges with caution. Set an anchor and belay across a suspect section of a glacier rather than using a long-rope-and-hope approach. Be proficient with snow belays so that you are not hesitant to set one up. Belaying off an anchor offers a much more reliable system for catching a fall than hoping your partner is able to self-arrest in time.

Paul Koubek is an IFMGA American mountain guide and member of the AMGA Instructor Team. Koubek has been leading groups in glaciated terrain in Alaska, Antarctica, the Alps, the Himalaya, the North Cascades, Patagonia, and the Waddington Range for the past three decades.

Figure 8-16. *To belay standing up using your ice axe:* **a**, *With your ice axe at the ready, take a large locking carabiner and clip the rope through it.* **b**, *Drive the shaft of the axe through the carabiner, with the narrower end of the carabiner pointing toward the anticipated load.* **c**, *Stand on and just barely forward of the axe in an athletic stance, with your feet perpendicular to the direction of the anticipated load (the person in this photo isn't quite there yet). You can then belay with a shoulder belay or a Munter on your harness.*

lead-belay in a more traditional manner; if the leader were to fall before they placed protection, they would slide down past the belayer, and the belayer would need to catch this very harsh fall in the downhill-facing position. This orientation is especially important on steep snow or easier ice, where climbers are often putting in very little protection.

Moats can serve as excellent, quite strong features for belaying, provided they are not undercut and you can find a secure position from behind them. Approach any moat with caution (ideally on belay). Try to get a view from the side if possible, and if it appears to

Figure 8-17. *Evan Miller is lowered into a moat on the Eldorado Ice Cap using a front-facing standing ice-axe belay.*

Figure 8-18. *To belay facing out while standing with an ice axe:* **a,** *Clip the rope into a large locking carabiner and slide the shaft of the ice axe through the carabiner.* **b,** *Drive the ice axe into the snow, with the axe head perpendicular to the load.* **c,** *Stand on the head of the ice axe, and then begin belaying.* (Photos by Ian Nicholson)

overhung or you cannot assess its stability, find another option.

SIDE-STANDING ICE-AXE BELAY

Another very common belay technique is the standing ice-axe belay, which is usually done in the sideways-facing position. It is great for belaying or lowering a second on steep snow or for climbing into or out of a crevasse. It is much faster to set up than a seated belay with a backup but isn't quite as strong, nor is it very good for belaying a lead climber, though it does have the advantage of not getting your bottom wet from sitting in the snow.

1. Clip the rope through a large locking carabiner, and then slide the shaft of your ice axe through the carabiner (fig. 8-16a). Keep the rope as close as you can to the head of the ice axe—this reduces leverage and increases the anchor's strength.
2. Drive the ice axe into the snow (fig. 8-16b).
3. Stand on the ice axe with your feet roughly shoulder width or a little wider apart, pressing into the axe with the foot farthest from the load.
4. Take the brake-side strand of rope coming from the ice axe and put it on belay with a Munter or through a belay device (fig. 8-16c). You can also use a shoulder belay, but be sure to practice this technique before you use it.

FRONT-FACING STANDING ICE-AXE BELAY

This belay is a variation on the side-standing ice-axe belay that, while slightly stronger,

Figure 8-19. *Timberline technique:* **a,** *Bury a cabled picket.* **b,** *Attach a carabiner to the cable and drive your ice axe through the carabiner into the snow, and then clip the rope through it.* **c,** *Stand on the axe head with one foot and control the rope with your opposite hand.*

doesn't handle dynamic loads as well (fig. 8-17). It is better suited for lowering people or for belaying steeper but not quite vertical terrain where it is easy to keep the slack out of the rope. This belay method is more effective if the belayer is wearing crampons.

To carry it out, follow these steps:

1. Slide a locking carabiner from the bottom of the shaft to the head of the axe, or clip the locker into the axe-head eye and then clip the rope into it (fig. 8-18a).
2. Drive the axe pick-first into the snow, so that the narrow end of the carabiner faces forward (fig. 8-18b). The head should be across the fall line, perpendicular to the load.
3. Step onto the axe head, positioning it so that the pick and the adze sit between your crampon points under your arches.
4. Lastly, take the brake-side strand coming off the locking carabiner on the axe and put it in a belay device on your harness or use the Munter hitch (fig. 8-18c).

TIMBERLINE TECHNIQUE

The Timberline technique is essentially a side-standing belay on the front of a picket fence anchor (fig. 8-19). Timberline Mountain Guides developed it on Mount Hood to create strong anchors in the fragile, aerated rim ice that covers the peak during the bulk of the climbing season. This rim ice is suitable for belaying and lowering climbers down 50-degree slopes in often very windy conditions where efficiency is critical.

ECUADORIAN SEATED BELAY

The Ecuadorian seated belay, also known as a sitting ice-axe belay, was popularized in North America by the former Ecuadorian Mountain Guides Association's technical director Joshua

Figure 8-20. *Ecuadorian sitting ice axe belay:* **a,** *Clove hitch the rope going from the tie-in point on the harness to the head of the ice axe.* **b,** *Drive the ice axe spike-first into the snow and adjust the rope so that there is at most one foot of slack.* **c,** *Sit on the ice axe and use the V created by the rope going from the axe to your harness as a power point to belay from.*

Jarrin and for its use on the high volcanoes of Ecuador. It is very strong—stronger than either of the standing ice-axe techniques listed above. It does take longer to set up and does require the belayer to sit in the snow, which, depending on the conditions, could be wet or cold. However, it's strong enough to belay or lower climbers in steeper terrain, as it "splits" the load between the ice axe and the belayer quite effectively.

1. Take the strand of rope coming from your harness and make a clove hitch 1–1.5 feet from your attachment point (fig. 8-20a). Drive the shaft of your ice axe through the hitch into the snow, and adjust the slack (fig. 8-20b).
2. Sit on the ice axe. The sideways V of rope that runs between the ice axe and your harness is effectively the master point.
3. Clip a carabiner to this V stretch of rope to belay or lower from (fig. 8-20c).

BOOT-AXE BELAY

The boot-axe belay isn't as strong as many of the previously mentioned options. Plus, it's often mistakenly associated with the epic Pete Schoening six-person catch on K2 in 1953—where Schoening braced himself against a boulder and used a hip belay. Yet the boot-axe belay remains a solid technique where speed of anchor construction is important and you anticipate low loads, or you need to reel in large amounts of slack efficiently from a climber who is ascending quickly.

Follow these steps:

1. Drive your ice axe in to the head, with the rope threaded around it in a U shape that opens toward the load.

***Figure 8-21.** To execute a boot-axe belay, drive your ice axe into the snow and place your boot between the axe and the load. The rope should come from the load around the ice axe and then break over the belayer's ankle, as Chris Marshall demonstrates.*

2. Place either boot immediately in front of the axe.
3. Run the brake-side strand in front of your ankle so that the braking action happens near your heel and Achilles tendon area.

BELAYING WITH A DEVICE

If you know you'll be doing a fair amount of belaying, consider just bringing a belay device (fig. 8-22). It is easier to provide a good belay, with the right amount of slack, particularly if the leader is moving quickly, which is easy on a 45- to 55-degree slope. It will also result in fewer twists in the rope compared to belaying with a Munter hitch, making the rope easier to handle, particularly if there are multiple pitches in a row.

***Figure 8-22.** While a Munter or a hip belay works great in a pinch, carrying and using a traditional belay device may be worthwhile. Here, Anouk Erni belays out of a moat using such a device on the North Ridge of Eldorado Peak, North Cascades, Washington.*

In very steep terrain or any time there is a chance a climber will fall on vertical terrain, consider belaying directly off the anchor, with the belayer completely out of the system (fig. 8-23). This, of course, means the anchor needs to be strong and redundant—be it two pieces equalized or a Saxon's cross (see chapter 7)—because the belaying climber cannot take any of the load.

MUNTER HITCH ON AN ANCHOR

Munter hitches are strong, but holding a fall for prolonged periods of time will require more effort than with a belay device. Munter

Figure 8-23. *Jesse Selwyn belays off the anchor, a technique where the belayer is not in the belay system.*

hitches are, however, faster for hauling in slack, for example, on a long pitch where your second is cruising up a relatively low-angle snow slope after overcoming a steep glacial feature. Munter hitches are also far easier and faster to flip into lowering mode.

AUTOBLOCKING BELAY DEVICE

An autoblocking belay device is a device that, when clipped to an anchor, forces the rope to pinch on itself, catching the fall on its own—*autoblocking*. They're most commonly used while belaying a seconding climber from above. As there are a few situations in which these devices will not catch, they are not considered hands-free, but they will do most of the work for you.

Keep in mind that it's not as easy to pull slack through an autoblocking device as it is through a Munter hitch if a seconding climber is ascending an easier pitch, nor are autoblocking devices as easy to lower with. However, they have the advantage of stopping a fall immediately in many circumstances.

Opposite: *AMGA Climbing Instructor program manager Andrew Megas-Russell hauling on the Quien Sabe Glacier in Boston Basin, Washington's North Cascades.*

CHAPTER 9

Crevasse Rescue and Mechanical Advantage

Any climber traveling on a glacier needs to be able to catch a fall, transfer that load to an anchor, and then subsequently use various systems that utilize mechanical advantage to haul someone out of a crevasse. You may never need to use these skills, but you certainly *must* know them and stay practiced and current. While there are several systems, they incorporate subtle variations of the same skills. Once you become fluent with one, it's easy to learn the others—and well worth the time, as they may be better options for certain situations.

Figure 9-1. *Digging your feet in allows your legs to hold most of the load, as Tino Villanueva demonstrates here.*

HOLDING A FALL AND SECURING YOURSELF

Your ice axe helps you stop, but your feet are what hold you in place. If the snow is soft, once you have self-arrested and stopped a fall, create "foot buckets" or "footholds" that are as large as possible, to take the majority of the weight (fig. 9-1). The rope might be running over one hip, which is fine; many climbers find it easier to have it running between their legs, which helps spread the load more effectively between both legs and gives you a little more reach and range of motion.

DIGGING THE ANCHOR AND TRANSFERRING THE LOAD

Once you have established yourself and are able to consistently hold the fall without sliding, it's time to dig the anchor. The fallen climber's weight, subsequent strain on your legs, and quality of the snow will dictate which anchor system you construct.

As you start constructing the anchor, err on the side of building it close to you—if you slip, and it's difficult not to slip a few inches or more, you still need to be able to reach it (fig. 9-2). Once the anchor is built, clip it to the knot you used to attach the climbing rope (fig. 9-3) to your harness and slowly downclimb, "testing" the anchor as it becomes weighted.

Figure 9-2. *Sarah Janin digs an anchor close to her body while holding a fall. Be sure to dig the anchor close enough to yourself so that even if you slip a little, you'll still be able to reach it.*

Never attach the anchor to your belay loop or the carabiners connecting you to the rope, because you could become trapped and would need to block-and-tackle your way out of it.

If you are unsure whether the anchor is strong enough, go through the steps above but back up the first anchor with a second piece of protection. For example, you could use your ice axe, if you placed a vertically driven picket for your initial placement (see chapter 7 for more about equalizing anchors).

If you slip or build the anchor too far away and cannot clip it in to the knot attaching your harness to the rope, fear not: Just open up your coils, or pull the rope out of your backpack, and tie an overhand on a bight on this nonloaded side of rope coming off your harness knot, clipping this new knot to the anchor—which should still be within reach (fig. 9-4).

Figure 9-3. *For most crevasse-rescue techniques, you will start by clipping the anchor directly into your original tie-in knot.*

Figure 9-4. *When you can't reach the anchor, use the nonloaded side of the rope to tie a new overhand on a bight that does reach, as Grant Price does here.*

SECURING YOURSELF

Securing yourself after you've built an anchor takes only a few seconds.

Follow these steps:

1. Drop your coils, take the extra rope out of your backpack or wherever you have been storing it, and make it accessible.

Figure 9-5. *After you build your anchor and attach it to your clip-in knot, secure yourself:* **a**, *Tie a clove hitch, attach it to your harness, and then unclip from your original tie-in knot.* **b**, *Estimate your distance, adjust the amount of rope, and then attach a prusik.* **c**, *Adjust the clove and prusik hitches as you move toward the crevasse edge.*

2. Flake a few arm lengths of rope (depending on the distance you are from the known crevasse or other hazards) and clip yourself to it with a clove hitch on a new carabiner, or other "hard knot," like an overhand on a bight (fig. 9-5a).
3. Unclip from your original knot.
4. Estimate your distance to the edge of the crevasse. Adjust the amount of rope out between the anchor and the clove hitch to match this distance and then attach a prusik to this section of rope (fig. 9-5b).
5. Adjust both the clove and prusik hitches as necessary as you move out toward the crevasse edge (fig. 9-5c), where you can communicate with the fallen climber and make a plan to extract them.

For further security, attach a prusik hitch between the anchor and the hard knot. Note that the prusik is just a short-distance backup to the actual hard knot, and relying on a single friction hitch in the event of a crevasse fall is not setting yourself up for success!

DEALING WITH THE LIP

Cleaning the lip is a simple but incredibly important step. Failing to clean it adds friction to your system, making it much more strenuous to haul and more difficult for the fallen climber to turn the lip and get out and onto more horizontal terrain. Under most circumstances using some sort of drop-loop or drop-end system, you will be able to clear the lip 3–4 feet off to the side of where they fell in, limited by how much snow falls on them.

Figure 9-6. Not clearing the lip will add significant friction to your system, making hauling the person out more strenuous as well as climbing back onto the surface more difficult.

Figure 9-7. To safeguard against a fall, attach yourself to the rope if you are close to the lip even if you have probed the area to ensure there are no other crevasses.

APPROACHING THE LIP AND PROBING

As you approach a fallen climber, probe the snow with your ice axe or, better yet, your more-sensitive trekking pole, with the snow basket popped off the tip (see fig. 6-23). When probing, you are looking for consistent or progressively more resistant snow. If you feel hollow, airy, or otherwise less-resistant snow under you, then you're likely standing on a crevasse or near its fragile lip.

CLEARING THE LIP

Once you've figured out where the crevasse edge is, it is imperative to clear away any excess snow, which increases drag and makes hauling much more difficult (fig. 9-6). For most hauls, note that you are not limited to hauling a team member out exactly where they fell in; when selecting a hauling locale, if it's safe to do so, step 2–3 feet to one side of the original line (the weighted rope that's still holding the fall), and knock down the lip. Stepping aside helps you avoid knocking snow down on them.

If the fallen climber is able, encourage them to pull their hood up, put their helmet on if they aren't already wearing it, and—if they're wearing crampons—tension to the side to minimize how much snow is knocked down on them.

Then secure yourself and adjust the rope so that you have very little (or no) slack while you work at the lip. Since there's a very real

Figure 9-8. *To free the rope, Michael Yarnall removes a ton of snow, with most of it falling onto his father, John Yarnall, below.*

Figure 9-9. *Clear away most of the loose snow and then place an object (such as a backpack or ice axe) under the rope to keep it from digging into the snow. This step is critical for reducing friction enough to haul someone out of a crevasse.*

chance the crevasse lip might be severely overhanging or there might be another buried crevasse in the area, attach yourself to the anchor (fig. 9-7) to safeguard against a potential fall. Climbers commonly attach themselves with enough slack to reach the crevasse edge, using a prusik to manage the slack.

If you are attempting a direct line haul, then you must clear the weighted rope out of the snow to minimize friction for your hauling system. Although it is straightforward, this process takes time, care, and caution (e.g., take your crampons off *first* to reduce the chance they will damage the rope) because all the snow you knock down is going to land on the person below unless they can swing out of the way (fig. 9-8). While it is harder to excavate the weighted rope for a direct line haul, it becomes more important than with other crevasse-rescue systems.

PADDING THE LIP

Once the lip is clean, pad it so that the rope doesn't cut farther into the snow (fig. 9-9). Padding drastically reduces friction and will make hauling notably easier. It also helps reduce the chance that the rope will cut in so far that the fallen climber gets jammed against the lip on their way out of the crevasse.

Several objects work great as padding. On a summit climb with a mostly empty backpack, a pack can work fantastically and has the advantage of coming with clip-in or daisy-chain points that can be clipped around the rope to keep from losing it as the fallen climber comes over the lip. An ice axe or trekking poles can also work; secure them so they don't inadvertently fall into the crevasse, potentially injuring the fallen climber and disappearing (fig. 9-10).

TIPS FOR THE FALLEN CLIMBER

If you're the fallen climber, make it easier for your rescuers by doing whatever you can to unweight the rope. For example, place an ice screw if you have one and can reach the

Figure 9-10. *Michael Yarnall has used an ice axe as padding at the crevasse lip, securing it with a sling connecting the head of the axe to the rope (noted in photo) to keep it from falling in.*

Figure 9-11. *If you fall into a crevasse and are near one of the walls, place an ice screw and clip yourself into it.* (Photo by Sarah Janin)

crevasse wall, and clip in to it (fig. 9-11). This will make it easier for your rescuers to place an anchor, preventing them from slipping down or even experiencing a larger, more catastrophic slide. You can also stem with your legs if you can bridge the crevasse walls. If there are features in the walls you can use like footholds, kick a foot in.

MECHANICAL ADVANTAGE

Mechanical advantage is a type of simple machine that reduces the effective weight of a mass by moving it a greater distance. Simple machines include things like ramps, pulleys, or levers, but they all work on the same principle of moving a portion of the mass's weight some greater distance (fig. 9-12).

One of the simplest machines is a ramp (fig. 9-13). Say you want to lift a mass 1 foot. If you just lift it straight up with a rope, you pull the rope up 1 foot and thus the object moves up 1 foot (1:1). If you use a 3-foot-long ramp to help raise the mass 1 foot (3:1), you have to move the objective farther (3 feet of horizontal distance plus 1 foot of vertical distance) than with the 1:1 haul (1 total foot of movement), but you only have to push one-third of the object's weight up the ramp.

DROP-END 3:1 HAUL

The drop-end 3:1 haul (a.k.a. new-strand 3:1 haul) has become the new standard in hauling systems, as it lets the rope team use knots in the rope and take advantage of the reduced friction and easier hauling associated with a fresh lip. It also doesn't require both ends of the rope team to carry twice the distance of rope as the distance between climbers, as with the 6:1 drop-loop system. This technique is also sometimes called a "new-strand 3:1 haul" because it does not utilize the rope that the climber fell in on; instead it uses "extra" rope from one end of the group. However, it does require that you have rope left that is similar

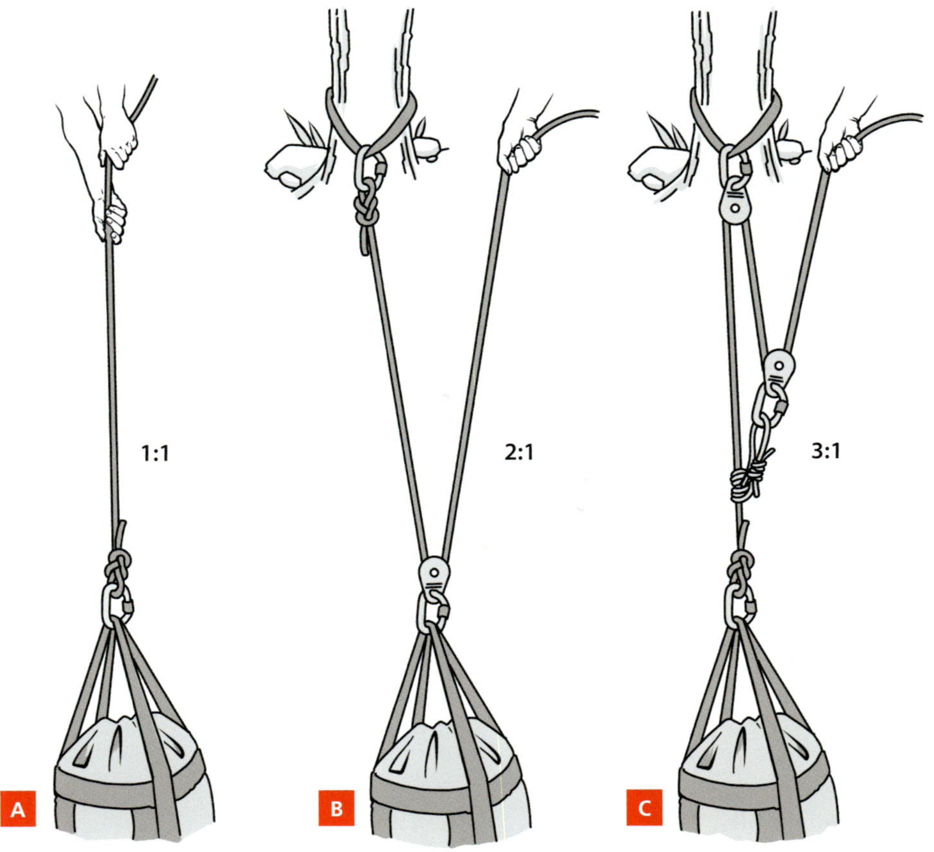

Figure 9-12. *Comparing mechanical advantage:* **a,** *In a 1:1 hauling system, either the anchor holds all of the load's weight or you haul all of the load's weight.* **b,** *In a hauling system with a 2:1 mechanical advantage, when you haul the load, you pull half its weight and the anchor holds the other half.* **c,** *In a 3:1 hauling system, when you haul on the load, you pull a third of the load's weight and the anchor holds the rest.*

to the length between the climbers on the rope team. For example, if you have 35 feet of rope between climbers, you need a little more than 35 feet to build the haul system.

This system is also best if the fallen climber is conscious and able to clip themselves in to the new strand of rope. While it is uncommon for people to get knocked out cold by falling into a crevasse, it does happen. If this happens, the rescuer would either have to rappel to the fallen climber and clip them in to the new strand and then ascend, or perform a direct-line 3:1 haul (see below).

To build this system:

1. After arresting the fall and building an anchor, clip the anchor in to the knot with

MISCONCEPTIONS ABOUT MECHANICAL ADVANTAGE

A common misconception is that increased mechanical advantage puts huge loads on the anchor, but under most circumstances, that's simply not true. When you build a 3:1 system and a fallen climber is weighting the anchor, the anchor is loaded with 100 percent of their weight. Say the fallen climber weighs 150 pounds; the anchor holds 100 percent of that weight. When you, the rescuer, start hauling with your 3:1 system, you are pulling 50 pounds (one-third of the load), while the anchor holds the other two-thirds, or 100 pounds. Most hauling systems experience the most weight when you aren't hauling.

A *big* exception is when your load gets stuck—for example, your fallen climber gets pinned against the lip. The main risk is not the anchor failing but the climber getting crushed (at least one person has died in this scenario on Mount Rainier). When the load runs up against something and stops moving, it can hypothetically weigh close to infinity, which means the load on the anchor increases radically as well.

Keep in mind that these examples take place in a hypothetical, frictionless world. In the real world, the ropes traveling across the snow and being redirected by carabiners, pulleys, the crevasse lip, and so on all introduce friction. Meanwhile, other factors—including whether you're hauling or not—affect the loads as well, but not enough to put three to six times the weight of the climber on the anchor.

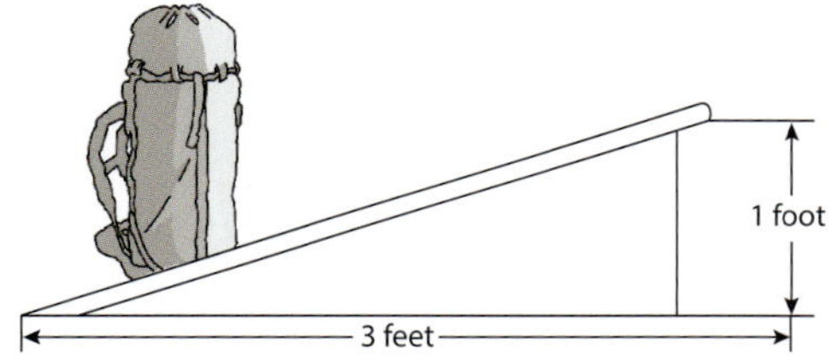

***Figure 9-13.** A ramp is a simple machine that increases mechanical advantage. Here, you have to move the pack 3 feet horizontally in order to raise it 1 foot vertically, but you will be pushing only about a third of the pack's weight.*

which you were originally clipped in to the rope or in to a new knot on the slack side of the rope (fig. 9-14a–b).

2. Weight the anchor to test it (fig. 9-14c). Attach yourself farther down the rope with a clove hitch and a locking carabiner, at the distance you need to investigate the lip (fig. 9-14d). For example, if the lip is 10 feet away, clip in with around 10 feet of slack. While not required, it is best to add a prusik to avoid falling farther than you need to, especially if you have a lot of rope in your system (e.g., you climb in with more than 20 feet of slack).
3. Unclip yourself from the knot or bight of rope you were originally in when you caught the fall and that, presumably, the anchor is now clipped to.
4. Work your way toward the crevasse edge; use your ice axe or pole (basket removed) to probe the crevasse.
5. Drop the free rope end to the fallen climber and have them clip in with a locking carabiner (fig. 9-14g).
6. Clear and then pad the lip using your backpack or other (fig. 9-14h).
7. Walk back up to the anchor, pulling the rope to the fallen climber taut to keep track of which end is which.
8. Clip this end through a Petzl Micro Traxion, Garda hitch, or similar ratchet (see chapter 2 for options) such that the rope is running from the back side of the original knot down to the fallen climber

Figure 9-14. *Drop-end 3:1 haul:* **a**, *Arrest the fall, and build an anchor.* **b**, *Clip the anchor to the same knot the rescuer is clipped in with; take care not to clip the rescuer's clip-in carabiner.* **c**, *Let the anchor take the weight of the fallen climber and access the rescuer's extra rope.* **d**, *Approximate the distance to the edge of the crevasse and tie a clove hitch at this distance.* **e**, *Attach a prusik hitch near the anchor on the slack side of the knot. The rescuer can now unclip and move toward the edge.* **f**, *Communicate with the fallen climber.* **g**, *Tie a knot in the end of the rope, attach a locking carabiner to it, and lower it down to the fallen*

climber. **h**, *Clean and pad the lip of the crevasse.* **i**, *Walk back up toward the anchor. Pull the rope taut that leads to the fallen climber and clip it to the anchor through some sort of progress capture ratchet.* **j**, *Attach a tractor to the rope between the fallen climber and the ratchet.* **k**, *Brake and haul, resetting the tractor as necessary, and taking in slack from time to time by tying overhand knots on the strand of rope the climber fell in on.*

and then back up to your ratchet (fig. 9-14i–j).

9. Next, build the tractor: walk back down toward the lip and attach a friction hitch like a prusik on the front side of the ratchet or use a mechanical ratchet like a Petzl Tibloc to the strand of rope coming out of the crevasse, clipping the long end of the rope to it so that it's now redirected a second instance, which eventually ends at you.
10. Back up the haul system: Return to the anchor again and use a clove hitch in the rope end that's traveling from the tractor to the anchor. It will catch if either the rope-grabbing hitches or mechanical ratchets fail.
11. Haul, managing the ratchet and resetting the tractor and lip padding as necessary (fig. 9-14k).

DROP-END 6:1 HAUL

The drop-end 6:1 haul (a.k.a. new-strand 6:1 haul) builds immediately off the 3:1 haul but increases the mechanical advantage with just one more carabiner and one more hitch. As such, it is the most common way people increase mechanical advantage if they find themselves needing more pulling power.

1. Starting from the previous drop-end 3:1 haul, with your backup clove hitch on the anchor, take the rope on the haul-side strand of the tractor (the prusik) and tie on another prusik, attaching a nonlocking carabiner to it (fig. 9-15a–b).
2. Take the brake-side strand of the clove-hitch backup on the anchor and clip it to the clove hitch you just made (fig. 9-15c–d). Voilá, you just turned your 3:1 into a 6:1!

DIRECT-LINE 3:1 HAUL

The direct-line 3:1 haul (a.k.a. original-strand 3:1 haul) is the traditional method of crevasse rescue. It has the disadvantages of having a more challenging load transfer—as there is much more friction in the system even after the lip has been cleared—and the rope team cannot use knots, but it offers one main advantage: It needs just a bit of extra rope that's not under tension. Note that groups planning on using this haul often have a single prusik riding just in front of each rope team member, prerigged on the rope to facilitate transferring the load.

If you are the rescuer, take these steps:

1. After arresting the fall and building an anchor, clip the long end of the prerigged prusik to the anchor (fig. 9-16a–b).
2. Downclimb to make sure the anchor takes the weight (fig. 9-16c).
3. Take a locking carabiner and clip a clove hitch to it and then attach it to the anchor. This serves as a backup should the prusik hitch holding the weight start to fail (fig. 9-16d).
4. Access the rest of your rope and clip yourself into it with a clove hitch roughly the travel distance to the lip of the crevasse. For example, if the lip is 10 feet away, clip in with 10 feet of slack. To shorten any potential fall, use a prusik kept snug to the anchor as you move out. Conversely, clip a modern tool like a Petzl Micro Traxion device onto the rope below the knot to facilitate the load transfer (fig. 9-16e).
5. Go to the lip and communicate the plan with the fallen climber and then dig out and pad the tensioned rope holding the fallen climber (fig. 9-16f–g).

Figure 9-15. *To create a drop-end 6:1 haul:* **a**, *Starting with a 3:1 hauling system, tie a clove hitch behind the hauling system if there is not already one there.* **b**, *On the hauling side of the tractor, tie a clove hitch in the rope as close as possible and attach a nonlocking carabiner to it.* **c**, *Take the free end (back side) of the clove hitch backup on the anchor and clip it to the clove hitch you just tied.* **d**, *Haul, resetting the prusik (tractor) and clove hitch as necessary.*

6. Walk back toward the anchor and attach a prusik or a mechanical prusik such as a Petzl Tibloc to the tensioned rope (fig. 9-16h).
7. Take the back side of the clove hitch that is on the anchor and clip it to this prusik—this will be the tractor (fig. 9-16i).
8. Walking back up to the anchor, take the back side of this stand and attach a clove hitch on a locking carabiner—this will be the new backup (fig. 9-16j). You cannot start hauling yet because you need to remove the previous backup, which is by far the most overlooked step and thus the one in this sequence you should practice the most.
9. Once the new backup is on, either open up the "old" backup and take out one

Figure 9-16. *Step-by-step of a 3:1 direct line haul:* **a**, *Arrest the fall and build an anchor.* **b**, *Tie a prusik hitch to the rope between the rescuer and the fallen climber.* **c**, *Attach the prusik hitch to the anchor, and down climb to test and let the anchor take the weight of the fallen climber.* **d**, *Tie a clove hitch on the slack side of the prusik hitch, and attach it to the anchor to back up the prusik hitch.* **e**, *From this clove, approximate the distance to the edge of the crevasse and tie another clove hitch. Tie a prusik hitch closer to the anchor and clip it to yourself to limit the distance you can fall.* **f**, *Adjust the prusik and clove hitch to keep yourself*

safe as you move out toward the lip of the crevasse then communicate with the fallen climber. **g**, *Clean and pad the lip.* **h**, *Move back toward the anchor, attach a tractor, and clip the back side of the clove hitch on the anchor to it.* **i**, *Tie and attach a clove hitch on the back side of the tractor where it meets the anchor; this will eventually be the new backup.* **j**, *Attach a locking carabiner between the two clove hitches on the anchor.* **k**, *Clip the back side of the original clove hitch running free (not in a knot) to the middle locking carabiner. Once it's clipped, undo the clove hitch and remove that locking carabiner.* **l**, *Haul.*

TRANSFERRING THE INITIAL LOAD WITH A MECHANICAL RATCHET

If you are carrying a mechanical ratchet like a Petzl Micro Traxion, you can use it instead of a prusik to transfer the load for direct line or original strand hauls. You still need to make sure not to build your anchor too far away just like when using a prusik. Keep in mind that the mechanical ratchet has less "play," so you need to be even more careful to set it up close enough. The advantages are many. Not only is the mechanical ratchet far less likely to slip than a traditional prusik, but it also saves you several steps later on in this rescue sequence and makes it easier to haul past knots in the rope should you need to do that.

If you are carrying one and planning to do a direct line haul rescue, using a mechanical ratchet to transfer the load offers a lot of advantages and will significantly simplify the steps to set up a rescue system.

strand of rope so it can flow freely, or add a second carabiner clipped to the anchor and the rope before removing the old backup and locking carabiner (fig. 9-16k).

10. Haul while managing the ratchet and resetting the tractor and padding as necessary (fig. 9-16l).

If you don't have enough rope or aren't using a new-strand system, and you don't suspect the rope has cut into the crevasse lip too deeply, then you can use a modern tool like a Petzl Micro Traxion device, instead of the more traditional prusik, to transfer the load. Clip the mechanical ratchet directly from the rope onto the load side of the rescuer's knot, giving them some "slack" once the anchor has taken the weight and setting the rescuer up to use the ratchet.

Hauling Past Knots in a Direct-Line System

If you tied knots in your rope, have no fear. It is possible to haul past them with just a few extra steps in your hauling system:

1. Rig your hauling system.
2. Use a double-length sling or similar material with one end attached to the anchor, attaching the other end with a mechanical prusik or another friction hitch to the load strand leading directly to the fallen climber.
3. Haul until the knot gets close to the ratchet in your haul system. Pass the knot with your friction-hitch and sling combination, and then push this combo tight so that it can take and hold the weight (fig. 9-17a–c).
4. Loosen your ratchet so you have slack to untie the knot (fig. 9-17d–e).
5. Repeat as needed (fig. 9-17f).

Figure 9-17. *To haul past knots:* **a**, *Haul until the knot you want to pass is right in front of your tractor.* **b**, *Attach a friction hitch or mechanical prusik on to a sling to the side of the knot that is farthest from the anchor. Clip the other side of the sling (minimum recommended length is 120 centimeters) in to the anchor.* **c**, *Haul slightly until you can open your ratchet and let a little slack into the system to tension the sling and let it take the load.* **d**, *Let the sling take the weight and the rope becomes slack.* **e**, *Untie the knot.* **f**, *Haul and repeat as needed.*

DRAGGED INTO THE ABYSS

BY JONATHON SPITZER

In late June, I flew into the Alaska Range to lead an expedition on Denali with Rachel Greenberg and six clients. We left our base camp that evening after sorting gear and reviewing crevasse rescue. While traveling on the well-established path out of camp, our snowshoes were sinking in only a few inches. At the bottom of Heartbreak Hill, an independent climbing team of two passed us.

As we crested a small dip in the glacier, we heard screams for help. As we approached, we saw that a climber had fallen into a crevasse, and it was his friend on the surface screaming. I immediately noticed how close the individual up top was to the crevasse lip—his partner had taken a substantial fall, dragging the climber to the edge. Sure enough, when I looked into the crevasse, I could see the fallen climber 30 feet down, his heavy sled tied directly to his harness. He was responsive, but he was getting soaked by water dripping from above; meanwhile, his taut rope had cut deeply into the massive crevasse lip.

Rachel and I determined that there was no way to use their rope for an extraction, so we quickly probed out another area for our clients to stand and built an anchor we then clipped them to. I returned to the edge to get a better look at the climber. He was still responsive but now shivering as he became drenched. The sled was also pulling on his body, causing him excruciating pain. With the size of the crevasse lip, we would not be able to haul both him and his sled out at the same time.

I rappelled into the crevasse. Rachel, up on the surface with our climbing rope, used it to set up a drop-loop haul system. I helped the climber get out of the dripping water and then put a jacket on; I also cut his sled free and clipped it to the bottom of my rappel line. We then transferred the fallen climber onto the drop loop; Rachel and our clients hauled him out. Once the climber was back up top, the team set up another drop loop to haul his sled out. Finally, I ascended back out of the crevasse under my own power.

KEY TAKEAWAYS: Not all crevasse falls or crevasses are the same; a simple haul on the loaded strand may not be possible. If the crevasse lip is massive, before dropping a fallen climber a new line, consider digging through the overhang 3–6 feet off to the side so as to not crush them with falling debris. Use the correct sled configuration while traveling on a glacier: Attach the sled to the rope with a clove hitch or a prusik loop (see chapter 13). Finally, train to be self-sufficient. Your team members may be the only ones you can rely on.

Jonathon Spitzer is an IFMGA mountain guide, member of the AMGA National Instructor Team and the director of guide service for Alpine Ascents International. Jonathon has been climbing and guiding on glaciers for more than two decades and lives in North Bend, Washington, with his wife, Rachel, and son, Ari.

Figure 9-18. *The drop-loop 6:1 system is one of the most efficient systems for crevasse rescue because, besides your choice of backup, only one tractor needs resetting.*

DROP-LOOP 6:1 HAUL

The drop-loop 6:1 haul (a.k.a. Canadian drop loop) gained its nickname because of its popularity among the Association of Canadian Mountain Guides. If you happen to have enough rope, it's the most efficient form of crevasse rescue, as it lets you use a new strand of rope and only "reset" on a tractor on a 6:1 (fig. 9-18). The primary downside is that, up on the surface, you need roughly twice the amount of rope between you and the fallen climber available. This makes the drop-loop 6:1 a good technique should the situation allow, but it should not be the only tool in your toolbox. If you are the rescuer, follow these steps:

1. After arresting the fall and building an anchor, clip the anchor in to your clip-in point or just past it on the side of the rope that is not holding the fall (fig. 9-19a).
2. Attach yourself farther down the rope with a locking carabiner and a clove hitch, leaving enough slack to investigate the crevasse lip. For example, if the lip is 10 feet away, clip in with around 10 feet of slack. While not required, place a prusik to avoid falling farther than you need to, especially if you have a lot of rope in your system (e.g., you fall in with more than 20 feet of slack).
3. Unclip yourself from the bight of rope that you were originally in when you caught the fall and that, presumably, the anchor is now clipped to.
4. Work your way toward the edge of the crevasse; use your ice axe or pole to probe the crevasse.
5. Once you're at the lip, clear the edge of snow.
6. Drop a bight of rope (with one end coming from the brake-side strand of the knot holding the load) down to the fallen climber. Have them clip in to this bight with a locking carabiner.
7. Walk back up to the anchor and pull the rope up so it comes taut to help you keep track of the strands. If you lose track of which strand to pull, start with the end that is attached to you or where it's clipped in to you, and then work back toward the system (fig. 9-19b).
8. Attach a Petzl Micro Traxion device or other ratchet (see chapter 2) to the anchor, such that the rope's long end goes into the ratchet, which helps you keep track of the ends.
9. Now walk down and attach a tractor to the strand emerging from the crevasse and that leads to the ratchet you just put on.
10. Clip the tractor with a nonlocking carabiner.

Figure 9-19. *To use a drop-loop 6:1:* **a**, *Build an anchor, transfer the load, clip in with a clove hitch, and work your way out toward the edge; toss down a bight of the rope and have the fallen climber clip in.* **b**, *Walk back up to the anchor and rig a ratchet (i.e., a progress capture system like a Garda Hitch or a mechanical ratchet like a Petzl Micro Traxion). Walk back down and attach your tractor and clip its brake-side strand with a nonlocking carabiner.* **c**, *Back up the system (e.g., by managing slack on the original end as shown here). Haul, resetting as necessary.*

11. Back up the system: You can manage slack on the original strand by regularly tying knots; otherwise, clip a clove hitch to the anchor or your harness.
12. Start hauling, resetting the tractor and backups as needed (fig. 9-19c).

EDGE HAUL 2:1

The edge haul 2:1 (a.k.a. loose-pull method) is shockingly effective in certain situations despite its low relative mechanical advantage. There is no tractor or ratchet to manage, and it's quick to set up. It is best done with a ratcheting pulley like a Petzl Micro Traxion device, Edelrid Spoc, or similar, as this technique maximizes hauling power by minimizing friction. It is also "committing" in the sense that once you start hauling the fallen climber, it becomes difficult to release them, as they are on a ratcheting pulley that will be tough to access. While this is rarely a problem, it means you likely shouldn't attempt the edge haul 2:1 with someone who is hurt, unconscious, or under a sizable lip. Fortunately, if you need more oomph, you can always convert this haul into a different technique, assuming you don't need the Micro Traxion device or to lower the fallen climber.

1. After arresting the fall and building an anchor, clip the anchor into your (the rescuer's) clip-in point or just past it on the side of the rope not holding the fall.
2. Attach yourself farther down the rope with a locker and clove hitch, and access

Figure 9-20. *To execute an edge haul:* **a**, *Build an anchor and attach the anchor to your clip-in knot. Attach yourself to a new clove hitch, unclip from the original knot, and down climb to test the anchor. Then access your extra rope and work your way toward the lip of the crevasse.* **b**, *Create a bight of rope on the nonanchor side of rope and attach a mechanical ratchet to it with the load side going toward the anchor and haul side being the free end. Setting the ratchet up correctly is critical. Lower this ratchet to the fallen climber and have them attach themselves to it.* **c**, *Pull up on the brake strand coming out of the ratchet that is on the fallen climber. Run the rope from the crevasse up your side, across your back, and over your opposite shoulder.* **d**, *Haul using a squatting motion that allows you to rely primarily on your legs. Squat-pull the slack in over your shoulder and then hold the rope in the brake position and stand up.*

THROW THEM 'BOWS

If you are being hauled out of a crevasse, it is imperative that you prevent your knot and upper body from getting jammed into the lip of the crevasse. A stuck knot could prevent the hauling team from pulling you over the lip, or it could result in injury to you as you get pulled into the lip. In the last few decades, there has been at least one known fatality from this scenario on Mount Rainier. As you are hauled upward and get close to the lip of the crevasse, use your elbows and knees to keep yourself out and away from the wall, particularly as you transition from the vertical terrain in the crevasse to the horizontal terrain on the surface. This technique also often reduces friction, reducing the effort the hauling team must exert to pull you out.

With your elbows out, push your forearms into the lip of the crevasse to keep from getting pulled into it as your rescuers haul you up and over.

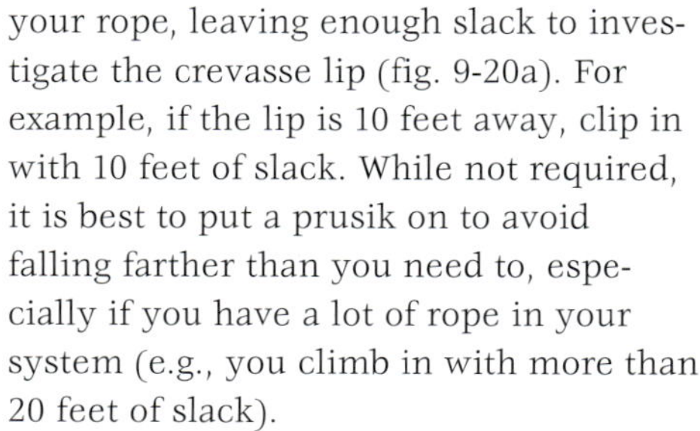

your rope, leaving enough slack to investigate the crevasse lip (fig. 9-20a). For example, if the lip is 10 feet away, clip in with 10 feet of slack. While not required, it is best to put a prusik on to avoid falling farther than you need to, especially if you have a lot of rope in your system (e.g., you climb in with more than 20 feet of slack).

3. Unclip yourself from the bight of rope that you were originally in when you caught the fall and that, presumably, the anchor is now clipped to.
4. Work your way toward the crevasse edge; use your ice axe or pole to probe the crevasse. Ensure you maintain your security, utilizing a longer clip-in with a clove hitch (based on the distance from the anchor to the lip) and a friction hitch to manage the slack if needed.
5. Once at the lip, clear the edge of snow.
6. On the long-end side of your clip-in clove hitch, form a bight of rope (with one end coming from the brake-side strand of the knot holding the load) and clip in a Petzl Micro Traxion device, Edelrid Spoc, or similar device situated such that the rope's long end (not going to the anchor) becomes the "hauling" end. Lower the bight and ratchet to the fallen climber and have them clip in to the ratchet with a locking carabiner (fig. 9-20b).
7. Cinch yourself tight to your clove hitch, as this form of crevasse rescue requires that you stand right on the crevasse lip to minimize friction.

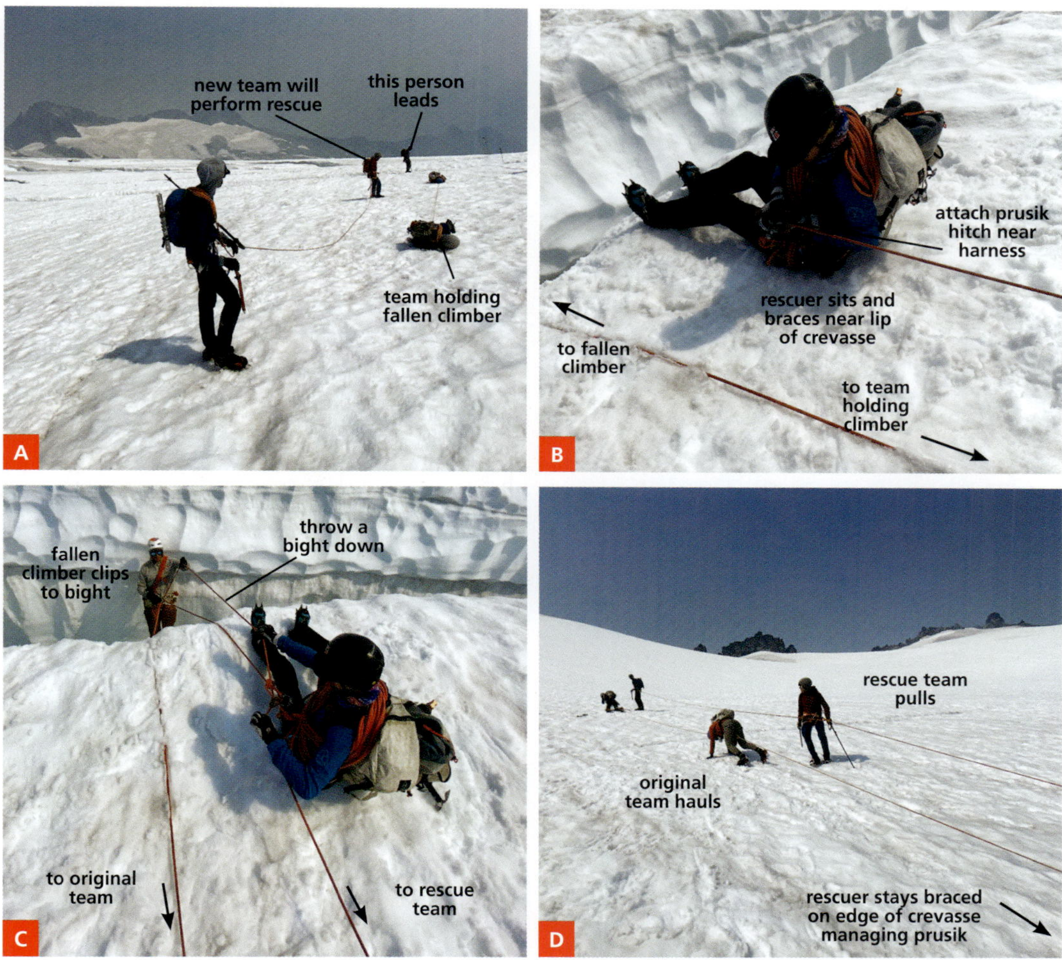

Figure 9-21. *How to perform the team C crevasse-rescue system:* **a,** *Step 1: After the first team (right) has arrested the fall, the second team (left) should slowly approach the crevasse lip.* **b,** *Step 2: The leader of the second rope team should sit down and brace their feet, leaning off tension from their rope team. They should then put a friction hitch on the rope between them and the second climber on their rope team. They might need to access their coils (extra rope) and adjust their clip-in point if the fallen climber is super deep.* **c,** *Step 3: The second rope team's leader should then pull rope through the prusik until they have enough rope to throw a bight to the fallen climber, who then clips into it.* **d,** *Steps 4–7: The second rope team's leader, on the crevasse edge, should manage their prusik and kick their feet into the snow to brace themselves, all while their rope team hauls out the fallen climber on their rope by walking away from the crevasse. Simultaneously, the first rope team's climbers, who caught the fall, can both help and serve as a backup by crawling away from the crevasse.*

Figure 9-22. Consider clove-hitching the rope to your harness and crawling uphill so your legs do the work. Bear-crawling lets you rely primarily on your stronger leg muscles to haul.

8. While you can use any hauling method, one of the most effective is a shoulder belay. Pull out the slack and drape the rope over your shoulders; the rope should pass over you and then cross behind your back before coming off the opposite shoulder (fig. 9-20c).
9. Do squats to haul the fallen person out: bend your legs, pull the rope taut, and lock it off as in a shoulder belay; stand up with a straight back, using your legs to haul (fig. 9-20d).
10. Repeat, letting the Micro Traxion device take in the slack.

TEAM C (2:1)

For groups that are traveling with more than one rope team, there is no faster, easier, or more effective crevasse-rescue system than the team C—the big caveat being that you need a completely separate rope team on hand. However, if this is the case, you can perform crevasse rescue without needing to ever attach the load directly to an anchor; the original team can provide the "backup" by crawling as the second team hauls out the fallen climber:

1. If a climber has fallen into a crevasse and a rope team is holding them, then the leader of the second rope team should cautiously approach the crevasse to establish both the location of the crevasse's edge and communication with the fallen climber (fig. 9-21a).
2. If the decision is made to haul, the second rope team's leader can put a prusik on the rope leading to their rope team (fig. 9-21b). This will protect them while they drop down a U of rope between themselves and the next person on their rope team, as in the next step.
3. After establishing how far down the fallen climber is and accessing rope they have stored in their pack or in coils, the second rope team's leader should then drop a U of slack down to the fallen climber and have them clip in to the U (not a knot) with a locking carabiner (fig. 9-21c).
4. The second rope team's leader should now prep the lip, knock down excess snow, and pad the lip (e.g., with a backpack, foam pad, ice axe, or similar to keep the rope from cutting in).
5. The second rope team's leader should then sit down and kick their feet in; if the terrain slopes downhill or they are lighter than the fallen climber, they could use an ice axe or a picket as a backup, with the goal of feeling only half the weight of the fallen climber (fig. 9-21d).

6. Have the second rope team walk away from the crevasse edge. They are pulling with a 2:1 mechanical advantage.
7. The original rope team that caught the fall should also crawl away from the crevasse. This helps "back up" the fallen climber and acts as a safeguard for the second rope team's leader, keeping them from getting pulled down more than a foot or two toward the crevasse.

Note that this system uses crawling as a backup. Hauling can be a lot of work, depending on the weight of the fallen climber (plus their backpack). This works in other systems as well. Instead of just pulling with your arms and back, try clipping a clove hitch to your belay loop or harness and crawling up the slope, using the strength of your legs (fig. 9-22). This can sometimes mean the difference between being able to haul someone out easily and barely being able to budge them.

Opposite: *Sarah Janin ascends out of a steep crevasse on the Eldorado Ice Cap, Washington.*

CHAPTER 10

Self-Rescue

Figure 10-1. *While you should be prepared to rescue yourself by ascending a rope, unlike in hauling scenarios, escaping a crevasse this way isn't always an option.*

Self-rescue refers to the fallen climber ascending out of a crevasse under their own power. Generally, a fallen climber ascends their climbing rope—the one they fell in on—but self-rescue can also include any number of methods that don't depend on climbers on the surface creating a rescue system. Some methods include belaying the fallen climber out if they can climb up with one axe, or stem between the crevasse walls, and lowering a second ice axe or ice tool when practical. In rare circumstances, fallen climbers have been lowered to the "floor" of the crevasse, where they could then walk, scramble, or climb out via a less steep egress.

Every climber should be prepared to self-rescue and ascend a rope using the tools on their harness. However, you shouldn't rely on rope ascents for self-rescue, because climbers who fall into hidden (trapdoor) crevasses are rarely able to ascend the rope back to the surface, not because the rope ascent is difficult, but because the final 2–7 feet where the rope cuts into the lip are extremely tough to navigate (i.e., it's exceptionally difficult to clean the rope out from below even on a small overhanging lip; fig. 10-1). A mechanical prusik like a Petzl Tibloc or a Micro Traxion device is certainly better than just using prusiks, but if you are only going to be

Figure 10-2. *Grant Price battles through a small lip, showing just how strenuous self-rescue can be.*

proficient with one aspect of crevasse rescue, self-rescue is secondary to the rope team crevasse-rescue techniques covered in chapter 9. For example, when you are being hauled by a rope team, you can push yourself up and away from the obstacle, which is nearly impossible to do while moving your ascending tools up the rope (fig. 10-2).

Thus while self-rescue is unquestionably an important skill, the likelihood of it being your method of choice is low. The fallen climber can be most helpful to their team by, first, unweighting the rope (see chapter 9 and fig. 10-3). As such, spend the bulk of your time practicing building solid anchors and rope team crevasse rescue techniques so you can execute them quickly, reliably, and efficiently.

ASCENDING

One of the hardest parts of ascending a rope out of a crevasse is getting started. The rope is taut to your harness, meaning the ascent will be strenuous at least until you get up a bit and

Figure 10-3. *When you initially fall in, the rescuer on the surface should immediately start building an anchor. Unweighting the rope, even if just for a little while, will make their job easier, as Wade Spiner does here while stemming with his legs across a crevasse.*

can use the tools you have available more efficiently (fig. 10-4).

To begin, you will need to attach two friction hitches (or mechanical prusiks) to the rope. One of these hitches will clip to your belay loop as a "waist prusik," a term used here generically to describe a mechanical prusik like a Petzl Tibloc or Wild Country Ropeman. You don't necessarily need to use a locking carabiner, since you should never rely solely on a friction hitch, as it will likely slip badly as you try to turn the lip.

The second hitch or ascender will need to have some sort of cord or loop—generally 3.5

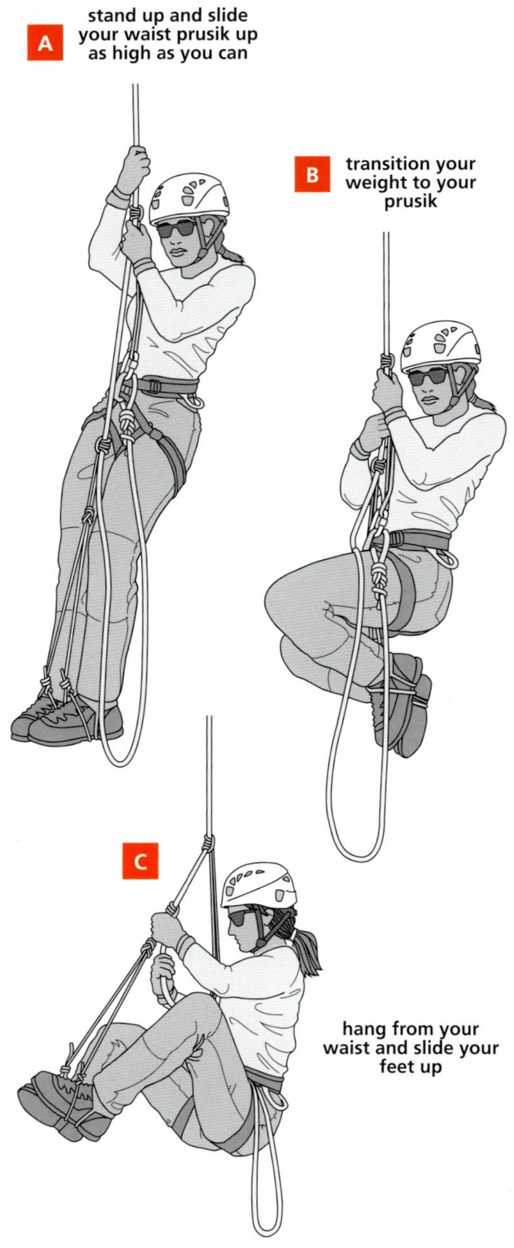

to 5 feet long—for one or both of your feet to stand in. This is your "foot prusik."

Your goal in a rope ascent is to transition back and forth between hanging on your waist prusik and standing in your foot prusik. You "weight" one prusik and then push up the other, unweighted prusik, alternating them back and forth as you ascend the rope:

1. Put a foot prusik on the rope (fig. 10-5b).
2. Put a mechanical ratchet on the rope and clip it to your belay loop (fig. 10-5c).
3. 3. Step up onto your foot loop, and attach the mechanical ratchet to your belay loop (fig. 10-5d).
4. Alternate between pushing the foot prusik up and weighting it, and pushing up the waist prusik and weighting it (fig. 10-5e).

Contrary to popular belief, it is more efficient to put your foot-prusik attachment *above* the waist-prusik attachment. This setup allows for greater "throw" (the vertical distance gained with each ascension rep). To practice this method, hang on your waist prusik and bend your knees toward your chest while raising your feet; this allows you to push your foot prusik quite high up the rope. Then, once your

Figure 10-4. *The basic principle of ascending a rope is to alternate between sliding, weighting, and then unweighting hitches and/or devices connected to the rope. To follow the method shown here:* ***a****, Use a longer piece of material (such as a 120-centimeter sling) to tie a friction hitch on the rope above you, and then use the open end as a foot loop. Tie a shorter prusik (roughly 60-centimeter loop) below the foot prusik and clip it to your harness. Stand up on your foot loop, and slide your slack waist prusik up the rope.* ***b****, Sit down in your harness, weighting your waist prusik.* ***c****, Slide your foot prusik up, and repeat.*

Figure 10-5. *Ascending a rope inside a crevasse:* **a**, *This climber is hanging from his tie-in knot inside a crevasse.* **b**, *To ascend, first tie a friction hitch on the rope above you, using a longer piece of material (such as a 120-centimeter sling), and use the open end as a foot loop.* **c**, *Attach a mechanical ratchet to the rope between the friction hitch and your tie-in knot.* **d**, *Step up onto your foot loop and clip the mechanical prusik to your belay loop. Wrapping your arm around the taut rope can help you stabilize your body.* **e**, *Standing on your foot loop, pull up on the rope between the mechanical prusik and your tie-in knot, and then sit and weigh the ratchet. Slide your foot loop up, weight it, and repeat.*

feet weight the now-taut foot prusik, "climb" it, sliding your waist prusik up until this latter is (ideally) just below your foot prusik.

BACKING YOURSELF UP

The cams or teeth of mechanical rope-ascending devices can often get jammed with snow, and there is a very real chance that as you try to push your hitches or mechanical prusiks through the crevasse lip, they will slip or not grab at all. So don't rely solely on hitches or devices for self-rescue. To back yourself up, clip a hard knot—like an overhand or figure-eight on a bight, or a clove hitch you can adjust on the fly—into your belay loop (fig. 10-6), ideally with a locking carabiner. If one or both of your ascent tools slip or fail catastrophically, you will still be securely attached to the rope. Note that both the hitches and devices are *far* more likely to slip on skinny, wet, or icy ropes, a common scenario in a snowy environment, especially when trying to surmount a crevasse lip. It's thus also a good idea to back yourself up every 6–10 feet (2–3 meters) to minimize the potential falling distance.

Figure 10-6. *Back yourself up as you ascend out of a crevasse. Clip a hard knot to your belay loop so that you don't fall the entire length of the rope.* (Photo by Zack McGill)

ASCENDING WITH A 3:1 ADVANTAGE

For less steep ascents, a 3:1 setup is likely overkill. But for truly steep or physical ascents, it's useful as an assist. This setup redirects the rope so that you can pull down with your arm as you stand up, which in turn helps "lift" your body. However, you'll need some sort of rope capture on your waist—ideally a progress-capture pulley like the Petzl Micro Traxion device or Edelrid Spoc, but you could also use a Garda hitch, a belay device in guide mode (i.e., autoblocking mode), a GriGri, or similar assisted-belay device. In setting up a 3:1 ascent system, you use a ratchet on your waist that is redirected through your foot attachment, allowing you to pull "down" on yourself to create the advantage (figs. 10-7 and 10-8):

1. Start from a traditional setup, with your foot prusik attached high and your waist prusik attached low.
2. Clip the rope so that it's redirected on your waist. A progress-capture pulley like a Petzl Micro Traxion, Edelrid Spoc, or similar works fantastically here.
3. The brake strand continues up and is then redirected again off the foot prusik. Note that you might need to tie an additional overhand on a bight or similar knot to create a place to clip the brake strand to.

MECHANICAL PRUSIKS MAKE THINGS EASIER

Ascending out of a crevasse is shockingly physical, and if you happen to not be wearing crampons and are hanging against a very slick, icy wall or, worse, are suspended out in space, it is easy to underestimate how physically demanding it can be. This is potentially compounded by a heavy pack and the need to breach the soft crevasse lip. This is where mechanical prusiks come in! Mechanical prusiks allow you to ascend more fluidly, as you can directly put your energy into going upward without having to fight with prusiks or other hitches.

Tools in this genre include the Petzl Tibloc and Wild Country Ropeman as well as progress-capture pulleys like the Petzl Micro or Nano Traxion devices and the Edelrid Spoc. These devices take a lot of the strain out of rope ascent. They add a little weight to your kit (an ounce or two depending on the model), but most of these devices still weigh less than a single locking carabiner. They can be used for both self-rescue (the fallen climber ascending out) and building mechanical-advantage systems on the surface. Consider traveling with at least one progress-capture pulley and one mechanical prusik—the weight is minimal, but the savings in safety and efficiency are immeasurable.

Using mechanical prusiks: **a**, *Peter Broback (top climber) uses a Petzl Micro Traxion device as his waist prusik and a Petzl Tibloc as his foot prusik.* **b**, *He pulls on the rope as it comes through the Micro Traxion device and simultaneously presses down with his foot on the Tibloc, maximizing efficiency.*

Figure 10-7. *To ascend out of steeper crevasses—or even lower-angle ones if you don't have crampons on—it can be quite helpful to use a 3:1 mechanical advantage, as Lyra Pierotti does here.*

4. If you have a traditional waist prusik on, remove it now.
5. As you ascend, hang on your waist redirect and push your foot prusik upward as you would with a more traditional ascent method; however, also pull down on the brake end as you step up on your foot loop. You are essentially ascending with a 3:1 mechanical advantage.

Being able to ascend the rope is a valuable tool that should be part of every mountaineer's toolkit (fig. 10-9). While you should not rely on it as your only technique for crevasse rescue, it is a valuable skill for both self-rescue and for rappelling into a crevasse to help an injured climber and ascending back out.

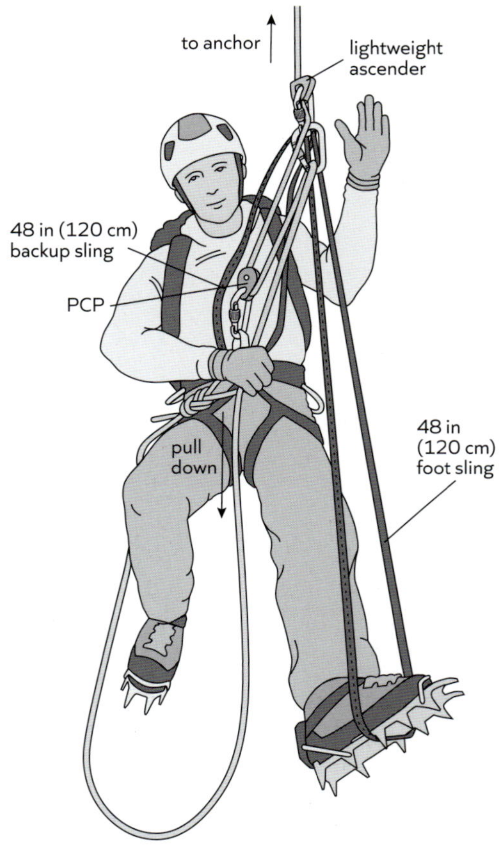

Figure 10-8. *Improvised ascension with a 3:1 mechanical advantage using a mechanical ratchet like a Petzl Micro Traxion on your waist*

DEALING WITH YOUR BACKPACK

Depending on the weight and size of your backpack, wearing it while performing self-rescue can be anything from a nonissue to extremely problematic. If you plan to carry an overnight pack of significant weight (more than thirty pounds), consider tying a "ditch loop," to make it significantly easier to take your backpack off without the risk of dropping

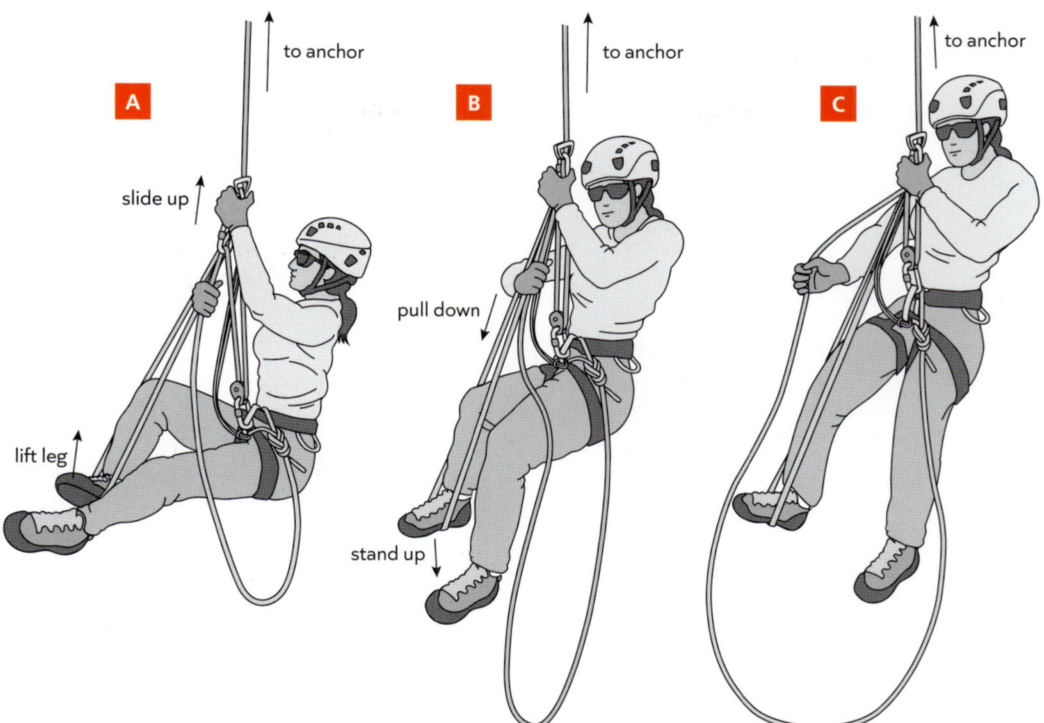

Figure 10-9. *To ascend a rope using a ratchet,* **a**, *Hang on the Micro traxion so your foot prusik is slack and you can slide it up the rope.* **b**, *Stand on the foot loop while pulling down.* **c**, *Hang on the Micro Traxion on your waist once again, slide your foot prusik up, and repeat.*

it. For lighter summit-day loads, a ditch loop is unnecessary—either because the pack's light enough that its weight on your back won't be an issue, or you can just clip it off to your harness with the grab loop or a daisy-chain attachment point (if available).

1. To rig a ditch loop, take some cord (5- to 6-millimeter cord works great) and capture both the pack's grab loop and one shoulder strap. Tie a bowline with a backup or a rewoven overhand (a.k.a. water knot).
2. Tie an overhand on a bight on the other end of the cord. Depending on the situation, you can pre-clip this to your harness or just have it ready to clip.

If you fall into a crevasse, you can clip your pack to your belay loop—or, if you are in the middle of the rope, tie a knot in the slack side of the rope and hang the pack off this.

If you expect to carry a heavy pack on a glacier, consider rigging a ditch loop on your backpack. If you find yourself in a crevasse, however, with a pack that feels too heavy to ascend with, you have options. One approach is to take a sling off your harness and thread it through both the pack haul loop and a

RESCUING MY HELMET

BY IAN NICHOLSON

On our fourth full day in the Kichatna Spires in the western Alaska Range in 2007, Graham Zimmerman, Ryan O'Connell, and I attempted the Northwest Face of Kichatna Spire, a roughly 3,000-foot route that starts with 2,000 feet of ice and mixed climbing capped by a headwall of mostly steep rock and ridge climbing. We began by ascending twelve long pitches to the headwall, but with weather moving in and the climbing difficulty increasing—plus, we were a little scared—we decided to bail.

We rappelled to the base on a mix of V-threads, nuts, and pin anchors. After nearly twenty-four hours on the move, we pulled the ropes from the final rappel, tired but excited to spend another two and a half weeks in the Alaska Range.

As we packed up to travel down the glacier to base camp, I removed my helmet to adjust my beanie and carelessly set it down next to me—only to watch it slide 50 feet downhill and flip over the lip of a massive crevasse. Ryan, Graham, and I stared. For a moment, no one moved. This was early in our trip, and when you are trying to climb massive new routes in a remote corner of the Alaska Range, helmets are essential. So I built an anchor, and Ryan and Graham belayed me to the lip to look for my helmet. By some miracle, it was sitting on a narrow ledge 80 feet down the otherwise-bottomless crevasse.

All of us were exhausted, but with snow falling and a storm in the forecast, we knew we had to act. I set another anchor and made the free-hanging rappel into the abyss to snag my helmet, taking care not to knock it any deeper. I then ascended back out using a GriGri as my waist prusik and a small prusik attached to a double-length sling as my foot prusik. While it was a bit physical, the process was far quicker than expected, and we could continue the trip safely.

This self-rescue technique had come in more than handy, and I'm still grateful to this day that I knew it.

KEY TAKEAWAYS: Knowing how to ascend a rope is an essential skill. Also don't set loose gear and equipment down next to you on a glacier—you never know where it may end up.

Looking down at the crevasse below the route, where I would eventually drop my helmet.

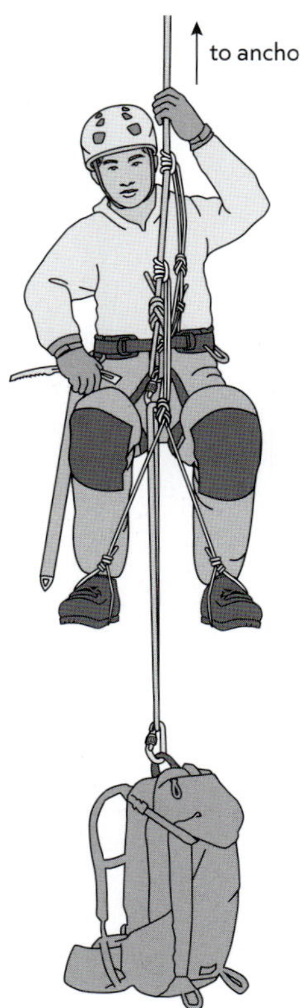

Figure 10-10. *A pack clipped in below a climber ready to ascend. If your backpack is heavy, consider hanging it off your harness with a sling so that you don't have to fight its weight, which may try to tip you over when it's on your back.*

shoulder strap; you can always clip the haul loop in afterward if you can't reach it. Clip the other end of the sling to your belay loop and then slide off your pack. Or you can attach a sling to your harness and the pack haul loop using a carabiner (fig. 10-10).

TEXAS KICK SYSTEM

While the Texas kick system (table 10-1), which uses two foot loops tied on a longer foot prusik instead of just one, is a tried-and-true method that is simple to use, it's fallen out of favor as other, better tools that also set up the rescuer to build a mechanical-advantage hauling system have become available.

TABLE 10-1. ROUGH TEXAS KICK LENGTHS

Climber's height	Foot prusik	Waist prusik
5'	11' (3.4 m)	5' (1.5 m)
5'6"	11'6" (3.5 m)	5'6" (1.7 m)
6'	12' (3.7 m)	6' (1.8 m)
6'6"	13' (4 m)	6'6" (2 m)

To rig the Texas kick system (fig. 10-11a–b):

1. Rig the waist prusik and foot prusik (tying two foot loops) on the rope, with the foot prusik tied above the waist prusik.
2. Hang on the waist prusik.
3. Push the foot prusik up the rope as far as you can.
4. Stand up on the foot prusik, unweighting the waist prusik.
5. Repeat the process, and back yourself up frequently with a hard knot like an overhand on a bight or a clove hitch on your harness.

BELAYING THE FALLEN CLIMBER

On occasion, if the lip doesn't overhang too far and the wall isn't too steep, the fallen climber can climb out (fig. 10-12). To do this, they simply swing their ice tool into the crevasse wall, kick in their front points, and then begin climbing. This is made easier if they have two ice tools or the crevasse is narrow enough for them to stem and chimney between the two walls. It's critical that the person or people holding the fall crawl away from the lip,

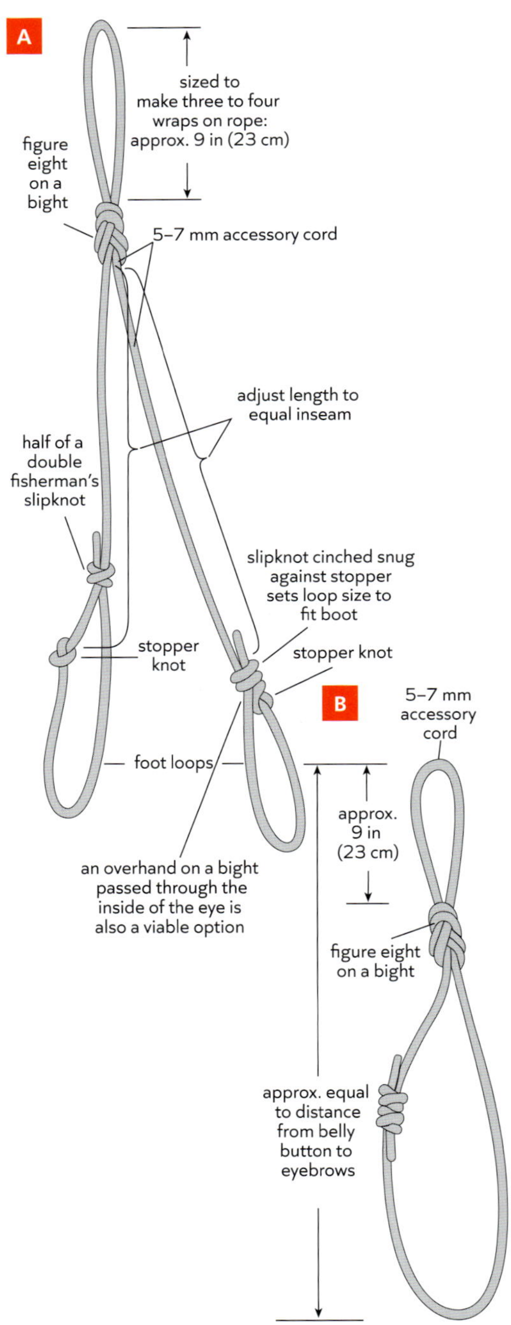

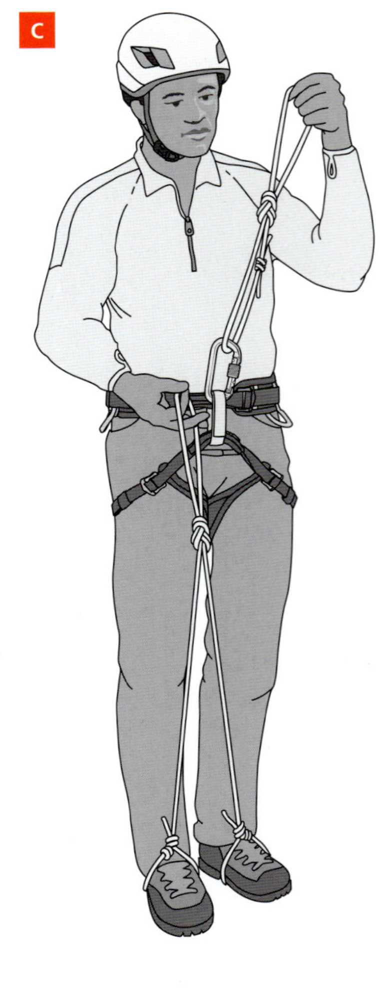

Figure 10-11. *Prusiks are quite useful for ascending a rope:* **a**, *foot prusik with a loop for each foot;* **b**, *waist prusik can be made of tied cord or a sewn sling;* **c**, *a climber with waist and foot prusiks adjusted to the correct length.*

Figure 10-12. *If the lip of the crevasse doesn't overhang too far, you may be able to belay the fallen climber out.*

keeping the rope taut and providing a "moving belay" (if not a mild assist) to safeguard the fallen climber.

Large overhangs (e.g., snowbridges) and thick sections of soft seasonal snow, which do not securely hold the axe's pick, will significantly reduce the effectiveness of these techniques.

LOWERING THE FALLEN CLIMBER

In the vast majority of cases, climbers who fall into crevasses will need to be pulled out or ascend out on their own. In extremely rare cases, however, it might be easier to lower the fallen climber deeper into the crevasse because there is a floor or some sort of feature that lets them more easily climb out. Keep in mind that a lot of the "floors" you might see in crevasses are actually quite unstable, and any climber you lower onto should be kept on a reasonably snug belay to protect them from unexpectedly dropping farther down—creating a very scary and dangerous situation. In yet other situations, climbers occasionally may take refuge in a crevasse with a solid floor (fig. 10-13).

Figure 10-13. *Sometimes you can walk around on the floor of a crevasse, as Colin Haley is doing here while waiting out a vicious storm on Mount Foraker, Alaska, after climbing the Infinite Spur.* (Photo by Rob Smith)

There are various lowering techniques you could use, but the trickiest part will be transitioning your fallen climber from hanging on the rope to being lowered. The easiest way to accomplish this is with a block-and-tackle (see chapter 7):

1. Go out to the lip of the crevasse as described in the techniques in chapter 9 and let the fallen climber know you're going to lower them.
2. On the non-weighted side of the knot holding the fallen climber's weight, build a new lowering system—like a Munter hitch or a redirected belay device in lowering mode—and then tie it off with a mule hitch. You'll use this system later.
3. Attach a friction hitch to the weighted side. Using whatever material you used to tie the friction hitch, add a second knot close to the hitch. This will eventually become the hauling point for your block-and-tackle.
4. Clip a carabiner to the knot next to the friction hitch.
5. Clip another, new carabiner onto the anchor. This is the other carabiner you are going to block-and-tackle with.
6. Clip a cordelette or other piece of long material to that new carabiner.
7. Now clip in a circular fashion, alternating between the friction-hitch carabiner and the anchor carabiners you just added, creating the block-and-tackle.
8. Haul on the material until you can untie the knot in the rope that was initially attached to the anchor after you self-arrested and transferred the load. This is the knot that has been holding the fallen climber's weight.
9. Lower the climber using the lowering system you created earlier, using a friction-hitch backup.

Although someone who falls into a crevasse will likely be hauled out by their team members or other rescuers, knowing how to ascend out of a crevasse is important for a multitude of reasons. It is a simple solution, especially if the fallen climber is only a few feet below the surface. If the fallen climber is hurt or incapacitated, rescuers have no other option than to rappel down to and ascend out before hauling them out. Knowing how to climb out of a crevasse may help you save someone else someday.

Opposite: *Jared Darapla rappels in the Alaska Range.*

CHAPTER 11

Rappelling, Rappel Anchors, and Lowering

In mountaineering and alpinism, getting up is only half the battle. You also need to get back down the mountain, and with fatigue and an eagerness to "just be done" sometimes clouding your judgment or making you rush, this is where a fair share of climbing accidents happen. That's why it pays not only to have your rappel or lowering systems and anchors dialed but also to slow down and double- and triple-check them as you descend.

RAPPELLING

Rappelling is a basic skill, but it's also where most accidents occur. Unlike traveling on a glacier or belaying, where the rope essentially acts as a backup in a fall, while rappelling, the systems get weighted and tested every time. Furthermore, in the mountains and on glaciers, there are rarely existing rappel stations like you'd find at your local crag, and any stations already in situ are weathered and frequently suspect. Meanwhile, glaciers and other snow-covered terrain, plus the steep rock slabs exiting many glaciers, are tricky mediums to build anchors in. If you're rappelling in the context of a crevasse fall, something has likely gone terribly wrong and you're feeling the additional stress and pressure of needing to rescue someone.

RAPPELLING IN COMPLEX GLACIATED TERRAIN

Just like in the rock realm, some terrain you climb up is best rappelled (fig. 11-1). However, unlike in the rock realm, there is rarely a fixed or convenient anchor like a sling-able tree just sitting out in the middle of the glacier. Therefore you'll need to be more resourceful and self-sufficient when descending.

Rappelling has two applications in the context of glacier travel: The first is crevasse rescue, in which the rescuer may have to rappel into a crevasse to provide medical attention or otherwise assist in setting up the hauling system, especially if the fallen climber is hurt or unconscious and you need to descend and aid them before hauling them out. The second is descending glaciers, strange glacial features, steep slopes, or rock features that are too steep, slow, dangerous, or time-consuming to descend on foot or downclimb (fig. 11-2).

EXTENSIONS

A rappel extension (fig. 11-3) offers a lot of advantages over simply clipping the device to your belay loop. The extension more effectively lets you use a friction-hitch backup, referred to as a "third hand." Creating separation between the backup and your belay

Figure 11-1. Rather than attempt to walk down a steep section of pure glacial ice or other challenging feature, it can be easier, faster, and safer to rappel, as Dan Corn does over a section of pure glacier ice on Green Creek Glacier, North Cascades, Washington. (Photo by Jason Antin)

device is advantageous when rappelling off a crevasse lip, down a rock slab, into a dark moat, or down other strange glacial features. It also makes it infinitely easier to transition from rappelling to ascent during a crevasse rescue.

There is no perfect extension. As long as your extension provides the necessary amount of length and offers a secure connection, it is okay. Below are three of the most common belay extensions, all of which can be made with a 120-centimeter sling, an item most climbers traveling on glaciers will already have. Prefabricated options include the Petzl Connect and Metolius PAS.

BACKUPS

A friction-hitch backup, also known as a third hand, is placed on the brake side of the belay device to allow the rappelling climber to go hands-free (fig. 11-4). This lets them more easily build and/or clip in to the next anchor, deal with a tangled or stuck rope, and/or swing around to look for the next rappel station. It also provides additional security in the

Figure 11-2. Rappelling can be used not only to descend difficult sections of terrain but also in crevasse rescue. Here, Peter Broback rappels into a crevasse.

Figure 11-3. A rappel extension makes it easier to go from rappelling to ascending, as in a crevasse-rescue situation. Here, Hannah McGowan rappels on extension with an autoblock as a third hand or backup.

Figure 11-4. *Test your third-hand friction-hitch backup to make sure it holds firmly. If it does, it can allow you to go hands-free to work on other tasks, though caution is still advised.*

event that the rappelling climber is struck by falling ice, snow, rock, or otherwise suffers from an accident that causes them to let go of the rope.

KNOTTING THE ENDS OF THE ROPE

A once greatly debated topic in climbing is now decisively swinging toward using stopper knots at the rope ends (fig. 11-5). The argument for not using knots is the fear of the rope getting stuck, which is still possible, though far less likely on snow than on rock. The argument for using them is that stopper knots protect the rappelling climber from unintentionally rappelling off one (or both) strands.

Even in the worst case, you'll most likely be merely inconvenienced by the knots getting stuck in some moat or lip of snow. At the time of this writing, no one has died directly from their ropes getting stuck on a glacier, yet climbers die every single year from rappelling off the rope ends in *all* venues: alpine, rock, big wall, sport climbing, you name it.

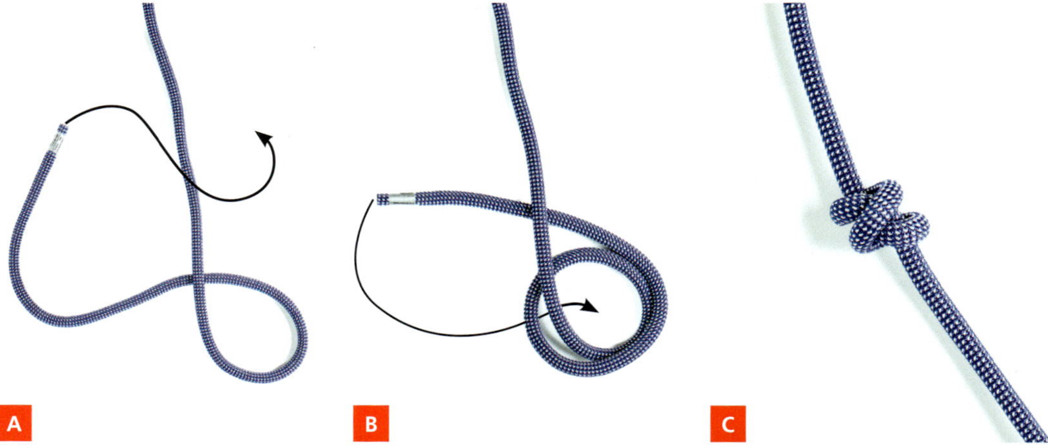

Figure 11-5. *To tie a barrel knot:* **a**, *Fold the rope in your hand, creating a bight, with itself.* **b**, *Make two complete wraps trending back toward the longer end of the rope. Poke the end of the rope back down through the wraps you just made.* **c**, *Tighten each strand to dress the knot.* (Photos by Truc Allen)

Figure 11-6. *Jake Skeen rappels off Sharkfin Tower, Washington, using a double-locking-carabiner rappel. If you don't have a belay device, this is the best technique for rappelling, as it's much smoother and puts far fewer twists in the rope than a Munter hitch.*

IMPROVISED RAPPELS

If you or your partner accidentally drops, forgets, or neglects to bring a belay device, you still have a few rappelling options. For example, you could simply lower the climber to the ground, through the steeper terrain, or to the next anchor. This is a straightforward solution, but it isn't always possible, particularly if you have several rappels remaining or you don't have a good idea of where you're going. (See Lowering, later in this chapter.)

Double-Locking-Carabiner Rappel

The simplest improvised option is the double-locking carabiner rappel (fig. 11-6), essentially a quicker, cleaner version of the classic double-carabiner brake rappel (not covered in this book). While this rappel setup doesn't offer nearly as much friction as a double-carabiner brake rappel, climbers using 8-millimeter and thicker ropes will find it

Figure 11-7. *To set up a carabiner brake rappel:* **a**, *Pass a bight through a locking carabiner.* **b**, *Clip a second locking carabiner to both the strands in the bight as well as both strands coming out from the either side of the locking carabiner (it can be either side as long as it's both).* **c**, *Clip a third locking carabiner or two nonlocking carabiners opposite and opposed to your rappel extension or belay loop. Do not clip both locking carabiners directly to your rappel extension. Also, position the two locking carabiners you are using for friction with either the big or small ends facing each other.*

acceptable even for dead-vertical rappels on single strands.

To set it up, you will need two similar-sized locking carabiners and a third locking carabiner (or two nonlocking carabiners that you will use opposite and opposed) to attach the first two locking carabiners to your extension or your belay loop.

1. First, pass a bight from the rope(s) through the closed first locking carabiner (fig. 11-7a).
2. Take the second locking carabiner and clip it through the bight you just made *plus* through the strands above the first locking carabiner (without clipping the two carabiners together). It is helpful to think of making an S shape that the two carabiners will clip in to (fig. 11-7b).
3. Attach these two locking carabiners to your harness with a third locking carabiner (or two nonlocking carabiners that are clipped opposite and opposed) to your belay loop or rappel extension (fig. 11-7c).

BEWARE THE ROPE-SNARLING MUNTER!

In general, rappelling with a Munter hitch is discouraged unless you have no other option. It isn't that the hitch won't provide enough friction, but that it invariably puts twists in the rope that, with long, near-vertical rappels, will likely be dramatic in number and will require repeated flaking of the rope to remove. Also, it is much more difficult to rappel with an extension, and the effectiveness of a third-hand backup is compromised because the Munter braking position is in the parallel position (or upward when rappelling), while the third hand creates friction in the lower, "open position."

If you're making a single rappel, you can get away with using a Munter, as you can choose to flake the rope once you are back in mellower terrain. But if you have three or more rappels, go with a double-locking-carabiner rappel or lower the climber.

TRANSITIONING FROM RAPPELLING TO ASCENDING

One of the trickier maneuvers is rappelling into a crevasse and then ascending back out. There are countless reasons you'd need to do this: to administer first aid, retrieve a fallen climber's backpack or other equipment, or put an unconscious climber in a chest harness or clip them into a drop-loop system.

Here's how:

1. Rig your rappel with an extension and a third-hand backup. Make sure the system is closed (knots in the rope ends, rope clipped back to the person rappelling, etc.). When you rig the rappel, make sure the extension is short enough that you can access the rope above the belay device, which you'll need to do for the ascent. Ideally, your extension runs 3–5 feet between your harness and the belay device.
2. Rappel to the fallen climber, clipping a clove hitch from the loose rope below your device to your harness to provide a "hard backup" in case you lose track of the rope (fig. 11-8a). You are dealing with a rescue and a possibly injured person, all in a deep, dark crevasse where anything can happen; cloving the rope off helps keep you connected to it. Once you are backed up to the rope, keeping a little bit of slack behind your third hand, initiate your rescue.
3. To ascend, take a single-length or double-length runner or similar material and put a friction hitch on the rope above your belay device, sliding it down to within an inch or so of the device.

AN EQUAL MEASURE OF LUCK AND SKILL

BY ALAN ROUSSEAU

In April one year, I guided the Southwest Ridge of Peak 11,300 in the West Fork of the Ruth Gorge, Alaska. Despite a slightly unsettling forecast, I began up the route with one strong, experienced guest. Around 2 p.m. on the first day, it began to snow, and spindrift started blasting down the South Couloir, where we were climbing, forcing us to quit early. Fortunately, we found a protected spot to spend the night at the "gray rocks bivy."

The next morning, we woke up to clear skies and started climbing quickly, knowing there would be afternoon snow showers. The climbing went smoothly, but on the last couple of pitches to the summit, we were engulfed in a cloud and visibility dropped to around 100 feet, just as we were to begin the complex standard descent down the East Ridge.

Once you're established on the East Ridge, the terrain gets progressively steeper the lower you go. In some conditions, it's soft enough to plunge-step down; other times, you V-thread glacial ice. Unfortunately, we hit it somewhere in between: The snow was too firm to kick steps in to make any sort of reasonably efficient progress. However, it was also too soft for V-threads—even when I chopped a few feet down, I couldn't find solid ice.

Eventually, I decided to chop a series of ten bollards into the "snice" (snow ice). While this was a fairly time-consuming and process, it was less risky and still faster than attempting to downclimb the insecure terrain.

We ended up stopping for the night on a perch just before the rock rappels, since our descent was taking longer than anticipated. As we were setting up our tent, an earthquake shook the gorge, releasing a large serac below us that threatened the end of the descent. It made us wonder, had we descended more quickly down the East Ridge, might we have been in harm's way when the earthquake occurred? Some days, luck might be more helpful than skill—but it's always advantageous to have both!

KEY TAKEAWAYS: Take the time to set up protection when descending. A little luck never hurts!

Alan Rousseau on one of the last rappels down Peak 11,300, Alaska, before climbers must cross under incredibly large seracs and the start of the objective hazard (Photo by Alex Beattie)

Alan Rousseau is an IFMGA mountain guide based in Salt Lake City. He has focused on big technical climbs in Alaska and the Himalayas, establishing several of the most cutting-edge alpine climbs of the last several decades. Alan has received the Piolet d'Or twice for his first ascents in Nepal.

clove hitch
on the
harness
A
add friction
hitch above
belay
device
then knot in
sling clipped
to belay loop
and then clip
long end of
sling into
belay loop
B
rappel until hitch
takes weight and
device becomes slack
C
remove belay
device
clove backup
D

Figure 11-8. *To transition from rappelling to ascending using prusiks:* **a**, *Tie a clove hitch or similar knot to serve as a backup while you switch systems.* **b**, *Use a sling or similar material to tie a friction hitch on the rope above your belay device. Then tie an overhand knot lower down in the material so you can just barely clip it to your belay loop.* **c**, *Rappel down until the new friction hitch and the sling take the weight and your belay device becomes slack.* **d**, *Remove your belay device and third-hand backup.* **e**, *Clip a Micro Traxion or similar device to the rope and then to your harness.* **f**, *Rock up on the Micro Traxion, pulling down and up simultaneously to shift the weight onto the ratchet and create slack in the sling attached to the friction hitch.* **g**, *Use the sling or add material to lengthen it and use as a foot loop to ascend (see fig. 10-9).*

Figure 11-9. *Unlike on rock, there aren't always fixed or convenient rap anchors on snow. Climbers often need to improvise. Here, Tagg Cole backs up Mike Pond, who is rappelling off a bollard on South Twin Sister in Washington's North Cascades.*

4. Measure the runner out to your belay loop and then tie a knot in it (e.g., an overhand on a bight) between the friction hitch and your harness, such that the runner is nearly tight once you clip this new knot (fig. 11-8b).
5. Rappel until the sling you just added takes your weight (fig. 11-8c).
6. Once the sling has taken the weight, remove your belay device (fig. 11-8d).
7. At this point, choose your mode of ascent. If you're using a Petzl Micro Traxion (or similar) on your harness, run the rope through it and tug on it so that you have enough slack to unclip the runner you used to remove your belay device. You can now attach one or more slings to this runner to build a foot loop(s), depending on its length (fig. 11-8e–f).
8. You can also ascend the rope using two prusiks. Simply put the foot prusik on the rope and stand up in it, allowing you to unweight the original piece of material and slide it up, alternating and repeating as necessary (fig. 11-8g).

RAPPEL ANCHORS

Besides rappelling into a crevasse, you may need to travel downhill or descend on the glacier surface itself (fig. 11-9). This could be to reverse steep, firm sections of snow or bare glacial ice, or to navigate moats, strange glacial features, icefalls, or recently exposed slabs below glaciers, which are typically smooth and slippery.

SNOW PICKETS

You can always leave a snow picket if you have no other viable options. However,aside from the fact they can be costly ($40–50), the average rope team often brings only two to four pickets, even for more challenging routes; unlike rock protection, you likely don't carry many of them with you and you might need them later in the day.

SNOW BOLLARDS

Snow bollards are one of the most useful rappel anchors for navigating complex glaciated terrain, as you can build an anchor without having to leave anything behind—it's just the rope, buried in a trench in the snow (fig. 11-10). However, they can be time-consuming to set up and difficult to assess. Like any other anchor, snow bollards are only as good as the medium they're built in—the stronger the snow, the better. Bollards typically range from 3 to 10 feet in diameter, depending on snow consistency (looser snow

Figure 11-10. *To make a bollard three different ways:* **a**, *Hold the lower shaft, use the spike as the pivot point and, with the pick, scribe in a half circle that will be the top of the teardrop.* **b**, *Hold the lower part of the shaft of the axe, use your elbow as the pivot point, and scribe the half-circle template with your pick.* **c**, *Sit on your knees, hold the ice axe by the lower shaft and use your entire arm to create the half-circle side of the tear rope by dragging your pick in the snow.*

requiring a larger diameter); moreover, you should take the time to work-harden the snow and compact it as needed (see chapter 7).

Bollard Sizing and Scribing

It's important to get a fairly uniform curve with your bollard, as this helps distribute the force of the rope more evenly across the snow, making for a stronger anchor. Shaping your bollard properly holds particularly true with smaller bollards, where every bit of strength matters. A good way to get a uniform teardrop shape is to first scribe out your bollard's imprint with your ice axe. Depending on the firmness of the snow, you can use one of three techniques:

- In very firm snow, use your wrist as the center or pivot point of the compass (fig. 11-10a).
- In moderately firm snow or névé, hold your axe in your hand by its shaft and use your elbow as a pivot point, drawing a half circle like you would with a compass (fig. 11-10b).
- In softer snow, sit in the middle of your intended bollard, facing away from the direction of the rappel with your arm fully extended and just below torso level, holding the axe by its shaft. Drag the pick in an arc until it's straight up from you in the twelve o'clock position; switch hands and continue dragging the pick until it's behind you (fig. 11-10c).

Besides making sure the bollard is big enough in diameter, it is important you undercut it slightly on all its uphill sides. Doing so will keep the rope from "jumping out" once you place it inside the bollard trench. Equally important is the taper where the rope comes out of the bollard; this should match the terrain such that neither of the long ends of the rope emerging from the narrow part of the teardrop—leading to the person rappelling—can lift out or otherwise compromise the bollard. Remember, bollards don't typically require you to leave a cord, sling, or webbing behind, as the most common application involves simply placing the rope in the bollard trench.

Testing a Snow Bollard

Due to the inherent and highly variable nature of snow, you should always test and back up a snow bollard before committing to it. To properly test, first situate your rope in the exit point from the bollard's teardrop, orienting it in the direction of pull. Now give the rope a moderate seesaw, pulling it back and forth a few times to see how the snow reacts. Then pull down on both ends, progressively increasing the load. To a very limited extent, the rope is work-hardening the sliver of snow it's sitting in. If there is any question, consider having two people pull, each on one end of the rope. Check out how deeply the rope has cut in—if it cuts significantly into the top of the snow bollard, dig your bollard deeper. Note that, in general, snow responds better to slow loading versus aggressive, sudden loading.

Backing Up a Snow Bollard

Since the team will be trusting their lives to the bollard, all but the last person rappelling should get a backup. This way, if the bollard fails during its first loading, there is redundancy in the system and the backup should take the load. The final climber to rappel can, before removing the backup, observe how the bollard reacted to the rappels and make any adjustments. A backup can simply be a snow picket or T-trenched axe with a sling clipped loosely to the rope at the peak of the teardrop

THE HUMBLE BOLLARD

BY IAN NICHOLSON

Graham McDowell, Ryan O'Connell, and I flew into the Waddington Range in the Coast Range of British Columbia with White Saddle Air to attempt a few of the unclimbed west faces in the Stiletto Group above the Tiedemann Glacier, across from Mount Waddington. Due to my busy summer guiding schedule, we had to fly in at the end of August, with much of our expedition taking place in September. The rock routes would most likely be free of snow, but we'd face involved glacier travel to get to the towers.

After landing at Sunny Knob, we spent the entire first day and half the second looking for a route from camp up to the immense rock walls of the Stiletto Group. There were several difficult glacial features to navigate that forced us to belay and pitch out, the largest being a crevasse that crossed the entire glacier right below the towers themselves. After walking along the entire length of the monster crevasse, we discovered a large swath of glacier in the middle that had collapsed upon itself, offering a chance of passage. I took a belay and started working my way across. Though hardly extreme, the climbing warranted two tools and was quite steep. *How will we get down?* I wondered as I climbed. I got to the top of the feature, built a belay, and brought Ryan and Graham up. Success! We had figured out a path to our objective, though now, of course, we needed to get back to camp.

Graham, an experienced ice climber, now based in Canmore, Alberta, started digging into the snow before declaring, "There is no ice—there's no way we're getting a V-thread in." I asked if we could chop a bollard. Graham and Ryan simultaneously asked if that would actually work.

I had taught rappelling off snow bollards while instructing glacier-travel and mountaineering courses but had yet to use one in real life. "I teach them all the time. I've had many students pull on them with great success," I said. I began digging the bollard, likely making it bigger and deeper than necessary. I also volunteered to back it up with my ice axe while the others rappelled, since it was my idea. Voila, it worked!

We would go on to rappel this section three more times on our trip, as well as make a free-hanging, bollard-anchor rappel off a much steeper section of glacier below a peak called the Blade. I would go on to use bollards in Patagonia, the North Cascades, Alaska, and the Alps.

KEY TAKEAWAYS: You may not employ bollards all the time, but they could prove useful just often enough—and in places where nothing else seems to work—that they become a key tool in your toolkit.

Graham McDowell rappels off a snow bollard over a very large crevasse, with the author standing on an ice axe to back it up, Waddington Range, British Columbia. (Photo by Ryan O'Connell)

Figure 11-11. It's standard practice to back up a bollard for all but the last person rappelling, who removes the backup. In this photo, the backup is the red picket on the right.

shape, poised to catch if the rope starts to cut the bollard too much (fig. 11-11).

Reinforcing a Snow Bollard

It is possible to greatly increase a snow bollard's strength in certain circumstances. One of the best and easiest ways is to collect rocks or sticks, lining the uphill side of the bollard with them (fig. 11-12). This precaution greatly increases the bollard's strength by both spreading the weight across more snow and greatly reducing the odds of the rope cutting through the snow. It also makes it easier to pull the rope. If you have the option, flatter rocks will facilitate a much smoother pull and help minimize the chances of the rope sliding off them during loading.

Figure 11-12. If rocks or sticks are available, you can line the uphill wall of the bollard with them, placing them between the rope and the snow to increase the bollard's holding power, as Graham McDowell has done here while rappelling over a large bergschrund on the Tiedemann Glacier, British Columbia. (Photo by Ryan O'Connell)

ICE BOLLARDS

An ice bollard is nearly the same as a snow bollard, with the big exception being that the harder medium lets you build a much smaller bollard, usually 1–3 feet in diameter. To begin, look for any feature that sticks up from the surrounding ice, giving you a head start with construction. Similar to how you construct a snow bollard, undercut the ice bollard to keep the rope in place. Also, as with a snow bollard, thoroughly test prior to committing, and back up the first person(s) rappelling with an ice screw clipped to the rope with a little slack.

MOAT BOLLARDS

The moat bollard (fig. 11-13) is similar to a traditional snow bollard, except that it's most

Figure 11-13. *Moat bollards are a fast and effective way to rappel couloirs or other features with moats. Most moats' overhanging and undercut nature makes it very easy to create a reliable bollard.*

Figure 11-14. *Jason Broman manages the rope from inside the moat on the Silver Star Glacier, North Cascades, Washington.*

frequently chopped into the snow immediately above a moat. As the moat is almost always undercut, just chopping down a few inches lets you create a rappel anchor in less than a minute. Even vertical moats along the edges of couloirs might have small, 2- to 3-foot sections where the moat is horizontal—look to build your moat bollard here. As with all improvised rappel anchors, thoroughly assess and test the anchor prior to committing to it, and back it up as needed.

While you can leave a sling as you would for a traditional rappel, you can often just run the rope right over the moat itself, which lets you keep more gear with you and minimizes leaving trash on the mountain. One tip is that between each person rapping, give the rope some seesaw action to make sure it isn't freezing in place, which can happen even with temperatures above freezing. Approach all moats with caution, in case they are too overhanging and/or undercut or work needs to be done to ensure that the rope doesn't slip off unexpectedly (fig. 11-14).

V-THREADS

The V-thread is also known as an Abalakov, for Vitaly Abalakov, a prolific Soviet climber who was the first person to climb the 23,000-foot Lenin Peak and has been credited with popularizing the technique. When building a V-thread anchor, look for the best ice possible: solid blue ice. In midsummer on a glacier, this usually means digging down through at least a few inches of rotten, aerated white ice first. While it is possible to build a V-thread with a shorter screw (16–17 centimeters), it takes more precision than with a longer screw (19–21 centimeters). V-thread tools are crucial when building a V-thread anchor (fig. 11-15).

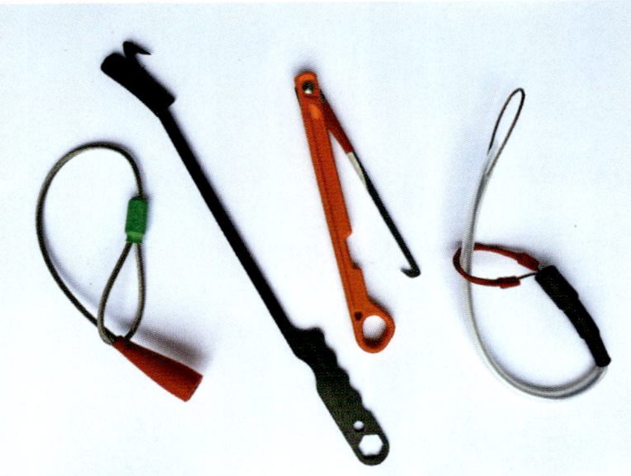

Figure 11-15. Different types of V-thread tools: from left to right, a wire model that's lighter and more compact, a stiffer one that's easier to hook material with, a V-threader designed to fit in your ice screws and assist with cleaning them out, and a Jsnare for zero threads (a.k.a. naked threads)

To use a V-thread:

1. Put the first screw in at roughly a 60-degree angle to the surface of the ice and rotate it all the way to the hanger (fig. 11-16a).
2. If you have two screws, back the first one halfway out to get a visual of what you're aiming for in terms of distance and angle. If you have only one screw, remove it all the way.
3. Use your screw to measure a second hole spaced laterally one screw-length away.
4. As you rotate this second screw in, sight it in relation to the first screw so that the two screws meet at a 90-degree angle at their deepest part (fig. 11-16b).
5. Drill this second screw all the way in, feeling for when it reaches the first hole—this should be at a point where the screw is well over halfway in. Now remove your screw(s).
6. Pass a piece of cord through one hole and hook it out the other with your V-thread tool (fig. 11-16c).
7. Tie a double fisherman's knot to join the two ends of cord (fig. 11-16d).
8. Ensure that the V-thread has adequate slack—if the cord is too tight, it creates a sharp angle between the V-thread holes, which puts unnecessary stress on the anchor.
9. Back up the V-thread for the first rappeler with an ice screw and a loose sling not taking the load (fig. 11-16e).

Tip: While vertical V-threads are stronger, they are much harder to drill accurately than horizontally constructed ones. In reliable ice, horizontally constructed V-threads have an average strength of 11 kilonewtons (more than enough to hold even the heaviest rappelling climber), while vertical threads are only slightly stronger, at around 14 kilonewtons.

ZERO THREADS

Zero threads (a.k.a. naked threads) are V-thread rappels that don't involve passing a piece of cord through the hole but instead pass the rope itself through, the advantage being that you don't have to leave any gear behind. However, they should not be done in super-cold temps—approximately 0°F (–18°C) and below—or in really wet, drippy ice, as the rope can freeze in place. Also, be aware that while traditional V-thread tools work fine, they can be hard on your rope; it's better to use a rope-specific tool like the Jsnare, which pinches the rope rather than hooking it (fig. 11-17).

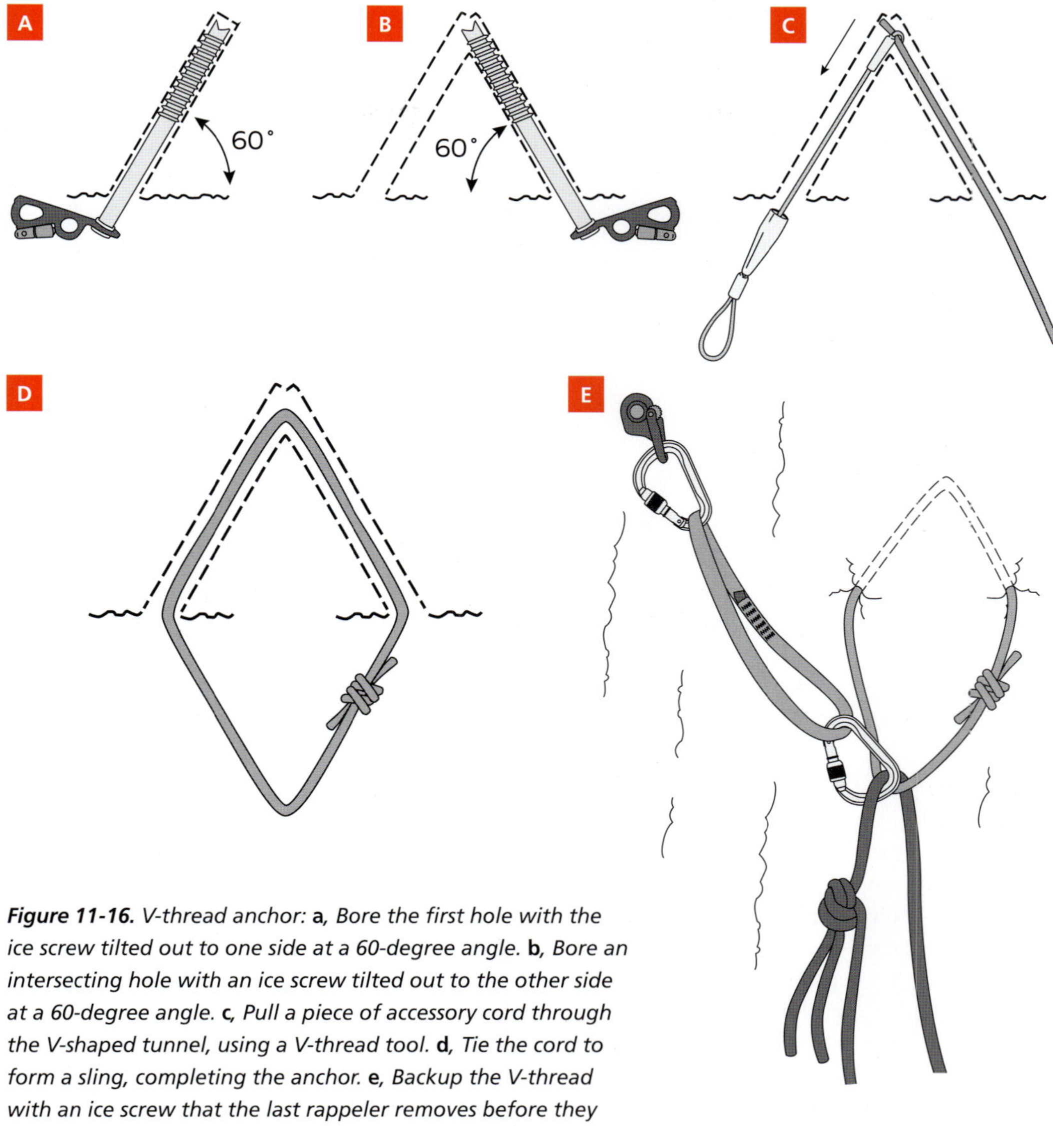

Figure 11-16. *V-thread anchor:* **a**, *Bore the first hole with the ice screw tilted out to one side at a 60-degree angle.* **b**, *Bore an intersecting hole with an ice screw tilted out to the other side at a 60-degree angle.* **c**, *Pull a piece of accessory cord through the V-shaped tunnel, using a V-thread tool.* **d**, *Tie the cord to form a sling, completing the anchor.* **e**, *Backup the V-thread with an ice screw that the last rappeler removes before they descend.*

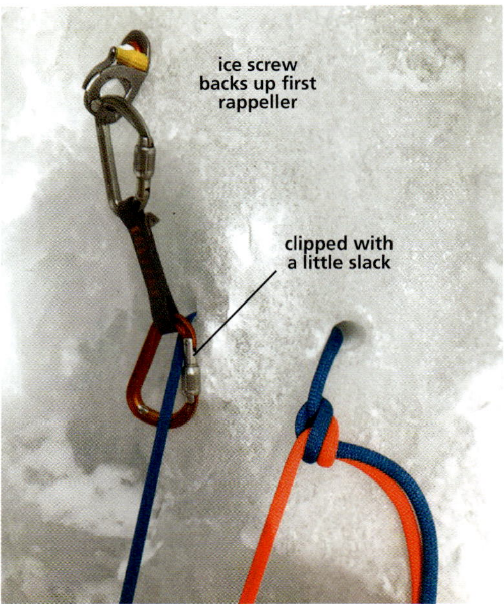

Figure 11-17. A zero-thread is a V-thread in which the rope is threaded and subsequently pulled out after the rappel. It does not require any cord or webbing. (Photo by Dale Remsberg)

Using an Improvised V-Thread Tool

It is useful to be able to drill and thread a V-thread without a specific tool—maybe you dropped it or forgot it in camp. Two helpful tools you'll likely have on hand are a skinny Dyneema sling and a wired nut. While you'll follow all the same steps outlined above for constructing your V-thread, the one caveat is that the more squarely the holes are angled toward each other (the more they overlap), the easier this improvised process will be (fig. 11-18).

1. While drilling your V-thread, identify which hole is "deeper" (it is often the first one but could be intentionally done on the second).
2. Then take the loop side of the nut or the Dyneema sling and push it into the deeper hole. (With the sling, keep the loop "open" by pushing the sling down with one hand on each strand.)
3. Now push the rope or cord into the other hole, just to where the tip of the rope should go into the sling's or nut's loop. The key to pulling it out is speed—pull the sling or nut out as quickly as possible, trying to have it "catch" the rope you're threading. You might not nail it the first time, but give it a few goes, paying attention to how the material goes in to decipher why it might not be catching.

NATURAL T-SLOT

The final improvised anchor you may have access to is the natural T-slot, which relies on a rock or other object buried in the snow. To build this anchor, girth-hitch or clove-hitch a sling around a rock and bury it as a T-slot. The size of the rock required depends on the strength of the snow. While it may be tempting to simply run the rope around the rock, leaving a sling attached to the rock is far less likely to shift the rock while you are rappelling and will make it much easier to pull the rope down.

STUFF-SACK T-SLOT

While this method does force you to leave behind litter on the mountain, you can, in a pinch, fill a stuff sack with snow and girth-hitch or clove-hitch the center of it (so it looks loosely like a dumbbell) to form your T-slot anchor. Be aware that the stuff sack isn't that strong, so you must sufficiently work-harden the snow to make this anchor reliable. Therefore, consider other, stronger options for longer and/or steeper rappels, reserving the stuff-sack rappel for things like getting over a short, steep roll or past a piece of exposed glacial ice.

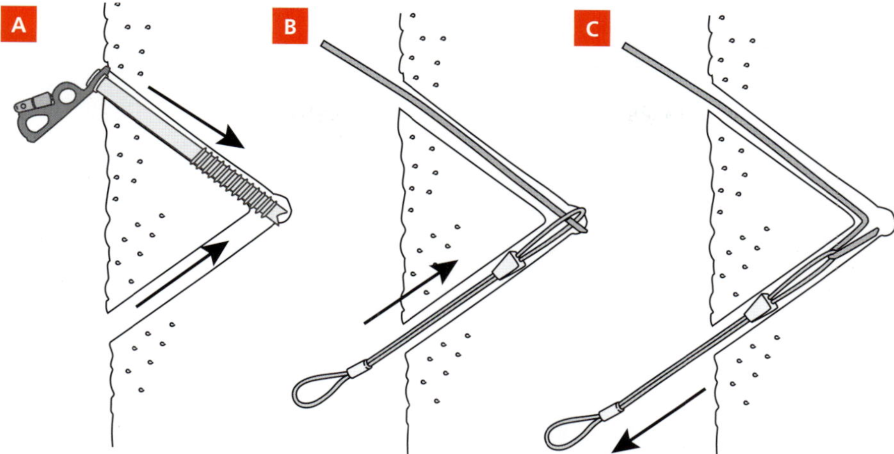

Figure 11-18. *To create an V-thread anchor without a V-thread tool:* **a,** *Drill both sides of the anchor with an ice screw.* **b,** *Use the loop side of a nut to push it into the deeper of the two holes. Then push the rope or cord into the other hole, and use the nut loop to grab it.* **c,** *Pull the rope or cord through the other side.*

RETRIEVABLE ICE-AXE RAPPEL

The retrievable ice-axe rappel may seem like a party trick, but it has a real-world applications (fig. 11-19). It is faster to rig than a snow bollard and can be useful in softer conditions; however, it forces the first rappeller to descend without an axe (if there are two people in the team). You might also be wondering about the likelihood that your axe will get stuck. The reality is that axes used to rig this rappel free *very* easily—so easily, in fact, that the real danger is them flying down the hill and hitting you during anchor retrieval. While there are many ways to rig this anchor, this is by far the best (in my experience):

1. Dig a T-slot and pre-drive a hole for an ice axe in front of the T-slot, as with the Saxon's cross anchor (see chapter 7).
2. Next, pass the rope end through the spike of one ice axe and then tie an overhand on a bight around the spike such that the rope captures the ice axe. After you finish the overhand, you should have around 2 feet of tail, which you'll attach to the second axe. (This first axe with the knot in the spike will eventually be your vertically driven ice axe.)
3. With the tail, tie a clove hitch around the adze of the second axe, leaving almost no tail. If your axe does not have an adze, run it through the eye in the head and tie a barrel knot.
4. Drive the first axe (with the knot in the spike) vertically into the hole you previously created.
5. Tie an overhand on a bight and slide it onto the shaft of the second ice axe, which you'll place horizontally as a T-slot. The strand of rope that leads to the overhand will be the rappel strand.
6. Ensure that the anchor is strong enough, but don't undercut the horizontal ice-axe placement or it will be too difficult to free from below.

Figure 11-19. *The retrievable ice-axe rappel can be fast to rig and useful in soft conditions. In this example, the rock and sling will be left behind, and the climbing partner is standing on the other side of the ridge weighting the sling to back it up.*

7. Rappel off the knot with the bight around the horizontal ice axe.
8. At the bottom of your rappel, identify the strand that leads up to the spike of the ice axe (and is subsequently clove-hitched around the adze). Give an aggressive pull, ideally while standing to the side or down a lower-angle section of the glacier, as the axe can come shooting out of the snow. Mind yourself!

PITONS

As glaciers recede, they often leave behind smooth rock slabs with minimal protection opportunities and that present potentially difficult downclimbing. The best way to descend these is by leaving a rock anchor and rappelling. However, because these slabs have, in some cases, been covered for centuries, the rock is often very compact, with only a few thin cracks. That's why it's helpful to bring a handful of

Figure 11-20. *Mike Pond rappels off two freshly placed pitons and a tied-off knob below the Green Creek Glacier, Twin Sisters Range, Washington. As glaciers recede, pitons are often the most viable solution for rappelling over the slabs left behind.*

pitons, especially in less traveled areas, to leave behind as rappel anchors (fig. 11-20).

Tip: While in early and midsummer, an adze is a superior tool for digging T-trenches and chopping or cutting bollards, consider bringing a hammer later in the summer when the surface is firmer. Notably, it will be easier to place pickets. Harder snow makes it more likely you'll be driving pickets vertically. You'll also have to deal with moats or rock slabs on the edge of a receding glacier, where a hammer lets you place pitons.

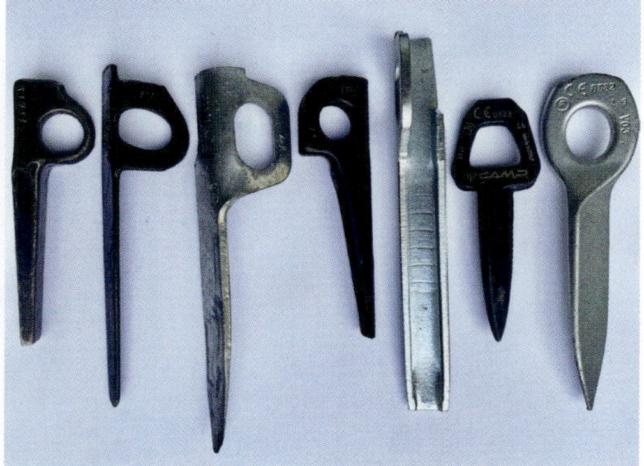

Figure 11-21. *A selection of soft and hard pitons.*

When making your piton selection, lean toward "full-sized" pitons like universal pitons, Knifeblades, angles, or Lost Arrows, generally avoiding aid-focused models like bird beaks, RURPs (realized ultimate reality pitons), and so on. Also, unlike big-wall climbing—where you generally only bring more-durable chromoly-steel pitons—consider bringing soft-steel pitons (often more of a silver color versus the near black of chromoly; fig. 11-21). Soft-steel pitons are designed to be left in place as anchors—they deform more quickly, making them less durable for repeated use but stronger in irregular cracks.

LOWERING

There are countless reasons to lower someone. It's an excellent way to get the rope down if it's windy or if you need to stop and build the next rappel station (i.e., the team is retreating downward). It can be faster or more efficient than having both climbers downclimb depending on the terrain (fig. 11-22). Also, it may be the best or only option for those less experienced with rappelling.

Figure 11-22. Here, Sarah Janin lowers Grant Price because it is faster and safer than having both climbers downclimb.

THE REDIRECTED PLATE

As a rule, rather than lowering from your harness through a redirect up above you, try a redirected plate. It is far easier to provide a smooth lower, puts less force on the anchor, and introduces fewer twists into the rope (fig. 11-23). This method has two disadvantages, however: It's marginally slower to set up than just using a Munter and requires a second locking carabiner (fig. 11-24).

1. As with any lower, strongly consider a friction-hitch backup.
2. Thread the rope into the device as you would to belay a leader, but instead of clipping it to your harness, clip it to the anchor such that both rope strands are traveling parallel toward the load.
3. To create the redirect, clip a second locking carabiner to the anchor and attach the brake side of the rope. It is helpful if this second locking carabiner (which creates

Figure 11-23. A redirected plate is the smoothest, least rope-twisting method of lowering. Here, Lyra Pierotti lowers her partner off a moat on the No Name Glacier, Washington, while using a friction-hitch backup.

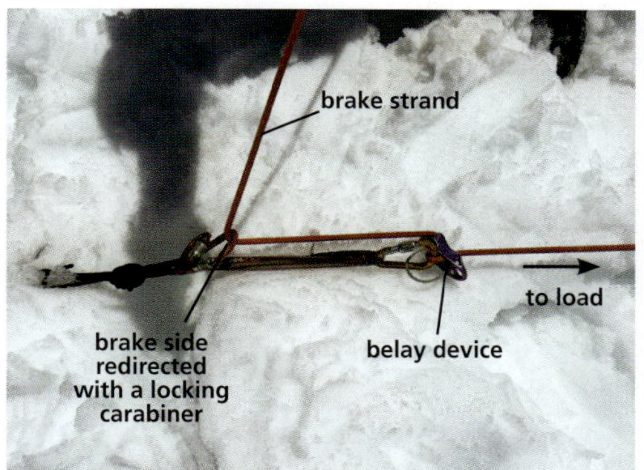

Figure 11-24. *Clip your belay device to the anchor such that both rope strands are traveling parallel toward the load. Then, clip the brake-side strand to a second locking carabiner equal to or smaller in size than the one holding the belay device.* (Photo by Truc Allen)

the redirect) is similar in size to or smaller than the one on the belay device.

LOWERING WITH A SINGLE REDIRECTED LOCKER

Using a redirected single locking carabiner is a fast and easy way to lower off an anchor (fig. 11-25). It takes a little more care to avoid putting twists into the rope but requires less gear and is slightly quicker to set up than the redirected plate.

1. Start with the belay device clipped to the anchor, with the rope threaded through it as if setting up for the redirected-plate lower (as described above).
2. Instead of clipping a second locking carabiner to the anchor to bend the rope over the device to create friction, wrap the brake-side strand around the front side of the carabiner from which you're lowering and reclip the belay-device locking carabiner to the anchor, forcing the rope to bend over the device when the load is applied to the other side.

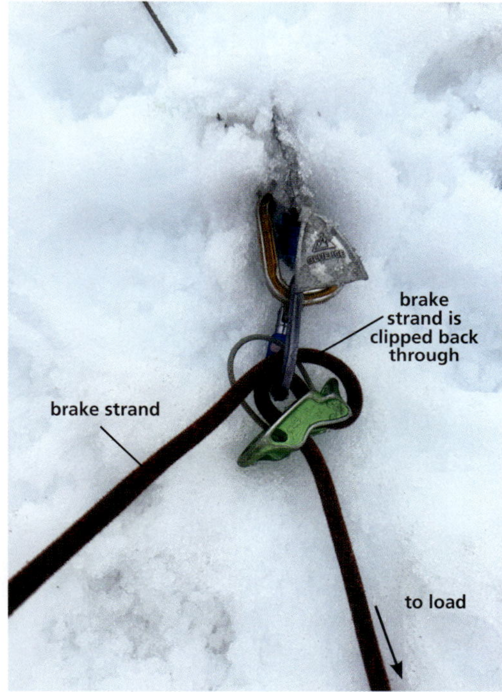

Figure 11-25. *To lower using a redirected single locking carabiner, thread the belay device normally and clip it to the anchor. Then clip the brake strand back through this primary locking carabiner so that it is redirected.*

LOWERING WITH A MUNTER HITCH

Knowing how to lower with a Munter hitch is a great skill, and all it takes is a single locking carabiner. Plus, contrary to popular belief, the Munter can provide a tremendous amount of friction. However, it is very hard to avoid twisting the rope; therefore, the Munter is best for short lowers or even a single longer lower, but not for several consecutive long Munter lowers in a row, which

Figure 11-26. *A Munter hitch offers plenty of friction to lower, but you must take care to minimize twists. Hold the brake strand fairly parallel to the load strand to form a narrow, upside-down V.* (Photo by Truc Allen)

will result in an extremely twisty rope, which not only is annoying but also has the potential of becoming so snarled it's a safety hazard.

To minimize twists, keep the load strands as close as possible to form a narrow, upside-down V (fig. 11-26). Additionally, keep an eye on the rope—you can see it twisting as it passes through the Munter hitch—and correct any twisting by forcing your own twists into the rope going in the opposite direction.

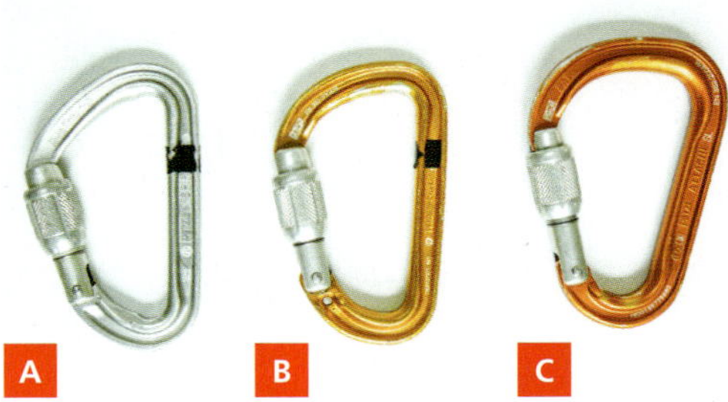

Figure 11-27. *While you can use nearly any locking carabiner with a Munter hitch, some types are better because they will put fewer twists in the rope and more easily flip back and forth, depending on if you are belaying or lowering:* **a**, *a poor option for a Munter;* **b**, *a middling option for a Munter;* **c**, *an HMS locking carabiner, an excellent option for a Munter.* (Photo by Truc Allen)

HMS Carabiner for Munter Hitches

With the Munter hitch, an HMS locking carabiner is the best option because it results in fewer snarls and twists (fig. 11-27). HMS stands for the German *Halbmastwurfsicherung*, which means "half clove-hitch belay"—that is, the Munter hitch. An HMS-style locking carabiner provides enough "room" for the Munter to flip freely and will reduce twists compared to a smaller or more heavily tapered locking carabiner, where one or both strands will ride (and subsequently twist) on the spine and/or the gate.

Opposite: *Skiing down off the back side of Girls Mountain above the Hoodoo Glacier in the Chugach Mountains near Valdez, Alaska* (Photo by Alexis Kane)

CHAPTER 12

Glacier Travel and Crevasse Rescue for Skiers and Snowboarders

While skiers and climbers traveling on glaciers use many of the same or similar techniques as climbers, there are differences, primarily because skiers tend to travel during the late winter, spring, or very early summer when there's more snow (fig. 12-1). These conditions, coupled with the improved flotation of skis, significantly reduces, but does not eliminate, the chances of falling into a crevasse. As such, skiers commonly carry ropes but are far less likely to rope up on the way up and even less often on the way down.

Nowadays, many people use tools like CalTopo, Gaia GPS, and Google Earth to plan tours, tools that are invaluable for drawing an intended route on a glacier. Even though crevasses move from season to season and decade to decade, these tools' satellite imagery can show you where the most problematic, heavily crevassed sections of the glacier are.

ROPING UP

Unroped skiers traveling on glaciers always need to carry two ropes spread out among the

Figure 12-1. *Doug Poortenga, Ken Boggs, and Nate Helweg skinning on the 50-mile Ptarmigan Traverse across Washington's North Cascades—skiing in the high mountains can take you to some wild places.*

***Figure 12-2.** Skiers are not roped up most of the time while traveling on glaciers. However, because any member of the team could fall into a crevasse, most ski-mountaineering groups carry two shorter ropes spread out among the group.*

party, because if one team member carrying a rope falls in, there will still be a second rope on the surface (fig. 12-2). Depending on the demands and nature of the route, a common tactic is to bring two ropes approximately 30 to 40 meters long, letting you split the weight up (versus carrying a single 60- or 70-meter line).

You can, of course, bring a full-strength, standard-sized cord (9 to 11 millimeters in diameter) for each rope, but these will weigh more. So, to save weight, you might consider two half-ropes, which generally run from 7.5 to 8.5 millimeters in diameter. A half rope (*not* a twin rope) is not technically rated for single use in steep terrain, but many rope manufacturers will list it as acceptable for single-strand usage for steep snow climbing or crevasse rescue so long as there are no sharp edges. Meanwhile, a twin rope is typically lighter but isn't as strong as a half-rope and is therefore *not* intended for single-strand usage; it must *always* be paired with another twin rope.

You'll next need to consider whether to bring dynamic or static rope (fig. 12-3). If there's a reasonable chance you'll have to belay, bring a dynamic rope (fig. 12-4). If there isn't, you might opt for a hyperstatic rope—a rope designed for glacier travel, rappelling, crevasse rescue, and other applications that don't involve a belay from a fixed point (e.g., an anchor), such as the ultra-strong Petzl RAD line, a 6-millimeter rope weighing only 22 grams per meter but rated to 12 kilonewtons.

When choosing between 30-meter and 40-meter ropes, consider bringing at least one longer rope for a bigger team; a route with more complex glaciated challenges; a route with more traditional snow, ice, or mixed pitches; or a route with short pitches of belayed booting or skiing. This lets you keep the 30-meter rope

Figure 12-3. Alex Kittrell opts to rope up on a suspect series of glacial features on the Klawatti Glacier, Washington. Carrying two 30- or 40-meter ropes in a group skiing on glaciers is nearly mandatory, but whether they are static or dynamic depends on the nature of the tour and the terrain.

as the "secondary rope" for crevasse rescue if the person carrying the long rope is unlucky enough to fall in. For example, a combination of one 30-meter RAD line and one 30-meter or 40-meter dynamic half rope lets you use either rope for crevasse rescue, with some weight and space savings from the RAD line, but you still get to use the dynamic rope to belay any sections that might require it.

WHEN TO ROPE UP

Most of the time while traveling on glaciers with skis or splitboards, ski-tour team members won't be roped up. The fat spring snowpack and the added flotation combined with good visibility, letting you see strange-looking features on a macro and micro level, allow you to spend most of the day unroped.

Figure 12-4. Manufacturers do not recommend using hyperstatic rope to belay someone off a fixed anchor. If you think you'll need to belay someone for climbing or skiing, bring a dynamic rope. Ian Nicholson belays Becky Frederick with a dynamic rope down the steep entrance into Thunder Creek drainage. (Photo by Ryan O'Connell)

However, if visibility decreases or there are several suspect or irregular-looking features in the snow, strongly consider roping up (fig. 12-5). Another reason to rope up is "hot-punchy" snow—snow you can easily punch through because it's been weakened by a day of warm weather after a cool period, a scenario that can be worsened if the snow is in the direct sun or the surface is not freezing overnight. Lastly, rope up if you are traveling in known crevasse zones or see bridges, cracks, or other features that lead you to believe there is a greater chance of falling into a hidden crevasse (fig. 12-6).

ASCENDING VS. DESCENDING

While skinning up, you should be quicker to put on the rope, as waiting a little longer at turns and managing slack are relatively minor downsides.

A ski descent, however, has its own dangers that need to be managed and weighed against the inherent hazards of the glacier when deciding whether to rope up (figs. 12-7 and 12-8). Roping up while skiing or snowboarding can lead to serious injury—imagine two or more people tied together, moving at speed, turning at different times and in different directions, with the chance of someone unexpectedly pulling very hard if they fall or while turning.

This essentially means that you should rope up only when the threat of falling into a hidden crevasse is greater than the danger posed by skiing while tied to another person. This also means that once it is time to rope up, everyone attached to the rope must ski or snowboard much, much slower, taking very conservative, predictable, extremely controlled, snowplow-type turns. In specific circumstances, it might be a reasonable option to rope only two people together and have others

Figure 12-5. *Poor visibility is one of the most common reasons skiers and snowboards rope up to travel on a glacier. In such conditions, it can be easy to miss even big features, let alone the often more subtle clues that you are crossing a suspect snow bridge or near a possible crevasse. You may even wander off an established route without realizing it.*

Figure 12-6. *A group opts to put the rope on because of low light and some sneakily large crevasses on the Southeast Fork of the Kahiltna Glacier in the Alaska Range.* (Photo by Jared Drapala)

WHEN TO ROPE UP WHILE SKI-TOURING ON GLACIERS

BY MIKE SOUCY

Maybe you've been here before. Staring at the blank canvas that is a smooth, snowy glacier, you wonder, *Do we need to rope up here?*

Human nature often points us toward shortcuts; this is made easier by most skiers' lack of fluidity with rope management and resistance to stopping. Without practice, it can also feel cumbersome to manage a rope team moving up or down a slope. Most of the time, things will probably work out. But if you're wrong, the consequences of an unroped crevasse fall are serious.

Make it a goal as a ski-mountaineer to improve your technical skills so you can deploy them rapidly in this situation as well as improve your ability to accurately gauge the likelihood of a crevasse fall. From a rock climber's perspective, you would consider the steepness of the terrain, exposure to a significant fall, and difficulty of climbing before deciding to rope up and belay. Ski-mountaineers have a similar list of observable factors. Here are a handful of questions to help you make the call:

Are there visible crevasses? Depending on the size and steepness of the glacier, you may or may not find crevasses large enough to present a hazard, and those crevasses may be well-covered by the season's snowpack. Look not only for open cracks but also for sagging areas that suggest deteriorating bridges. Pull out your avalanche probe to investigate hard-to-identify features, probe around in search of any sudden changes in resistance in the layers.

How much visibility do you have? You don't know what you can't see. Traveling on a glacier in flat light or whiteout conditions can be disorienting enough from a navigational perspective, as it diminishes your capability to routefind.

What are the depth and hardness of the seasonal snow overlaying the glacial ice? Snowpack peaks at different times.

Ryan O'Connell skinning up the south-central fork of the Coffee Glacier in the Alaska Range

You may think of midspring as the most reliable time to ski over well-covered crevasses, but every season is different in different places. Pull out your avalanche probe to get a feel for variations in depth and resistance; 2 meters of snow is the target for adequate coverage. Consider the snowpack's hardness. A well-consolidated 2 meters of 1F or pencil-hard snow is more reliable than a freshly deposited fist to 4F. Learn the hand-hardness test (R), perhaps from an avalanche course, if this terminology is unfamiliar.

Stephen Inman skis down the Forbidden Glacier on Forbidden Peak in Washington's North Cascades.

Do you have experience on that specific slope? Are you intimately familiar with the route and where crevasses exist? Have you set a recent track and gathered enough information to make an informed decision?

Are you traveling uphill or downhill? The slower pace and ability to assess the route and conditions on the fly make the decision to skin uphill as a ropeteam far more common. However, on the descent, consider the factors listed above and do not shy away from roping up and snowplowing when it's called for.

What is your team's confidence in assessing all the above factors? If you and your team are new to ski-mountaineering on a glacier or if you face some unfamiliar situation, increase your safety margin by adding the protection of the rope. It's common for this uncertainty to manifest in the form of disagreement (or silence!) within the team. Stick with the simple solution.

This is by no means an exhaustive list of considerations, but it's a great place to start.

Choose simple routes in good condition to build experience. Have everyone in your party put on a harness, and make rescue equipment accessible as soon as you step on a crevassed glacier. Keep ropes with at least two team members, and stow them on top of the pack, where they can be deployed quickly. Practice measuring intervals between skiers, keeping appropriate rope tension, and making kick turns and transitions *before* you need these skills. It shouldn't be a big deal to ski roped as a team.

Finally, use the time going uphill roped up to gather information and gain confidence, so that when you remove the rope for the ride down, you feel confident about your decision.

Mike Soucy is an IFMGA mountain guide, guidebook author, and member of the AMGA National Instructor Team with over twenty-five years of experience climbing and skiing on remote glaciers worldwide. While his skills span various mountain disciplines, he specializes in guiding remote glaciated peaks in far-flung locations. Mike lives in Longmont, Colorado, with his wife, Jane.

Figure 12-7. When you take off your skis, consider taking out your rope, as Dan Corn and his crew do while making a rare ski descent of Peak 12,200 (a.k.a. Lisa Peak) in the Alaska Range.

Figure 12-8. An unroped Pete Keane skis down the Stockji Glacier in low light, Zermatt, Switzerland. Traveling roped during a ski descent has its own dangers that can lead to serious injury, but there are times it may be prudent to do so.

in the group ski unroped in the roped skiers' tracks—or, if there are four of you, to break into two rope teams that can more easily self-manage their speed and turns.

WHAT ROPING UP LOOKS LIKE

If you choose to rope up, use the same spacing discussed in chapter 6: Rig the rope and use the rule of 10, with an additional arm length or two to accommodate any knots (see below). Unlike splitting the rope up for more traditional glacier travel, where you have a longer rope and you start in the middle, with skiing you'll need to make sure both "ends" of your rope team have enough rope to perform a rescue.

Here are guidelines for splitting the rope between skiers for glacier travel:

- **two people:** One person, one coil, and then the second at the other end of the rope.
- **three people:** Middle person gets the ends.
- **four people:** One of the two middle people will get two ends, or the group can split and travel closely together in two groups of two. Consider using a 40-meter rope.
- **five people:** Split into a group of two and a group of three.

KNOTS IN THE ROPE

In general glacier mountaineering, in which climbers cross glaciers in a variety of conditions from very firm to very soft, an argument can be made for not using knots when traveling across terrain (firm snow or ice) where they are less effective. For the skier or snowboarder who's roping up, however, snow conditions in the winter through early summer are overwhelmingly the softer conditions in which knots will prove quite effective (fig. 12-9). Because self-arresting is more difficult with skis or a splitboard than with an ice axe, knots drastically improve the arresting skier's ability to halt a team member's fall. Depending on the number of people in the party, the configuration will be slightly different.

Figure 12-9. *A group uses knots while traveling across the Worthington Glacier near Thompson Pass in Alaska's Chugach Mountains. The snow that skiers travel on is most frequently winter or moist springtime snow—the type of snow in which knots are most effective.*

Two-person skier or rider rope teams: With two skiers or snowboarders traveling with two 30-meter ropes, instead of "splitting" one of those 30-meter ropes in half when roping up, one skier has one whole 30-meter rope coiled and stowed in their backpack and is clipped to the other skier's rope. In this case, the two team members would have roughly 13 meters of spacing between them, with just over half the 30-meter rope in their pack. While this isn't a lot of extra rope, it's still enough for a new-strand 3:1 bight drop (see below) if a skier falls in.

Three-person skier or rider rope teams: With three people, the middle person will get the ends and, according to the rule of 10, should have 11 to 12 meters of rope, plus a little extra for knots. This means each "end person" on the rope team carries 16 to 18 meters of rope—plenty for a new-strand 3:1 bight drop should someone fall in.

Four-person skier or rider rope teams: With a four-person rope team, one of the two middle people should tie in to the rope and use standard approximately 10-meter spacing with a little extra for knots, with one end person taking 20–23 meters of rope and the other (with three people attached to the rope) taking 10 to 13 meters. While you can still rescue each person from any side, one person in the middle of the rope may have to come out of the system. For this reason, as well as to better deal with other potential hazards, it is strongly advised that four-person rope teams bring at least one 40-meter rope and one 30-meter rope (instead of bringing two 30-meter ropes). It is also possible for the team to split into two groups of two and travel very near one another (fig. 12-10).

Five-person skier or rider rope teams: A five-person rope team should split into a group of two and a group of three, and strongly

Figure 12-10. *Pete Keane weighs whether to rope up while leading his group down a crevassed section of Mount Cevedale, Ortler Range, Italy.*

consider bringing a 40-meter rope as one of their lines.

SKINNING WITH SPACE

Even when you are traveling up a glacier unroped, consider traveling with a little space between you and your partners unless you know that particular glacier and/or route exceedingly well and are quite confident about its condition. Traveling with two to three ski lengths (10 to 15 feet, 3 to 5 meters) between climbers avoids putting unnecessary pressure on a snow bridge over a hidden crevasse and reduces the likelihood of two people falling in a crevasse (fig. 12-11).

Figure 12-11. *A group traveling with good spacing (two to three ski lengths) on a lesser traveled area of the Sulphide Glacier en route to a ski circumnavigation of Mount Shuksan in Washington's North Cascades.*

OTHER SAFETY CONSIDERATIONS

Climbers need to consider several safety precautions, including wearing harnesses, taking off one ski at a time, the option of a glacier tether, probing, and fishing.

***Figure 12-12.** Chris Marshall assesses conditions with the rope at the ready and harness on while skiing down the Matier Glacier in the Duffy Lake region, British Columbia.* (Photo by Josh Cole)

HARNESSES

When skiing or snowboarding on a glacier, every single member of the team should have their harness on and a few carabiners ready to go, no matter how benign the glacier seems (figs. 12-12 and 12-13). There are countless tales of experienced climbers and skiers who were taken completely by surprise and fell into small, hidden crevasses. While wearing a harness doesn't guarantee an injury-free outcome, having it on already makes crevasse rescue much easier.

ONE SKI AT A TIME

Another safety technique commonly implemented while traveling on glaciers is removing only one ski at a time (fig. 12-14). Our skis distribute our weight over a much larger area than our boots, which dramatically decreases (but doesn't eliminate) our chances of falling into a hidden crevasse. Numerous skiers have punched one foot into a dark, bottomless hole while still clipped in on their other foot, and at least one person was left hanging from a single ski. So when taking a break or ripping or reapplying skins, do so one ski at a time, staying completely clipped in to the first ski before removing the second.

***Figure 12-13.** Everyone in the group should wear a harness while skinning or skiing on a glacier—as a group does here while crossing the Coleman Glacier, Mount Baker, Washington. It makes hauling team members out of a crevasse much easier.*

GLACIER TETHERS

In many glaciated areas, primarily in the Alps, it is common practice to ski with a glacier tether. A tether is essentially a leash or belay extension attached to your harness, generally with a girth hitch around your harness tie-in points or belay loop that is clipped to a higher connection point on your backpack (fig. 12-15). The idea is that if you were to fall unroped into a crevasse and become wedged in a constriction, it doesn't matter whether rescuers can get to your harness because

Figure 12-14. *On a glacier, while transitioning from skiing to skinning or vice versa, take off only one ski at a time. Remember that your skis are your flotation; there are epic stories of people popping into crevasses right as they changed their skis, including one in which someone was left hanging by their toepiece.*

you have a full-strength attachment on your shoulder, which is nearly always accessible.

PROBING

Suppose you encounter strange-looking glacial features that are difficult to circumnavigate (fig. 12-16). In this case, probe the features before trusting them or, better yet, have your partner quickly put you on belay. When traveling in low light or through more complex sections of glacier—whether up or down—keep your probe jammed between your back and your backpack (in the collapsed position), ready to deploy at a moment's notice (fig. 12-17).

FISHING

Fishing is a technique used in low light and during poor visibility, where it can be

Figure 12-15. *Here, I have a commercial rappel extension girth hitched to my belay loop and clipped to a strap on my pack above my chest. This tether will make it easier to rescue me if I were to fall into and become wedged in a crevasse.* (Photo by Dakota Schlag)

Figure 12-16. *Probe strange-looking features before you choose to commit to them as Michael Hutchins does here.*

Figure 12-17. *Having your probe easily accessible to be able to deploy and use on a moment's notice makes it easy to probe suspect features or just feel around on an unfamiliar route can greatly increase you and your team's safety. You have several options for stashing it:* **a**, *One option is to stow it horizontally in the small of your back above your waist belt as Molly Massena does here.* **b**, *Another great option is to strap it together and clip it to your harness as Michael Hutchins has done here.*

challenging to see the angle of the terrain, if anything at all. It is most commonly done by tying your cordelette or another, similar piece of material to the basket of your pole and flicking it as you go; when the material lies

Figure 12-18. *If you ski on glaciers a lot, you'll eventually be forced to travel in a whiteout. When you are, consider fishing. Here, Ian Nicholson desperately fishes as he approaches a complex portion of the Neve Glacier on day four of the Isolation Traverse, Washington.* (Photo by Ken Boggs)

down, you can see the angle of the slope and at least the next fifteen or so feet of terrain, to avoid skiing off a small cliff or into a wind lip during a turn (fig. 12-18). While fishing in poor visibility is undoubtedly slower than skiing in good visibility, you can get into a very reasonable rhythm and move at a moderate pace of flick, turn, flick, turn, and repeat.

SKI-SPECIFIC BELAYS AND ANCHORS

Sometimes, the terrain is spotty, whether because it's steep, firm, or has a seemingly greater chance of a hidden crevasse. Rather than risk it, become proficient at providing a quick belay so that someone in the team can check things out with some level of security (fig. 12-19).

ATTACHING THE ROPE

If you need to be belayed with skis or a snowboard, the most common method is a double clip-in system (fig. 12-20). The first clip-in point is generally a single locking carabiner clipping a knot like an overhand or figure-eight on a bight to your belay loop. To form the second clip-in point, pay out enough rope from this knot that the rope reaches your midback (have your partner help with this measurement), tie a clove hitch here, and then clip it to your belay loop with a large non-locking carabiner. With this setup, in a fall, the rope will be a lot less twisty, reducing the odds of whoever is on belay getting hurt (most knee injuries in skiing are related to twisting falls).

ONE SKI WITH A HIP BELAY

One of the most common ski belays is for the belayer to remove one or both of their skis and jam them into the snow near their crotch,

Figure 12-19. *Occasionally while moving together roped up, you'll encounter glacial features too suspect to ski across, and it is harder to arrest on skis than in a more traditional mountaineering scenario. Consider belaying each other, as Caleb Merrill does here to cross a very suspect feature on the Park Glacier while skiing the Watson Traverse in Washington's North Cascades.*

bases facing toward the belayer (fig. 12-21). The skis ideally need to be buried to the point where the heel pieces touch the snow.

It is also crucial that the skis are tilted away from the load (onto the belayer) at a minimum of 15 degrees, 20 degrees being better. The belayer should use a hip belay, braking over the side against which the skis are leaning; if the belayer has one ski on, they should keep the brake-side strand on the same side as this ski.

Figure 12-20. *Classic belay setup on harness*

> **Tip:** To provide a smooth belay, have the skier or snowboarder use a preset series of commands so that you can be as ready as possible when belaying them—for example, "1, 2, 3, turn."

Though the Munter hitch might sound like a better idea than the hip belay because it's stronger if faced with catching a potentially large load, it is in fact rarely a good option because it is extremely difficult to pull slack through quickly enough to match your skier's rate of travel. Instead, the hip belay is generally a better option for belaying any sort of "real" turns.

I-ANCHOR

An I-anchor that backs up a stance is generally stronger than a single ski jammed between the belayer's legs. An I-anchor is, however, rarely strong enough to belay directly off without incorporating the belayer's body into the system.

To build an I-anchor, start with one ski nearly parallel to the snow surface and then drive the tail into the snow (fig. 12-22a). Starting with the ski so close to the angle of the snow's surface will allow the tail rocker to force the ski to "stand up," its final position at least 20 degrees from perpendicular to the snow's surface (fig. 12-22b).

Once the first ski is in, take the second ski and place its tail against the base of the first

Figure 12-21. *Tom Vogl uses a braced ski belay. Setting up the rope so that load strand is on the same side that the ski is braced on reduces the belayer's chances of being twisted out of position and lessens the chance that the brake strand will get loaded over the edge of the ski. The ski is tilted away from the direction of pull and sunk in to brace his upper body.*

Figure 12-22. *To set up an I-anchor with skis:* **a,** *Drive the first ski in with the base toward the load, because most skis have a tail rocker. Start at a much lower angle than you think you need to, as it will rotate toward vertical as you push it down. Once the ski is in, it will ideally be at least 20 degrees past perpendicular away from the direction of the load.* **b,** *Drive in the second ski, as Katie Koepke does here, making a V shape. Again, the tail rocker will bring the bases closer together as you drive the ski downward.* **c,** *Putting a ski strap around both skis once they are in the snow helps ensure the skis won't "scissor," possibly damaging the anchor material.* **d,** *Tie a clove hitch and put it around both skis.* **e,** *Sit in a position where the rope from your harness to the anchor is tight, kick your heels in, and use a hip belay or a Munter or belay device on your harness.*

Figure 12-23. *Make sure you choose an anchor strong enough for the anticipated load, as Arthur Baines does here while belaying Tracey Bernstein in the Cherry Couloir on the Python, Thompson Pass, Alaska.*

ski where the first ski meets the snow. Starting at nearly a 90-degree angle, drive the second ski into the snow; it should rotate into place, with the skis ending up base to base (fig. 12-22c). It is a good idea to throw a ski strap on the top of the skis to keep them from shifting and potentially scissoring the anchor material. Tie a clove hitch around the anchored skis and set up to belay (fig. 12-22d–e).

When belaying with the I-anchor as a backup, keep the load strand on the side of your body where the rope runs. This position keeps you from being twisted. Consider the direction an anchor would be loaded and its anticipated strength (fig. 12-23).

Figure 12-24. *An H-anchor is often stronger than an I-anchor but not as strong as a T-trench. To create an H-anchor, drive the base of both skis toward the load at least 20 degrees past perpendicular to the load (25 to 30 degrees is ideal). Next, clove, girth, or basket hitch the material to the balance point of the ice axe. Place the axe on the opposite side of the skis, pick facing down, and pull the sling between the skis.*

H-ANCHOR

In favorable snow conditions (i.e., denser snow), an H-anchor is often stronger than an I-anchor. In very firm snow it can be much faster to set up than a T-slot-style anchor and is often strong enough for similar tasks. To build an H-anchor, drive your skis into the snow with their bases facing toward the load, and then brace an ice axe between your skis (fig. 12-24).

CREVASSE-RESCUE PRACTICE MAKES PERFECT

BY IAN NICHOLSON

I have led more than twenty ski-tours across the Alps, guiding the Haute Route, the classic, weeklong traverse that travels over 100 miles across rugged and extremely mountainous terrain, from one alpine epicenter in Chamonix and Mont Blanc to the other in Zermatt and the Matterhorn. While I've had countless miniature epic and hair-raising moments on the Haute Route, one stands out the most.

It was the final day, and our group was making the grand and sweeping final 9,000-foot descent from the Col de Valpelline right under the North Face of the Matterhorn into Zermatt. We were halfway down—on the Stockjigletcher (a.k.a. the Stockji Glacier)—when we saw a man frantically waving his arms and yelling, *"Geeeede geeeeede!"*

"I am a guide. What's up?" I asked, after our group skied over to him.

His companion was on the phone (with the helicopter-rescue and flight company Air Zermatt, I would later learn), and though I couldn't make out the man's hurried Swiss German as he barked into the phone, I could tell he was panicked. The man who had been waving his arms pointed to a hole in the glacier and said, "My son."

The intensity of the situation washed over me. I pointed to a flat compression area in the glacier a few hundred feet down and instructed my clients to ski down to it. Autopilot kicked in: I quickly clipped my rope to the first man, whipped out my probe, and started feeling for the edge of the crevasse. I could see down 30 or 40 feet, but it was just black, with no sign of a human being. The man said his son's name was Max, and so I shouted his name into the abyss—but heard nothing in return.

The man's face made me tear up, but I tried to ignore his anguish and just focus on the task at hand. I walked a short distance from the crevasse, and fueled by adrenaline, I dug a T-trench, clipped a rope to it, and attached myself. I then walked back out to the edge, knowing I would either make contact or need to rappel in.

I decided to try one more thing; I took the 40-meter rope I had with me and folded it in half, lowered the U into the darkness, then pulled back up on it, only to lower it again, slightly more this time. Each time, I slowly let more and more rope slither into the blackness, the father watching my every move. Finally, as if it were a movie, with only a foot or so of slack left in my hands, the rope pulled back on me—*hard!*

"I am freaking getting you out of there, Max," I yelled into the hole, which I reiterated to his dad, who by now had started crying. I quickly threaded my Micro Traxion device on the anchor and, with a few hard pulls, gained just enough slack to attach a ratchet and a tractor and start hauling.

As I hauled and hauled, the distraught man's twenty-something son Max slowly came into the light, all 6 foot 4 inches and 230 pounds of him. (I don't remember the haul feeling difficult, but my biceps were very sore the next day.) Max had been unable to clip the rope in to his belay loop when I'd lowered it because of how he was pinned inside the crevasse; he could only clip the locking carabiner to his waist belt, which had pivoted to his hip. As I hauled, he hung horizontally.

Just as Max was getting to the surface, an Air Zermatt helicopter swung around overhead and landed. Two of their medics assisted me in pulling him to the surface. Max was crying, his dad and friend were crying, I was crying, and we all hugged.

The medic said they had only gotten the call fifteen minutes prior; they could not believe that I had gotten the fallen climber to the surface so quickly. And after a quick patient assessment (entirely in Swiss German), the medics and all three climbers jumped in the helicopter to go straight to a hospital in Sion. I wish I had gotten their names, but I am happy that things seemed to work out well for Max.

KEY TAKEAWAYS: With any actual rescue, there is no heads-up. Most of the time, things are going fine until they aren't; act surely, calmly, and efficiently. Just being able to react to the task at hand is imperative, not only because of the complexity of the technical systems you may need to use but also because someone could be in a life-threatening situation. To be ready, you need to practice, practice, and practice some more. Repetitive practice of crevasse-rescue drills can seem arduous, even unnecessary at times, but when it's time to act, it sure is nice to be ready.

Standing before the Matterhorn moments before happening upon the group who had a team member fall into a crevasse

Figure 12-25. *Building a T-trench anchor:* **a**, *Dig a trench in the snow big enough to fit your skis. In the middle of that trench, in the direction of the load, dig another trench connected to the first one. Your skis go in the trench across the slope, the anchor material goes in the other one.* **b**, *Use a ski strap to ensure that your skis won't scissor, possibly damaging the anchor material you are about to place on the skis. If your skis don't have breaks, you'll need to use two ski straps.* **c**, *Use a basket or clove hitch to attach the material to the skis. Avoid using a clove hitch as it can twist the skis, possibly affecting the integrity of your anchor.* **d**, *Place your skis in the top leg of the trench.* **e**, *Backfill snow from the back of the anchor (rather than the load side), filling the gaps between the skis and load side wall. Since skis are not flat, filling the spaces with snow ensures that force will be distributed evenly on the anchor.* (Photos by Tom Vogl)

Figure 12-26. *To build a Saxon's cross with skis:* **a,** *Attach the anchor material to one ski. Place that ski in T-trench fashion with the base toward the load, using your skins to pad the edges.* **b,** *Drive the second ski base-to-base perpendicular to the first one.* (Photos by Mike Soucy)

Depending on the size of the loads and the steepness of the terrain, you could potentially belay directly off an H-anchor or use it to back up a stance as you would with an I-anchor.

T-TRENCH

T-trenching your skis, a form of the T-slot anchor (see chapter 7), is the strongest, though also most time-consuming, of the ski-specific anchor options (fig. 12-25). Its strength makes it the default anchor for most situations in which you are performing crevasse rescue or belaying another skier directly off the anchor (rather than having your body in the system, as with the I-anchor belay).

When building the T-trench using two skis, it is considered best practice to use one ski strap just below the shovel if your skis have ski brakes—or two ski straps if they don't—before you put anchor material around the ski. This approach guarantees the skis won't pivot and potentially scissor the material.

If you are using only one ski in your T-trench (which in tests rates less than half the strength of using two skis), it is considered best practice to pad the ski so that its edges don't cut your anchoring material. The most common "pad" is made by opening your skins with glue side toward the ski and then wrapping the edges of the ski where the sling will rest. Lastly, keep in mind that a ski is slightly stronger when loaded with its base toward the load (the way you could envision a ski was meant to be loaded)—this is the preferred orientation.

Tip: Many ski-mountaineers don't bring pickets on glaciers because they can improvise with skis or shovels. As discussed in chapter 7, consider the weight of a given anchor and how strong it is versus your needs in the field. These ski-specific anchors can be connected—useful for larger loads such as those in crevasse rescue.

SAXON'S CROSS WITH SKIS

The Saxon's cross has the potential to be stronger than the T-trench depending on snow conditions and will be *far* stronger than a

Figure 12-27. *If someone falls in a crevasse, probe aggressively where you are and where you intend to build an anchor. It can be difficult to pinpoint the edge of the crevasse or evaluate whether there are other crevasses in the area. Tino Villanueva probing for the edge of a crevasse on the Mount Baker's Easton Glacier.*

single ski T-slotted into the snow. Plus, it's a fast upgrade if you have a ski already in the ground. After you T-trench one ski with a sling extending out, place the other ski with its base side facing toward the base of the T-slotted ski (i.e., bindings toward the load on the vertical ski (fig. 12-26). This vertical ski helps back up the "weakest" part of the T-trench: the excavated area where the sling emerges.

UNROPED SKI-ORIENTED CREVASSE RESCUE

Since skiers and snowboarders primarily travel unroped, it's not surprising that the majority of their crevasse falls are also unroped. While the victim has an increased chance of being hurt and/or sinking deeper into the crevasse than they would if they were roped, the one advantage for the rescuer is that the process of pulling them out is simplified.

IMMEDIATELY AFTER A FALL

If someone in your group falls into a crevasse, start with the same steps regardless of which rescue system you intend to use. First, probe out where you are and ensure you aren't standing atop another hidden crevasse (fig. 12-27). As you probe, feel for progressively more resistant snow—it's okay to feel short sections of less resistant snow as long as the snow increases in resistance again. If there is ever a stark reduction in resistance

Figure 12-28. *To rescue an unroped climber who has fallen into a crevasse, first probe the area you want to build an anchor in (see fig. 12-27).* **a,** *Start digging the main trench.* **b,** *Make the main leg large enough to hold the skis and handle a load toward the direction of the fallen skier.* **c,** *T-trench your skis and backfill the gap on the load side to maximize the surface area and distribute the pressure of the skis pressing into the snow. Work-harden the snow as necessary.* **d,** *Once the anchor is complete, clip one end of the rope to it with a figure eight on a bight.* **e,** *Estimate the distance to the edge of the crevasse and attach yourself with a clove hitch at around that point. Now clip a prusik or similar friction hitch to limit how far you will fall if you pop into a hidden crevasse.* **f,** *Probe toward the edge of the crevasse.*

A
clean channel and T trench
hole big enough for skis
B
throw snow from this side
to load
backfill between skis and front wall for even more loading
C
clip end of rope to anchor
D
clove hitch
prusik
E
probe to edge
F

WHY YOU SHOULD BACKFILL SKI-SPECIFIC T-SLOT ANCHORS

While backfilling most T-slot anchors doesn't significantly increase their strength, backfilling matters with skis. Skis generally don't have a flat surface that can press against the wall of the T-trench. They are rockered, have different-shaped bindings, and may be sitting in the snow at an angle other than with their sidewalls to the ground.

Backfilling matters more with T-trench ski anchors, especially on the load side, which allows the ski to distribute the force more evenly and along a much broader plane. They don't need to be fully buried.

for more than one foot (30 centimeters), be very careful, as you could be standing on a crevasse.

Once you have established a safe zone, pop your skis off and construct an anchor, generally a T-trench with both skis, but you could choose any of the above mentioned options (fig. 12-28). Once you've built the anchor with the T angled toward the fallen skier, clip the end of the rope to it with a figure-eight or overhand on a bight—this rope will let you get down to and eventually rescue the fallen skier.

Finally, it is critical you establish communication with the fallen party (fig. 12-29). Remember, snow has vital noise-absorption properties, so you may not be able to hear them back at the anchor. Thus, you'll want to get out to the edge—though if they've fallen in very deep, you still may not be able to hear them. The most common way to approach the edge is to estimate the distance from your anchor to the crevasse lip, tie a clove hitch, and clip it to a locking carabiner on your belay loop. Now, attach a friction hitch to the rope near the anchor. Adjust the friction hitch as necessary as you move toward the crevasse, probing as you go not only to make sure you both know where the lip is but also to determine if there are crevasses between your anchor and the crevasse your partner has fallen into.

Figure 12-29. *Tino Villanueva establishes communication with a fallen skier. Communicating with the fallen person and figuring out your plan is important. Most crevasse falls will require some sort of hauling system to extract the person, but you may need to rappel down to them to administer first aid, get their backpack or skis, or do something else. In some instances, they may be able to climb out by using the walls of the crevasse or ascending the rope.*

Figure 12-30. *You can clear away snow and pad the crevasse lip before or after you throw the end or the bight of rope down.* **a,** *Take a few steps off to the side of the fallen person to minimize how much snow falls on them. Knock down all the overhanging snow at the lip of the crevasse and even go so far as to make the top couple feet a slab or sloped toward the haul system.* **b,** *Once the snow is cleared away, pad the lip so that the rope doesn't cut in to the snow further, a backpack is what many people use but other shovels or ice axes can work great too.*

CLEARING AND PADDING THE LIP

Clearing away overhanging snow and padding the lip of a crevasse is essential to reducing friction and physically getting someone from the horizontal realm of a crevasse back onto the surface (fig. 12-30). Taking these steps can make the difference between successfully rescuing someone from a crevasse and needing to call for outside help. Once you have established a plan that involves hauling them out, the climber ascending a rope, or belaying them out while they climb, you need to clear away overhanging snow from the edge of the crevasse.

To minimize how much snow you knock down on the fallen climber, take a step or two to one side of them. If you have crampons on, take them off. Take the time to snug up your prusik and adjust the clove hitch that attaches you to the anchor to minimize slack. Then knock away all overhanging snow and ideally make the very lip of the crevasse a slab or sloped toward the haul system. A shovel

Figure 12-31. *A shovel is an excellent tool for clearing large lips.* (Photo by Paul Koubek)

can be very useful (fig. 12-31). Once the lip is clear, place and anchor an object to keep rope from cutting further into the snow at the edge of the crevasse when you start hauling. Backpacks are the most common, but shovels, ice axes, closed cell foam sleeping pads as well as any number of other items, can work well.

SETTING UP THE RESCUE SYSTEM

The rescue systems utilized by skiers and snowboarders in the event of an unexpected crevasse fall are very similar to those used by climbers and mountaineers, except that the team member who's fallen is unroped. Therefore, you'll need to get a bight or an end of rope to the person in the crevasse. If skiers and snowboarders are roped together, the process of building an anchor changes, as their skis or snowboards are usually incorporated into the anchor. Because removing your skis or snowboard and creating an anchor with these tools is a tricky process, it's best done in a specific order (see Skis-on-Feet Roped Escape, below).

You can also lower a strand of rope into the crevasse to see if it pulls back on you. Wiggle the rope around in case it's just out of the fallen person's reach, and listen closely. If you cannot hear them and you don't feel a pull on the rope, you may need to rappel in to assist them. Bring your backpack and a first-aid kit. The backpack will also allow you to bring up their skis if necessary.

Drop-End 3:1

This technique requires the least amount of rope and is the simplest, but it obviously has less mechanical advantage than the drop-loop 6:1. Once you have built an anchor, and probed to the edge of the crevasse while prusiked in or on belay, clear and pad the lip. Then establish your plan.

To execute a drop-end 3:1:

1. Drop a bight of rope with a locking carabiner down to the person, using the side of the rope not attached to the anchor (fig. 12-32a).
2. Walk back up to the anchor and pull the rope taut to help keep track of the longer end (fig. 12-32b).
3. Run the end that goes straight down to the fallen skier through a ratchete device like a Petzl Micro Traxion or similar device (or improvise with a Garda hitch or similar, fig. 12-2c).
4. Tie a friction hitch (or place a mechanical ratchet) on the strand coming out of the crevasse and clip the rope in. As a backup, tie a clove hitch and clip it to your harness to serve as a backup. Bear crawl to haul (fig. 12-32d).
5. An alternative backup is to tie a clove hitch on the anchor (fig. 12-32e).

Drop-Loop 6:1

Once you have built an anchor, move toward and probe the edge of the crevasse. Once you have established that there are no crevasses in the path of the hauling system, clear and pad the lip of the crevasse and establish communication with the fallen climber. If you have enough rope (twice as much rope as the distance from the surface to the fallen skier), using the drop-loop 6:1 system is the most efficient technique, as it has only one ratchet that needs a reset.

To set up a drop-loop 6:1 from the lip:

1. Drop a bight of rope down to the person with a locking carabiner on it (fig. 12-33a).

Figure 12-32. *To carry out a drop-end 3:1:* **a**, *Tie a knot on a bight (like a figure-eight or a flat overhang) in the open end of the rope, and attach a locking carabiner. Lower it to the fallen climber until they can clip into it.* **b**, *Clear and pad the lip and walk back to the anchor. Pull up all the slack so that the rope is taut to the fallen climber. Now clip it into a ratchet.* **c**, *Attach a tractor to the haul strand closer to the person in the crevasse. Clip the rope coming out the other side of the ratchet into the tractor.* **d**, *Clove hitch the rope to your harness, and bear crawl to haul.* **e**, *The clove on your harness is a backup. Alternatively, you can clip the haul strand to the anchor with a clove and locking carabiner.*

Figure 12-33. To execute a drop-loop 6:1 from the lip: **a**, *Drop a bight of rope down to the person in the crevasse.* **b**, *Clear and pad the lip and then walk back to the anchor, pulling the rope tight to the person in the crevasse so it is easier to keep track of the strands. Attach a rachet on the anchor.* **c**, *Attach a tractor to the front (load) side of the rachet, and clip the back (haul) side of the ratchet.* **d**, *Clove hitch to your harness, adjusting it from periodically to minimize excessive slack.* **e**, *Now that you have created a 6:1 (with a C on a Z), bear crawl to haul.*

Figure 12-34. *A person is more likely to be knocked out or injured while skiing or snowboarding than in traditional mountaineering because of the potential for more significant falls. Make sure you have the skills to rappel down, put a chest harness on them, ascend the rope, and then haul them out.*

2. Walk back up to the anchor and pull the rope taut to help keep track of the longer end (fig. 12-33b).
3. Run the longer end through a ratchet-type device like the Petzl Micro Traxion or improvise with a Garda hitch or similar (fig. 12-33c).
4. Place a friction hitch (or a mechanical ratchet like a Petzl Tibloc) on the strand coming out of the crevasse and clip the rope in.
5. Tie a clove hitch and clip it to your harness or the anchor to serve as a backup (fig. 12-33d).
6. Haul, remembering to back the fallen skier up and/or to remove slack in the back of the system every 2 meters or so (fig. 12-33e).

An Incapacitated Skier

There might be instances in which the fallen skier is unable to clip a rope that's been dropped to them. They could be seriously hurt, incapacitated, or have fallen into a tight constriction. If this is the case, you will need to rappel in to attach them to the rope—and strongly consider bringing medical supplies and a pack to take their skis and poles back up. If they are unconscious or seriously injured, you may need to put a chest harness on them (fig. 12-34).

Skis-on-Feet Roped Escape

While unroped crevasse falls are far more common in ski mountaineering, roped falls do happen, and you should be equally prepared to perform crevasse rescue and transfer the

Figure 12-35. *How to escape a loaded rope on skis:* **a**, *Arrest the fall (whether skiing or skinning) by turning to the side and getting your edges perpendicular to the fall line.* **b**, *Pop your uphill ski off and jam it between your legs so you can brace against it.* **c**, *Using a shovel or ice axe, dig two-thirds of a T-trench on the slope in the direction you are facing. Make sure to clean out the narrow leg of the T, where the anchor material will go toward the load.* **d**, *Remove your downhill ski, and attach your skin around it where the anchor material will go. Use a clove hitch or basket hitch to attach the material to the ski. Finally, jam the tail of the ski into the undug third of the long leg of the T, and push the other end into the open end of*

the trench. **e,** *Clip the rope from the T-trenched ski anchor to the rope.* **f,** *Down climb carefully and test the anchor. Then immediately attach yourself with a new clove hitch with just a few feet of slack.* **g,** *If the anchor appears to be holding, stand up and drive the ski that was your brace immediately in front of the T-trenched skis just to one side of the anchor, creating a Saxon's or iron cross.* **h,** *Attach a friction hitch between your clove and the anchor. Adjust your clove at a distance similar to that of the hole from you. Move toward the crevasse to establish communication, probing as you go, and haul the fallen person out using one of the techniques described earlier in this chapter.* (Photos by Mike Soucy)

load from your harness to your anchor (which might be made with your skis) when starting with your skis or splitboard on your feet.

1. While skiing, you will generally turn to a stop, with the rope tensioned perpendicular to the load on your skis. Dig your lower ski edge into the snow; this is the one that will do most of the holding work (fig. 12-35a).
2. Remove the upper ski and jam it into the snow tail-first, with the base toward your body and bindings away; it's easier to plunge the ski in deeper in this orientation (fig. 12-35b). You want the ski to overhang your body and be 15–20 degrees past perpendicular to the slope, as with other anchors previously covered in this chapter. Tilt slightly toward your back so you are "hooked" around the ski—this is uncomfortable, but when the ski is well-set, it is quite secure.
3. Remove your shovel from your backpack and dig a T-trench (fig. 12-35c). You can often get away with digging only 60 to 70 percent of the width needed, depending on how much tail rocker your skis have, because you can stab the tails backward into the snow and push them down into the T-trench (fig. 12-35d).
4. Pad the edges of your ski with a skin or other item to protect the anchor material you'll use.
5. Attach the anchor material and jam it into the snow (fig. 12-35e). Backfill as needed.
6. Clip the rope attached to your harness to the anchor and carefully crawl downslope to transfer the weight (fig. 12-35f). Be ready—and make sure the anchor you just built is holding.
7. Remove the second ski and stab it vertically into the snow like you would when building a Saxon's cross (fig. 12-35g). Equalize it and/or build backup anchor if necessary.
8. Attach a friction hitch between your clove and the anchor. Adjust it to roughly match how far the hole is from you. Move toward the crevasse to establish communication, probing as you go, and haul the fallen person out using one of the techniques described earlier in this chapter (fig. 12-35h).

DIGLOO EMERGENCY SHELTER

A digloo is a much faster emergency shelter option, for three people to lie down in, than a snow cave, taking only twenty to thirty minutes—instead of hours—to create. It is a skill that most skiers and snowboarders traveling above tree line, and certainly on glaciers, should know. To build a digloo, dig a trench that is wider at the bottom than the top and put skis and poles across the top to brace it (fig. 12-36a). Then put a tarp across the top and cover it with snow (fig. 12-36b). Enjoy your cozy shelter (fig. 12-36c).

Whatever kind of emergency shelter you rely on, practice building one ahead of time. When you find yourself in a situation where you need to bivy unexpectedly, shelter from a storm, or simply take a break for a few hours, you'll know that you have the necessary equipment and are prepared.

Skiers and snowboarders need to choose when to rope up while traveling on glaciers. It is crucial to know how to build ski-specific anchors

Figure 12-36. *To build a digloo:* **a**, *Dig a trench straight down about shoulder width across; avoid widening it until you have first dug down a foot. After you have dug down 2–3 feet and outward, lay your skis and poles across the top of the trench to create a "ceiling."* **b**, *Cover this framework with a silnylon tarp, and cover the tarp with snow.* **c**, *Enjoy hanging out in your cozy shelter like Brian Muller and Drew Daly are in theirs.*

and rescue systems and be familiar with appropriate belay techniques. Skiers are more likely to take bigger falls, often unroped, and so all party members should practice these skills ahead of time so they are ready when they need to apply them.

Opposite: *A group approaches the 7,800-foot camp on Denali, Alaska, while crossing the Kahiltna Glacier, looking up the Northeast Fork and at Denali's mighty south face.*

CHAPTER 13

Overnight and Expeditionary Glacier Travel Hazards

Climbing on many of the snowy, glaciated mountains of the world involves camping. Whether the trip is one night or thirty, overnight mountaineering requires preparation and planning: Where will you camp? How do you know it's safe to camp there? How much fuel will you need, and how will you get your water? While these simple questions can be answered with a little bit of research and planning, overlooking any of them can put a drastic end to your trip.

CAMPING ON OR NEAR GLACIERS

On a long alpine outing or mountaineering expedition, you'll commonly camp either on or near a glacier. While waking up perched on a sea of ice is a fantastic and beautiful experience, it also presents myriad problems compared to more traditional backpacking or camping. These hazards range from the possibility of pitching your tent on a hidden crevasse to the lack of easy access to running water. However, with a little forethought, planning, and skill, you can make the whole experience a lot smoother.

SITE SELECTION

It's preferable to pitch your tent on dirt or rocks versus snow or ice, because you'll have a warmer, drier experience—it can be worth traveling a little farther to reach these sites where possible (fig. 13-1). If you do sleep on snow, be aware that it will feel colder because ice and snow are nearly always colder than bare ground during the months that most climbers climb glaciated mountains (i.e., the summer season). You'll need to bring a warmer, more insulated sleeping pad to combat the conductive heat exchange with the ground.

Also, be aware that, even among the highest-quality waterproof tents, the floor will become damp with condensation when camping on snow. The tent floor touching the snow is cooler than the warmer air above, and when that warmer air gets close to the tent floor, it cools and condenses (just like a glass of ice water "sweats" on hot days).

While there is no guarantee of a crevasse-free location on a glacier, specific locations are more likely to form crevasses than others (see chapter 1). Concavities compress many of the crevasses that might have formed, reducing or eliminating them compared to convex rolls where the glacier is being pulled apart. Additionally, both the inside and outside of a distinct turn or change of direction in the glacier can be riddled with crevasses; in these areas, search for a less broken spot, more toward the middle of the glacier.

Figure 13-1. If there is a suitable dirt or rock campsite, it is usually warmer and drier than sleeping on snow.

LEAVE NO TRACE TRAVEL

When choosing a site, also keep the natural environment in mind. The nonprofit organization Leave No Trace (LNT) has seven principles for minimum-impact travel in the backcountry. LNT's second principle addresses traveling and camping on durable surfaces. Durable surfaces include established trails, campsites, rock, gravel, and dry grasses or snow. When you walk on snow, established trails, or bare rock, there is rarely anything your footsteps will destroy. On the flip side, plants and vegetation near and above tree line spend much of the year buried in snow and thus have very short growing seasons; they'll struggle to survive if even a small portion of their leaves or branches are broken or otherwise impacted by walking or camping.

Figure 13-2. Lyra Pierotti probes for a suitable camping location below Mount Crosson in the Alaska Range. (Photo by Bryce Hill)

PROBING YOUR CAMP

Regardless of where you camp on the glacier—even in a relatively safer compression zone—it is still critical that you probe the

THE UNSEEN DANGER

BY DAN CORN

You don't see most of the crevasses you fall into—plain and simple. When I worked as a park ranger in Denali National Park, I frequently saw people arrive at camps along the West Buttress route, unrope and wander around as if the camps and the surrounding areas were completely safe because there were no visible crevasses. Many don't realize that these camps are chosen for minimal exposure to overhead hazards or protection from the wind, not because they are free of crevasses.

I remember one rescue vividly. At the 7,800-foot camp, someone chose an old campsite without inspecting or probing it and fell into a hidden crevasse. While the crevasse was only about two feet wide, they became tightly wedged in an awkward and painful horizontal position. When we arrived, guides had been working to get to the fallen climber for hours, chipping downward with their ice axes. The narrow crevasse and climber's wedged position made a straightforward haul using traditional methods impossible. My fellow National Park rangers and I tried a chainsaw, but there was not enough space to get it in the crevasse. We ended up chipping away with an ice tool until a pneumatic chisel was flown in from Girdwood.

It took fifteen rescuers helping across more than twelve hours to extricate the climber. In the end, guide Kristie Kayl was the only person small enough to slither down to the fallen person in the crevasse and finish chiseling them out.

KEY TAKEAWAYS: Crevasses can lurk beneath the surface even in popular camping locations. Don't rely on the fact that someone else has camped there. Probe your campsite thoroughly and stay roped up until you have tested the site.

Dan Corn is an IFMGA guide and former ranger in Denali National Park, who has been on more than 30 expeditions on glaciated peaks across the globe. He received a Medal of Valor from the US government for saving more than a dozen people in a single incident on Grand Teton. Corn lives in Jackson, Wyoming.

site. Crevasses can be very difficult to notice, especially in an area with a lot of snowpack. In areas with more seasonal snow and early in the season (April through June in most of the Northern Hemisphere), you'll want to use an actual probe like you would use for companion rescue. Later in the summer or in areas with less seasonal snow, it can be perfectly acceptable to use a trekking pole with its basket removed to probe your camp rather than carrying a dedicated probe.

As you'll recall from chapter 6, probing is pretty simple: You want to feel progressively more resistant snow. A small hollow spot is okay if the snow quickly returns to gradually becoming more resistant. What you don't want to feel are larger, empty spaces—or consistently less-resistant snow. Systematically probe roughly every 3 feet (1 meter) around and across your camp. Once this is done, use markers around the perimeter so no one unintentionally wanders beyond the probed area (fig. 13-2).

TENTS, BIVY SACKS, AND SNOW WALLS

Climbers can choose from among many types of shelters while sleeping in the mountains. The length of the trip and anticipated weather often play the biggest roles in shelter selection. For shorter trips with better weather, a lighter-weight shelter will often suffice, but if the weather is poor or the trip is longer, then a heavy shelter can be worth its weight for its comfort, space, weather protection, and ability to help its occupants dry out.

TENT SELECTION

Many different tents are suitable for camping above the tree line. The best one for you mostly depends on what type of climbing you'll be doing—and where. The most common type of tent suitable for glacier travel is a "four-season" tent, meaning it can be used in conditions found across all four seasons. (The fourth season—winter—refers to the tent's ability to handle moderate amounts of wind and snowfall.) During optimal conditions, it is possible to use a three-season tent above tree line, but they are generally not as strong or resilient in a storm.

However, there is no standard for four-season tents either, though most manufacturers engineer them to be stronger for use in alpine terrain. Four-season tents typically fall into the following three categories, with some overlap between them.

Figure 13-3. *Sam Hennessey wakes up in a bivy tent on the East Face of Mount Dickey, Ruth Gorge, Alaska Range.* (Photo by Rob Smith)

Bivy Tents

Bivy tents, also frequently called "alpine tents," are generally lightweight, two- or three-pole designs that are single walled in construction and pack down small (fig. 13-3). They are generally tiny inside, with minimal headroom—not places you want to hang out in other than spending the night.

These tents are great for trips where weight and/or packed volume are at a premium, such as routes with long approaches or that require you to carry your shelter up and over technical terrain. They're also good for trips planned during stable, good weather. (Bivy tents are solid enough for many four-season trips but are generally a poor choice for truly extreme weather.)

Figure 13-4. *Forest McBrian hangs out in Sandy Camp below Mount Baker, Washington, by a hybrid tent. These tents strike a balance between comfort and weight, but are much weaker than expedition tents.*

Figure 13-5. *Expedition tents are much stronger and often roomier than their lighter counterparts but are usually around two to three times as heavy.* (Photo by Jacob Schmitz)

PITCHING A TENT IN WINDY CONDITIONS

If you are setting up camp in windy or stormy conditions, your tent is most prone to damage during the pitching process. When some—but not all—of the poles are inserted, the tent can take on sail- or kitelike characteristics and, in a gust, snap the inserted poles, which don't have the rest of the poles to brace against.

In this scenario, it's often best to, first, insert *all* the poles into their sleeves or clips before attaching the ends, while keeping the tent near the ground. Then, once all the poles are ready to go, position them as quickly as possible. In extreme wind, designate a person whose only job is to hang on to the tent to keep it from blowing away.

Bivy tents can also be good in small or cramped tent sites: A tiny, two-person bivy tent can fit just about anywhere two people can lie down side by side, where a hybrid or expedition tent might not fit.

Hybrid Four-Season Tents

Hybrid four-season tents (fig. 13-4) generally have two or more poles and are more frequently double walled in design. Hybrid tents generally offer the same level of strength and storm resistance as bivy tents but are a little bigger, have features like a vestibule and bug-mesh doors, and can handle a wider—and wetter—range of weather and conditions.

These tents are often a great choice for most mountain ranges in the Lower 48 and southern Canada, but they aren't robust enough for the more extreme weather found

DIG OUT THE VESTIBULE

Any tent with a vestibule from a bivy tent to a full-on expedition model can be made a lot more comfortable by digging out the vestibule. At minimum, it allows you to put your boots on in a more traditional sitting position but will also provide more storage space and even a place to cook. The key to digging out the vestibule is starting right below the door of the internal tent. Do not make the hole larger than the vestibule itself. In fact, leave yourself up to a half-foot margin between the edge of the hole and the vestibule fabric so that the excavated area is inside the vestibule once it's closed. Most of the time you will want to make your hole barely bigger than your boots are long.

Hanging out in comfort and style after having just easily put my boots on in a dug-out vestibule. (Photo by Erica Engle)

in places like the Alaska Range, Antarctica, or high Himalaya.

Expedition Tents

Expedition tents are the strongest and most capable type of four-season tents, but also the heaviest (fig. 13-5). These tents often incorporate three to five poles into their design as well as an additional "hooped-vestibule" pole to provide a larger covered area for cooking or equipment (fig. 13-6). Expedition tents can be overkill for many peaks in the Lower 48 or southern Canada, but they are among the few models that can handle more extreme alpine environments with regular high winds and heavy snow loads. These tents are also designed with a lot more space and comfort in mind, making them a nicer place to hang out when pinned down by weather.

TARP SHELTERS

While tarps have become commonplace among thru-hikers and other weight-focused packers, they are less useful for glacier travel and mountaineering. The reason is threefold. First, tarps are best when you have very strong anchor points such as trees or large rocks—only the latter of which you might find on a glacier. Second, tarps often require a camp with a particular configuration, which can be difficult to find in talus or other rocky areas. Third, tarp shelters are generally less

Figure 13-6. *Most expedition tents have either a hooped vestibule or one that's big enough to require a support pole.* (Photo by Matt Park)

wind resistant, a key consideration above tree line, where you are more exposed to the elements (fig. 13-7).

However, for weight-focused trips with good weather, a silnylon tarp will pack down smaller and weigh less than even the smallest bivy tent. This can make a tarp system better for certain objectives where you have a good, stable forecast and information about your potential campsite. If the weather and conditions allow, bivying out under the stars without nylon walls can be quite spectacular (fig. 13-8).

Figure 13-7. *Chris Simrell relaxes under a tarp on the Harvard Route on Mount Huntington, Alaska. Tarps are viable alpine shelters only for shorter trips where the weather forecast is good and low weight is paramount.* (Photo by Max Neale)

Tip: Keep sharp items like ice axes, crampons, ice screws, and snow pickets away from your tent, including your vestibule. Far too many tents have been shredded by these items. However, because you also don't want to lose this critical gear in a snowstorm, have everyone leave them in a "sharps area," with a few longer items driven into the snow to identify the cache if it snows heavily.

BIVY SACKS VS. BIVY TENTS

As bivy tents have gained popularity, bivy sacks—basically thin, very lightweight sleeping shells you can use alone or over a sleeping bag—have become less popular. The reason is that the weight of two bivy sacks is close to or even surpasses the weight of a lighter two-pole bivy tent, yet they are much less comfortable to hang out in. The advantage

Figure 13-8. *It can be nice just to sleep out under the stars. Here, Ian Nicholson gets ready to enjoy some fresh night air in Eldorado Creek, Washington's North Cascades.* (Photo by Peter Webb)

of bivy sacks is that you can sleep nearly anywhere you can lie down, including tight spaces like ledges, and still have some protection from the elements. The disadvantage is condensation, which can quickly accumulate in a bivy sack if it's raining or snowing, and like tarps, they don't stand up well to a storm (fig. 13-9).

ANCHORING A TENT

When it comes to most four-season tents, it's more important to anchor the guylines than the bottom corners. When the wind blows on the tent, it pries the tent away from the ground from below with greater force than it can exert on the tent's middle. Making sure the guylines are well anchored is the priority (fig. 13-10). In ideal conditions, they will be spread out

Figure 13-9. *Three bivy sacks after an unexpected storm high on the Tiedemann Glacier, British Columbia. The weight of the new snow not only crushed all the loft in the sleeping bags but also soaked them.*

SHELTER IS SURVIVAL

BY ROB SMITH

In May 2016, Colin Haley and I left Denali Base Camp with a week's worth of food and fuel and 120 wands. Our plan was to climb the Sultana Ridge of Mount Foraker, both as an objective and reconnaissance for a potential ascent of the South Face via the Infinite Spur. As is often the case in the Alaska Range, the weather was far worse than forecasted. Deep, unconsolidated snow made for slow progress, whether we were on skis or foot. On our second day, at about 12,000 feet as we crossed Mount Crosson, we found ourselves in a full-blown storm—nuking snow and temperatures plummeting to minus 25°F with 60 mile-per-hour wind gusts. Visibility was zero and frostbite became an imminent threat.

Pitching our tent would have required tall snow walls that we didn't have time to build, even if we could have found a suitable place. With no better option, we started descending. Suddenly, Colin vanished and the rope became taut—not as tight as it would have been had he fallen into a crevasse but rather as though he was moving fast. I followed the rope down into the largest crevasse I'd ever seen. Dark, cold, and intimidating, it offered protection from the relentless wind. We set up our tent and bivied.

After enduring relentless cold inside what we later dubbed "Freezy Nuts Castle" for six days, we were out of food and fuel. We knew that navigating the descent in low visibility was nearly impossible, with parallel crevasses that were hard to read. But ten days later, we realized our dream—climbing the 3,000-meter Infinite Spur in eighteen hours. With no food and extreme cold, we were eventually forced to descend to base camp.

KEY TAKEAWAYS: In extreme cold, protecting yourself from wind is just as critical as retaining warmth through insulation. If you can no longer move in a severe alpine storm, you need shelter to survive. Even a lightweight ten-ounce sil-nylon tarp can provide crucial shelter if you are forced to hunker down.

Rob Smith is an IFMGA guide and accomplished splitboarder, who has been climbing for more than three decades. His fast-and-light alpine style has led to speed records on iconic routes like the Infinite Spur and Slovak Direct, first ascents in Alaska and Patagonia, and redpoints up to 5.13c and M10. Rob lives in Chamonix with his wife Jackie and their cat Bugaboo.

in their respective directions from the tent's middle or angled so that some of them are anchored directly into the prevailing wind.

BUILDING SNOW WALLS

When camping in locales that are exposed to the wind, strongly consider building snow walls as a protective barrier (fig. 13-11). To do so, first pack down an area of snow (commonly called a quarry). Next, dig a trench roughly 1 foot wide, just over 1 foot deep, and as long as you need to cut blocks from.

Once the trench is exposed, create your blocks with a snow saw by cutting the four unexposed sides, including the bottom. Cut the blocks in long rows from the top before cutting them vertically into smaller pieces (fig. 13-12). This technique keeps the blocks

Figure 13-10. *Because they reduce the wind's leverage as it blows across the tent, securing a tent's guylines is key, as shown here at the 14,000-foot camp on Denali in the Alaska Range.* (Photo by Dallas Glass)

more uniform in size, which makes it easier to build a strong wall. Even after cutting the sides, you may still need to jam a shovel down vertically into the farthest cut to "pop" the blocks out.

Start laying the blocks around your tent to form the first layer, leaving plenty of room to walk around and potentially dig snow out during and after a storm. It's easy to underestimate how much room your tent will need, so err on the bigger side.

Now run your snow saw across the top of the first layer to ensure the blocks are uniform in height and to make the second layer more stable. Walk around and inspect your first layer, making sure there are no overlapping seams (fig. 13-13). If you find

Figure 13-11. *In ranges prone to extreme wind, snow walls can protect your tent.* (Photo by Dallas Glass)

Figure 13-12. *To get blocks for your snow wall, create a quarry. Then, dig a trench and cut blocks in rows.* (Photo by Brian Muller)

Figure 13-13. *The key to making a strong snow wall is preventing seams between the levels and cutting each level with a saw so that it's flat on top.* (Photo by Dallas Glass)

two blocks on different levels forming a seam, remove the irregular block and cut and situate a new one that fits. Now put the second layer down, and repeat the process of leveling the top with your saw. If any blocks have partially broken or collapsed, make small repairs with snow. Depending on your camp's wind exposure, walls ranging from half of to the full height of your tent usually work best.

WATER AND HYDRATION

You will, of course, also need to stay hydrated, as well as cook meals, up on a glacier, processes that can be complicated by the terrain and conditions. However, there are almost always workable solutions for finding water.

MELTING SNOW

Just like the famous line in Samuel Taylor Coleridge's famous poem *The Rime of the Ancient Mariner*, on a glacier there is "water, water, everywhere, nor any drop to drink." This situation is especially true earlier in the season, when even traditional camping areas on the edges of the glacier are covered in snow. Or you may find yourself in the middle of the glacier where running water is a rarity. Thus, if meltwater isn't readily available, you'll need to find other solutions.

Figure 13-14. *Bringing the right amount of fuel is an important part of planning a trip.*

The most common way to get water on a glacier is to melt snow or ice using a stove. The two most common stove types are canister stoves and white-gas stoves (fig. 13-14). Canister stoves are lighter, more compact, and easier to light; however, they don't work well in below-freezing conditions and create a lot of waste on extended trips, and their fuel can be harder to come by in more-remote places.

TABLE 13-1. FUEL PLANNING	
Stove Type	**Fuel Usage**
White-Gas Stoves	• 3 oz. per person per day, cooking but not melting snow • 6 oz. per person per day, cooking and melting snow for water • 8 oz. per person per day, cooking and melting snow in extremely cold environments (Alaska, Antarctica, etc.)
Canister Stoves	• 1.5 oz. per person per day, cooking but not melting snow for water • 2.5 oz. per person per day, cooking and melting snow for water • 3.0 oz. per person per day, cold, dry snow, and cooking and melting snow for water

Figure 13-15. *Create a solar still using a black garbage bag or cook pot. Start with a little water and a lot of snow, and let it melt in the sun.*

White-gas stoves are heavier and require more effort to prime, but they are more efficient for very big groups or extended trips and can burn a wide range of fuels, meaning they can be used in the more-remote corners of the globe.

Figure 13-16. *Although it's easy to dismiss stories of climbers desperately using an ice screw to funnel shallow flows off difficult-to-reach places, the technique definitely works.* (Photo by Jason Antin)

While some stoves are more fuel efficient than others, table 13-1 lists general guidelines for fuel planning.

Another great way to get water is to create a solar still. Although a still can be made in many ways, it always follows the same basic principle: placing snow someplace relatively "hot" so that when it melts, it is captured in a vessel (fig. 13-15). One of the most common methods is to fill a cook pot (or other container) with snow. Prime it by adding a little water to minimize sublimation, and place the stove in a black garbage bag or in your vestibule during the heat of the day. You can

Figure 13-17. *Brian Muller admiring a massive glacial lake on the Juneau Icefield, Alaska* (Photo by Sam Howell)

also speed up melting by insulating the pot of snow from the glacier and its cooling effects using a foam pad or other equipment.

Finally, if you are lucky, you may encounter slow or shallow flows of water running across slabs or down cracks or dihedrals below a snow patch. The ice screw you're already carrying for anchors or a crevasse fall provides a quick, easy way to "funnel" this water into your bottle, in these situations where you likely couldn't capture the water with the bottle alone, a convenience that saves you from having to melt snow (fig. 13-16).

GLACIAL PONDS AND MOULINS

In late season, when the glacier is bare ice and most or all the seasonal snow has melted off, you may see small streams flowing down the ice—a great way to collect water without having to melt snow. Eventually, these streams fill in depressions to form glacial ponds (fig. 13-17), or they find a weak point in the glacier and plunge deep into the ice as moulins, like much bigger versions of your bathtub drain.

While moulins can be beautiful—almost mythical—in appearance, their danger is very real, and they've caused a surprising number of fatalities. The ice under and around the moulin where the water drains into the glacier is often very hard, smooth, and slick (fig. 13-18). As such, if a person were to fall into the flow, they'd have little chance of stopping themselves on the ice, and if they were to fall into the moulin itself, the chances of a rescue are essentially zero.

EATING SNOW

There are a lot of myths around eating snow to rehydrate, so does eating snow *rehydrate* you or *dehydrate* you? Well, the answer is—depends on the snow! First, eating snow is not the same as consuming water, because snow is a solid that must melt before it becomes a liquid. You're not getting a 1:1 ratio of snow to water, which means just eating snow before letting it melt doesn't help as quickly as you think. Second, colder, more winterlike snow is often only 3–12 percent water by volume. This means you need to consume ten to twenty-plus times more snow to get the same amount of water you would with summer snow, which is frequently 50–75 percent water.

Meanwhile, putting too much snow in your mouth makes for inefficient melting, meaning

Figure 13-18. An ice climber emerges from a moulin that has mostly dried up. Moulins are often deeper than you think—be cautious around them. (Photo by Paul Koubek)

you can take only small amounts in at a time. Your mouth will also get colder with each mouthful, lessening your melting efficiency. The bottom line is that eating snow in winter will not help you avoid dehydration, and even in the summer with denser snow, it can only briefly quench your thirst—though at least it won't make you more dehydrated.

COOKING

Contrary to what you might think, you can set up a fairly sophisticated camp kitchen on a glacier, particularly if you're based out of a single camp for a longer duration. It can be well worth the time and effort to build a place to cook as it makes it easier and more comfortable—and creating snow kitchens can be fun!

Figure 13-19. Rob Smith enjoys cooking breakfast at 14,000 feet on Denali. Digging a seat and hole for your feet can make cooking far more enjoyable. (Photo by Ben Tibbetts)

SNOW KITCHENS

Unlike camping on dirt or in the forest where there are rocks and logs to sit on, glaciers are relatively smooth. Therefore, from digging a simple hole in the snow that allows you to sit and cook more comfortably to crafting something more elaborate, it's practical (and fun!) to build a snow kitchen. Too often climbers have spent a night or two on a glacier and just dealt with the discomfort of cooking on flat ground, only to realize that spending five minutes fashioning a seat (often just by digging a hole) and a table would have been well worth the effort (fig. 13-19).

You can make your snow kitchen as elaborate as you wish, depending on how much time you're willing to spend creating it. Don't underestimate how shaping the snow to your needs will make melting all that water and cooking significantly more enjoyable.

COOK TENTS

For extended trips on snow, a cook tent is easily worth the weight of packing it in (fig. 13-20). While there are a few different styles, all of them are floorless. This allows you to dig the snow out such that you can stand and walk around, while also having a "counter" on which to cook.

Cook tents generally come in two primary varieties. The first is the "mid" (named for the Black Diamond Megamid, which was one of the first designs), a pyramid-style tent (fig. 13-21). These models generally use one support in the middle, which you can either improvise with trekking poles and straps or use a pole dedicated for this task (consider an extendable painter's pole). With mids, it is *critical* not to dig the kitchen out bigger than the tent's footprint because snow will blow inside, making your cozy kitchen a lot less comfortable.

Figure 13-20. *Ian Nicholson, Travis Williams, and Brian Muller cook on the West Buttress of Denali. On longer trips, a floorless cook tent lets you build a comfortable, user-friendly snow kitchen.*

The second type is a floorless tunnel style, generically referred to as a Hilleberg style because that tentmaker repopularized them as cook tents. The advantage of a tunnel-style tent is that it's stronger and can fit more people, but it's also heavier and more expensive. It can be worth it for bigger groups, areas with harsher weather, or locations where you are going to be dropped off by plane or helicopter (and never have to move the tent once at base camp). But it's rarely worth it for a group of two to four people.

STOVE LOCATION

If you don't have bare rock to cook on, you will need to carry some sort of cook surface for your stove so it doesn't melt into the snow. On shorter trips, you can use the back side of

Figure 13-21. *Nick Shepard and Will Hockett show off their roomy pyramid-style cook tent, with bench seating in the snow around the edges.*

a shovel or a piece of closed-cell foam, but for more extended trips, you'll likely want something stiffer and tougher, like a 1-square-foot piece of wood.

Another option is to hang your stove (fig. 13-22), which has the advantage of increasing fuel efficiency—setting your canister stove directly on the snow can change a lot of the fuel to its solid state, meaning the canister will "run out" prior to actually being empty. Many canister stoves come with a kit that lets you hang your stove from one or more poles or (carefully) cook in your tent, as long as you keep your tent well ventilated.

Figure 13-22. *Steve Swenson and Scott Bennett rest after their summit push on the first ascent of Changi Tower (6,500 meters) in the Pakistani Karakoram.* (Photo by Graham Zimmerman)

SPECIAL TRAVEL CONSIDERATIONS

A few other items can be integral to glacier travel, particularly multiday outings, including large backpacks, sleds, and chest harnesses.

BIG PACKS AND DITCH LOOPS

If you're wearing an overnight pack (more than thirty pounds, or fifteen kilograms)—but not a lighter summit pack—consider adding a "ditch loop" that allows you to quickly remove your pack and hang it from your belay loop in a rescue situation (fig. 13-23).

A ditch loop is a piece of single-strand, 5- to 6-millimeter cord tied around your pack, a grab loop, and at least one shoulder strap that you then knot and clip to your belay loop with at least one locking carabiner. The shoulder strap acts as a backup so that you don't lose your pack if either of the other two attachment points blows out. In the event of a crevasse fall, in which a heavy pack could tip you over backward as you hang, you simply shift your pack off your shoulders and let it hang from

Figure 13-23. *To create a ditch loop:* **a,** *Thread some 5 or 6 millimeter cord through your grab loop and one shoulder strap.* **b,** *Tie a rewoven overhand or figure-eight.* **c,** *The cord should be long enough that you can clip the other end to your harness for travel.* (Photo by Matt Park)

WHEN TIMING IS EVERYTHING

BY JULIANA GARCIA

At 3 a.m., our team of four climbers prepared to make our first deposit of supplies at Camp 1 on Gasherbrum I above the Baltoro Glacier. Moving in two rope team pairs with very heavy packs loaded with food, tents, and equipment, we set off under the night's sky, traversing the chaotic landscape of seracs and crevasses on the jumbled glacier. The cold night air kept the snow surface firm and the snow bridges solid, allowing us to progress smoothly but the vastness of the glacier was humbling.

Five hours later, Marco Suárez and I arrived at Camp 1 under a clear, sunny sky. We unloaded our gear and rested while we took in the stunning views, and then prepared to descend and continue our acclimatization rotations. We began to descend around 10 a.m. The valley was unusually warm—downright hot for nearly 20,000 feet. We watched avalanches tumble down distant slopes and nearby peaks, none directly threatening our route, but the constant roar was a reminder that conditions were changing. Our descent route was now in the sunshine and as we reentered the glacier's maze, we discovered how much conditions had changed. The snow had softened considerably. With each step, our boots sank deeper—first to my knees, then to my waist. The firm snow surface we had cramponed up on our ascent was gone. I stopped to increase the rope distance between us and add several extra stopper knots. We moved cautiously, with the rope tight between us. The snow bridges that had been solid that morning would now be unreliable.

I could feel hollow, unconsolidated wet snow beneath my feet as I clawed my way out of each collapsing step. My partners struggled too. There was no safe place to stop, no way to regroup. We could only press forward. Exhaustion and fear mounted as hours passed. Every step we sank knee to hip deep in extremely wet snow. I radioed base camp: "The glacier is a death trap in this heat. We don't know whether to wait for cooler conditions or keep going." They could only listen.

Ready for the worst, we crawled and waded through the disintegrating snow on the glacier's surface. Ten hours later, we finally reached stable ice, where our teammates waited with food and water—relieved to see us safe.

That night, we reflected on what we could have changed and what we learned. The answer was clear: when conditions are warmer than normal, you need to leave earlier than normal. On average, a party moves downhill twice as fast as they ascend. We had taken five hours to go up and should have taken up to three hours to descend. Instead, it had taken us almost ten. The prolonged exposure not only increased our risk to avalanches but also made crevasse falls far more likely.

KEY TAKEAWAYS: Traveling on snow and glaciers is easiest when they are firm. Planning to do most of a climb during the cooler hours not only makes the ascent smoother, but also reduces the risk of crevasse falls, as the snow bridges will be stronger. Adjust your start time to reflect the conditions you expect to encounter.

Juliana Garcia has climbed and guided mountains and big walls throughout Alaska, the Alps, the Andes, Bolivia, Colombia, Pakistan, Peru, and the US. She is the first female Ecuadorian and Latin America IFMGA guide. Garcia is an instructor at the Ecuadorian School of Mountain Guides.

Figure 13-24. *A group makes their way back to the airstrip on the Kahiltna Glacier, ascending the infamous Heartbreak Hill, Alaska Range.*

your belay loop. Now you can stay upright and move into rescue or self-rescue mode.

SLEDS

On self-supported expeditions to Arctic and Antarctic regions such as the Alaska Range, Wrangells, Coast Range, and various ranges in Antarctica, dragging a sled can be an effective way to move a lot of weight, especially over long distances across large, mellow glaciers (table 13-2). In fact, strapping a duffle bag to a plastic sled to move across lower-angle expanses of snow and ice is undoubtedly the most effective method of transporting your food and equipment, when possible (fig. 13-24).

Sled Rigging

Rigging a sled is relatively simple, no matter which model you're using. First, securely attach your duffle bag (where the majority of your things go) and any loose items, such as fuel cans and large pots, so that they cannot be lost even if your sled tips over.

The most common way to tie things down is to have one or two long pieces of cord hanging off the sled that you then crisscross, ensuring the cord weaves through every items. Once you finish passing the cord through

TABLE 13-2. GUIDELINES FOR WEIGHT DISTRIBUTION WITH A SLED

Terrain	Distribution
On flat ground or going slightly downhill	30–40% in backpack, 60–70% in sled
Moderate uphill	50–60% in backpack, 40–50% in sled
Steep uphill	70–80% in backpack, 20–30% in sled

Figure 13-25. *To set up a loop for your sled:* **a**, *Run a piece of 5 or 6 millimeter cord through the same area as your pack waist belt.* **b**, *Tie a double fisherman's knot to close the loop, creating a place to tie in your sled.* (Photos by Matt Park)

everything, tie off the system with a mule hitch. For the pulling cord—the one you use to drag the sled—the most common method is to thread a piece of 5- to 6-millimeter cord through the channel that holds your pack's waist belt (fig. 13-25). Now tie a loop in this cord using a double fisherman's knot or similar secure closure, and then clip that to another piece of cord (4.5–6 feet) coming from the sled itself (fig. 13-26).

Sled Brakes

For steeper descents, you can use a "brake" so that the sled doesn't run (so hard) into the back of your legs. Fashion your brake by tying several overhand knots in a 3.5- to 5-foot piece of 5- to 6-millimeter cord. Attach the cord near the front of the sled. To deploy the brake, drop it in front of the sled and then attach the other side of the brake to the sled to form a U underneath, so that the sled is constantly running over the cord. The knots will drag in the snow because of the weight of the sled, slowing it down.

Sleds in the Rope Team

If you are traveling in a rope team with sleds, anchor the back of the sled to the rope both to minimize the odds of the sled slamming down on top of the person dragging it should they fall into a crevasse but also to allow you, the person behind the sled, to "brake" the sled to keep it from running into the back of your teammate's legs.

A clove hitch works well, but some people prefer a friction hitch like a prusik. If you use a friction hitch, tie it tightly so it won't slip. Self-rescue is extremely difficult with sleds. It's critical your team is proficient with various drop systems because of the greater

Figure 13-26. *To tie off a sled:* **a**, *Attach the cord to one end of the sled, zigzag or wrap the cord in a Z over the sled, making sure to run through several straps on the duffle to secure it.* **b**, *Use a truckers or mule hitch to tension and tie off the cord.* **c**, *Back up the hitch with an overhand knot.* **d**, *Attach the front of the sled to your pack and the back of the sled to the rope with a knot, clove, or other secure hitch to keep it from hitting the back of your ankles and minimize the chance that it will slam into you if you fall into a crevasse.*

loads. Though it is more complex, if you have enough resources, it can be worth it to haul the sled (and their backpack) out separately from the fallen climber.

CHEST HARNESS

Chest harnesses are useful tools that could certainly be used more often for glacier travel, as they can help you stay upright in a crevasse fall. (figs. 13-27 and 13-28).

However, people will occasionally rig the rope so that it runs from their clip-in knot up through the chest harness. If they're wearing a heavy pack, this setup minimizes their chances of being flipped upside down in a crevasse fall.

Figure 13-27. *Wearing a chest harness on Denali in the Alaska Range* (Photo by Brian Muller)

The disadvantage is that it can make self-arrest in firmer conditions tougher, as the rope running through the chest harness will quickly bring the harness to the clip-in knot, "crunching" the person—essentially folding them in half. This effect can be worsened if the climber clips the rope in both directions, with the two strands of rope from their harness (assuming they are in the middle and not the ends), making self-arrest even more awkward and difficult. There is no best way, so you'll want to personally weigh the pros and cons of glacier travel with a chest harness pre-clipped.

DISPOSING OF WASTE

While camping in alpine terrain, be it on a glacier, on snow, or in most areas near and

Figure 13-28. *Chest harnesses can be a good idea anytime you are wearing a big pack or have a heavy load. The debate over whether to clip in your chest harness for travel rages on. While it makes you more likely to be held up in a crevasse fall, it also makes self-arrest harder and more awkward.*

Figure 13-29. *Playing chess with Graham McDowell during a stormy stretch in the Waddington Range* (Photo by Ryan O'Connell)

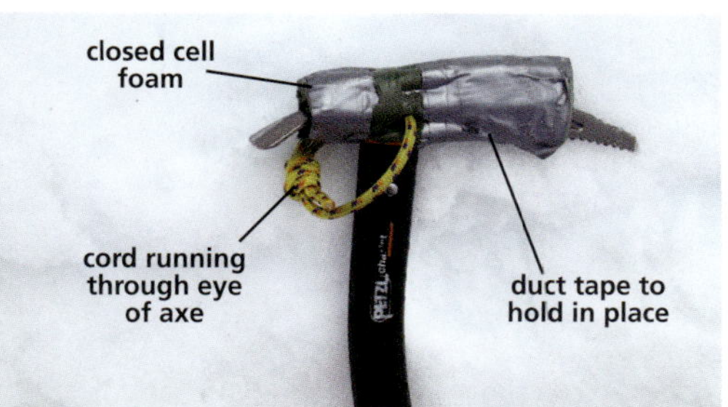

Figure 13-30. *Cut out some closed-cell foam in a rectangle, bend it over the axe head, trim, and tape it in place. For anchoring options, punch a hole in the tape and run some cord through the tape and eye. This insulated axe worked well on Denali in minus 42°F, my coldest summit yet.*

above tree line, you'll need to manage human waste. Below tree line, you can often dig a cat hole—a hole 6 to 8 inches deep and at least 200 feet from water—to deposit waste; in these environments, human waste can break down in a matter of weeks. However, in subalpine, alpine, and snowy environments, waste could take years to decades to break down. It is essential to have a plan to pack out your human waste if a depository is not available.

SPENDING TIME IN CAMP

Staying sane and being a good team player on an extended trip are skills just as critical as mastery of technical systems. Bring your favorite games, food, books, and the best attitude you can in case the weather or the conditions go south (fig. 13-29). For longer trips and expeditions, bringing supplies to entertain yourself is well worth it, both to pass the time and boost morale. Movies and shows downloaded to your phone or a small tablet are also nice, but these shouldn't be the only form of entertainment, as you may run out of power or things to watch.

On extended trips, don't underestimate the hours of diversion you'll get from simple games like chess or cards. Pick more thought- and skill-based games rather than chance-based games, which generally get boring quickly. Skill-based games are great on expeditions because they engage our brains when we would otherwise be hanging around camp doing nothing.

INSULATING YOUR AXE

For colder trips where you will be dealing with temperatures below zero Fahrenheit, it can be helpful to insulate your ice axe (fig. 13-30). Even if you are using very warm gloves or mittens, adding a little foam to your ice axe and duct-taping it in place will make a noticeable difference when it comes to holding onto a metal object for hours on end in Arctic temperatures.

ALTITUDE

As you gain elevation, the air gets thinner. There is less atmospheric pressure to

Figure 13-31. *This climber is about to enter the death zone on Geneva Spur, south side of Mount Everest, Nepal.* (Photo by Max Bond)

compress the oxygen molecules, causing the molecules to spread out and become less available. The decrease in atmospheric pressure isn't linear; therefore, it becomes more extreme the higher you get. At 10,000 feet (3,000 meters; e.g., high in the Tetons), there is roughly 75 percent of the effective oxygen in the air compared with sea level, and at 14,000 feet (4,300 meters; near the top of Mount Rainier), there is roughly 65 percent. At 18,000 feet (5,550 meters; high on Denali), there is only about 50 percent, and at 29,000 feet (8,800 meters; the summit of Mount Everest, fig. 13-31), there is less than 35 percent of the oxygen found at sea level.

ALTITUDE AND PERFORMANCE

Most people, even those who live at sea level, are relatively unaffected when ascending to altitudes of around 6,500 feet (2,000 meters). Above roughly 8,000 feet (2,400 meters), all climbers will experience a reduction in performance regardless of fitness, though the fitter and stronger you are, the higher you can go before you feel it.

While previous acclimatization might help, most people can get away without having acclimatized up to altitudes of around 13,500 feet (4,000 meters), especially if they aren't sleeping above 10,000 feet (3,000 meters). This is how many people attempt Mount Rainier (14,411 feet, or 4,392 meters) in Washington over only a two- or three-day stretch (fig. 13-32). This rapid-fire approach requires increased fitness compared to climbing subsequently higher mountains over the days prior or climbing more slowly, both of which give the body more time to adjust. Even with peaks just a little higher—for example, Mont Blanc (15,777 feet, or 4,807 meters)—most people who live at sea level will need to climb a few progressively higher mountains in the week or so prior. Many climbers going to the highest mountains in the world, such as the 8,000-meter peaks in the Himalaya and Karakoram, will most likely use supplemental oxygen and wear down suits (fig. 13-33).

THE ACCLIMATIZATION PROCESS

The body does several things to adapt to the reduction in atmospheric pressure and subsequently lowered volume of oxygen:

Breathing rate increases: To compensate for the lower oxygen levels, your body increases its breathing rate and depth. This is your body's immediate means of getting more oxygen into your bloodstream.

Heart rate increases: Your heart rate also increases to pump more oxygen-rich blood to your vital organs and muscles.

Red-blood-cell production increases: Over time, your body begins to produce

Figure 13-32. A team crosses Ingraham Flats at 11,000 feet on Mount Rainier. Most climbers, even those ascending to more moderate elevations such as Mount Rainier's 14,411-foot summit, will feel the effects of altitude. (Photo by Bryce Hill)

Figure 13-33. Climbers using supplemental oxygen close to 8,000 meters on Cho Oyu, China (Photo by Dallas Glass)

more red blood cells. Red blood cells contain hemoglobin, which carries oxygen from your lungs to your body's tissues. More red blood cells mean greater oxygen-carrying capacity.

Another effect is fluid retention, which can lead to swelling in the hands and feet. The lower air pressure causes fluid to leak from your capillaries into the surrounding tissues. You might experience digestive changes like nausea and reduced appetite as well.

TYPES OF ALTITUDE SICKNESS

Developing a basic understanding of the early signs and symptoms of altitude-related sickness is key to both preventing it and being able to recognize, monitor, and stop the sickness from getting worse. Being able to recognize these conditions becomes even more important at higher elevations where altitude sickness can be more severe and retreat can be difficult.

Acute mountain sickness: This is the mildest and most common form of altitude sickness. AMS symptoms include headache, vomiting, loss of appetite, mild nausea, difficulty sleeping, and shortness of breath. These symptoms can range from mild to severe, but generally, once these signs start, you should stop ascending; if they worsen or don't resolve, start descending.

High-altitude cerebral edema: HACE is the most severe form of AMS and occurs when the brain swells with fluid. HACE is life-threatening, and the person suffering from it needs to get to lower elevations and to medical attention immediately. They will often need treatment with drugs like dexamethasone. Common symptoms include the "umbles"—"the stumbles, bumbles, and mumbles," that is, the confusion, lack of coordination, and the inability to speak properly.

High altitude pulmonary edema: Like HACE, this is life-threatening. It can occur in the absence of AMS or HACE. HAPE causes a build-up of fluid in the lungs. Symptoms include coughing up blood-tinged sputum, shortness of breath, and crackling lung sounds—effects similar to pneumonia. Like HACE, this affliction does not correct as readily through descent, so take extra care to avoid it. The drug nifedipine should be administered immediately, and rapid descent and/or evacuation to a medical facility are a priority.

Opposite: *Climbing glaciated mountains takes an amalgam of skills; fortunately, most of these are learned skills that can be cultivated over a lifetime of adventure. In this photo, Dan Corn sets up a learning environment above a yawning crevasse on the Inspiration Glacier on Washington's Eldorado Peak.*

CHAPTER 14

Preparation and Practice

Like any other skills, glacier-travel and crevasse-rescue techniques require polishing to keep them sharp. Although you hardly need to practice these skills on a weekly basis, one refresher each spring or at the start of your glacier-travel season can go a long way toward ensuring you are well prepared to deal with the environment or a crevasse fall or related scenario that year.

SKILLS TO PRACTICE AT HOME

While many techniques are essential to practice on snow or, better yet, an actual glacier, you can also practice many of them in the comfort of your own home, on your computer, or at a nearby park.

TRIP PLANNING

Building digital trip plans not only helps you map out your route, hone your GPS skills, and review your resources to create the most well-placed GPS line possible before you go out into the wilderness, it also builds stoke for the trip planning and future adventures. Pick three to four "dream trips" and build complete and thorough tour plans (see chapter 3) for them. Like any other skill, the first few times can feel arduous, but this skill will quickly become second nature.

NAVIGATION PROFICIENCY CHECKLIST

Like trip planning, map-and-compass skills are also a learned, yet slightly perishable skill. Luckily, they are easy to practice, so you can maintain a high level of proficiency.

While it is great to practice these navigational skills in a high-alpine environment, don't underestimate how useful it is to practice closer to home, whether on a short hike or around your house, even if you live in a city (fig. 14-1). Simply print a map of your local area, including, for example, the area's Universal Transverse Mercator (UTM) lines and declination, and then practice these proficiencies.

Can you:

- Take a bearing in the field?
- Apply it to the map?
- Pull a bearing from the map and apply it to the field?
- Pull a UTM point off a map?
- Plot a UTM point from your phone or GPS device onto a map?

DEVELOPING PROFICIENCY WITH CREVASSE-RESCUE ESSENTIALS

While practicing crevasse rescue in a carefully orchestrated, life-load setting is important, it can be valuable to go over basic technical systems once a year in a nontechnical setting

Figure 14-1. *You don't need to be in a remote or wilderness environment to practice navigation skills. Take bearings from known points as I'm doing here using the Space Needle in Seattle.* (Photo by Henry Nicholson)

Figure 14-2. *Tracey Bernstein practices dry-land crevasse rescue at camp in the Southern Pickets in Washington's North Cascades.*

(fig 14-2). The hauling techniques that use mechanical advantage are, on the most foundational level, just technical systems, and while it is essential to practice them on snow at some point, don't underestimate how useful it is to learn and, at the start of each season, refresh these skills in your backyard or a local park.

While chapter 9 details the steps required for each technique, you can do some basic rescue practice by starting with a rope rigged with your team in glacier-travel mode. Start from a lying-down self-arrest position and use a tree, post, or other fixed object for your anchor. Note that while this simulation helps with the technical systems involved, it does not prepare you for the act of catching and holding a real-world crevasse fall and building a solid anchor under the duress of holding someone. Regardless, you should still ensure you are proficient at rigging these systems:

- Drop-end 3:1 haul
- Drop-end 6:1 haul
- Direct-line 3:1 haul
- Direct-line 6:1 haul

ASCENDING AND RIGGING A ROPE

Another skill that is easy to practice at your local park is ascending a rope (see chapter 10). Simply throw a rope over some monkey bars or similar playground equipment, and

THE IMPORTANCE OF ADAPTING TO CONDITIONS

BY ROB SMITH

After climbing the 10,000-foot Infinite Spur on Mount Foraker in May 2016, Colin Haley and I knew the real challenge had just begun: on-sighting the descent of the Sultana Ridge while utterly exhausted. Colin insisted that we rope up with around 80 feet between us, far more than the 40 to 50 feet commonly recommended for a two-person rope team. I initially thought that much distance was excessive, but it left us with just enough rope to set up a rescue system.

A few hours into the descent, I was leading what seemed like a solid path through massive crevasses. Without warning, the snow beneath me collapsed, and I fell 35 feet into a massive crevasse. Fortunately, I was uninjured, but my "swami" belt was painfully uncomfortable—I had cut my harness leg loops before the ascent to save weight. Colin positioned himself behind a massive wind drift, which acted as a natural anchor, making it much easier for him to secure himself and help me ascend out of the crevasse.

As it turned out, Colin's rope-spacing decision was perfect. Even after a dozen trips to the Alaska Range, I had underestimated the spacing needed for proper glacier travel in our circumstances. In the Alps, 40 feet of rope might suffice, but in this terrain, and without the ability to assess what angle we were crossing the crevasses at, it wasn't enough.

I did, however, lose both my ice tools—a major setback with a huge descent still ahead. In the end, descending the Sultana Ridge took longer than climbing the Infinite Spur. When we finally reached the West Buttress track on the lower Kahiltna Glacier, I felt an overwhelming sense of relief.

No matter how strong or fit a climber is, no amount of technical skill can help you completely avoid crevasses. Glacier travel is refined through years of experience. While standard guidelines provide a solid foundation, conditions and terrain demand judgment and adjustments. Trust your intuition. If a different technique seems to offer great security, use it. Guidelines exist for a reason, but the mountains do not follow rules.

KEY TAKEAWAYS: In big, glaciated terrain, err on the side of longer rope spacing for better protection. Proper rope management is just as important as fitness and technical skills in alpinism. Crevasse rescue can be learned quickly, but reading complex glaciers takes years—even decades—to master.

Rob Smith is an IFMGA guide and accomplished splitboarder, who has been climbing for more than three decades. His fast-and-light alpine style has led to speed records on iconic routes like the Infinite Spur and Slovak Direct, first ascents in Alaska and Patagonia, and redpoints up to 5.13c and M10. Rob lives in Chamonix with his wife Jackie and their cat Bugaboo.

Figure 14-3. *While practicing in a real crevasse may be the best classroom, don't underestimate how much you can learn from practicing regularly closer to home. Chris Marshall ascends a rope while I slowly lower him on playground equipment.* (Photo by Grant Price)

ascend one side of the rope as another person slowly pays out line through a belay device (fig. 14-3). This setup creates a kind of treadmill for the ascending climber, without creating the risks that come with being high off the ground.

From the comfort of your living room, you can also practice rigging the rope for glacier travel (fig. 14-4). Practice setting the distances between climbers; use your arm spans with two, three, and four climbers. Experiment with various ways to carry the rope, like the mountaineer's coil and Kiwi coil, as well as stuffing the rope into your pack.

Figure 14-4. *Rigging the rope for glacier travel is something you can practice on a mellow snow slope—or from the comfort of your own home!* (Photo by Bryce Hill)

SKILLS TO PRACTICE ON SNOW

When people talk about brushing up on skills related to glacier travel, they're often talking about technical haul systems and ascending fixed lines. However, understanding what it takes to create a good anchor is just as important, as a solid anchor is the foundation for any rescue or rappelling or lowering scenario. You can practice anchor building anywhere the snow is deep enough. Beyond knowing how to build an anchor, it is imperative that you know how to move efficiently and securely on snow. Practice movement on snow as well as the basics of self-arresting. Being proficient at all that, in addition to

Figure 14-5. The only way to get direct feedback about the strength of an anchor is to pull on it. (Photo by Paul Koubek)

knowing how to rig a crevasse-rescue system, could someday save your teammates' lives.

PLACING SNOW ANCHORS

Investigate the relative strengths of different anchors (see chapter 7). Pull-test them, standing far back in case the object comes flying out or, ideally, with someone holding them with a rope as a backup so the anchor doesn't fly out and hit you (fig. 14-5). Try classic T-slot (T-trenched) pickets, cabled pickets, and top-clipped pickets. Also, experiment with less traditional anchors like snow bollards and buried rocks in case you need to rappel or lower from them on a complex descent one day.

Figure 14-6. Take advantage of every opportunity to practice good technique while climbing snow—the more you do it, the more second nature it will become. (Photo by Jeff Ward)

Figure 14-7. Most climbers do a big, long self-arrest session when they first learn the skill, but it's a good idea—and fun—to refresh your skills every few years.

STRENGTHENING MOVEMENT SKILLS

Look for opportunities to strengthen your snow-movement and snow-climbing skills. This means practicing using the most secure, efficient technique for the terrain, even if you don't "have to." This practice gets your body used to the movement and technique for those

THE FIRST LESSON IS THE MOST IMPORTANT

BY CONRAD ANKER

Pete Carse, Mike Ruth, and I had just finished the winter season at Park West, Utah, a flannel shirt and jeans–type of ski resort at that time. Mike and Pete, older than me and with more reliable wheels, informed me that Mount Robson in Canada, our goal, was the crown of the Rockies.

At age sixteen, I had climbed Mount Rainier (a.k.a. Tahoma) in Washington, which felt like a snow trail with Merit Badge-sized gaps. This was going to be my first real expedition. First climbed in 1913 by guide Conrad Kain, Mount Robson's northeast face (a.k.a. the Kain Face) remains a test piece. With our radio tuned to the Stanley Cup, we hopscotched north from one crag and campground to the next and eventually to the trailhead.

Pete, our leader, had Denali experience along with crevasse- and self-rescue knowledge. We practiced rescue systems several times in the trailhead parking lot using parking pylons and picnic tables before setting off. As we wrapped around the impressive northern aspect of Robson via Berg Lake, we gazed at the Emperor and North Faces. At each successive camp, the mountain came more alive. The changes in temperature, precipitation, and wind and snow were the personality of this peak. These caves, chasms, and contortions of snow and ice were as surreal and intimidating as the ones I'd imagined.

One afternoon, as we skied toward the Dome, a buttress that splits the shorter Kain and North Faces, we could see that we were on leftover early spring snow. Pete set up the rope, while Mike and I made sure our skis functioned. The exercise was worth the effort; good, fun turns brought us a bit closer to our objective.

On the return, within sight of camp, a trapdoor underneath me suddenly gave way. I fell into an icy chasm. My skis—barely attached to my boots in the best of conditions—popped off and were left hanging from a small leash. Once I checked to see I wasn't hurt and shouted up to my partners that I was fine, I got to work attaching my prusiks to the rope and slowly started sliding them upward, alternating my weight, which eventually led me up to the lip of the crevasse. The recent snow hadn't set up enough to provide a hard edge, nor was the lip too overhanging to negotiate. Between prusiking, pulling on a ski pole, and a bit of wallowing, I made it out.

The rehearsals Pete had led us through had paid off. How we handled that fall was a reminder not only of the danger that lives even in seemingly innocuous terrain but also of how valuable training is.

KEY TAKEAWAYS: Glacier travel is a rare and wondrous activity. You are walking on water, albeit in a frozen state, that has sculpted the dynamic alpine landscape. By treating the glacier with respect—roping up and training for the unknown—you'll have a chance to return time and time again.

Conrad Anker is an American alpinist known for his bold first ascents, high-altitude expeditions, and decades as a leader in the climbing community. A former longtime captain of The North Face athlete team, he made significant expeditions worldwide, including the discovery of George Mallory's body on Mount Everest in 1999 and first ascents in Antarctica, Patagonia, and the Himalaya.

Figure 14-8. *Doug Poortenga, Ken Boggs, and Nate Helweg travel up the Formidable Glacier on the Ptarmigan Traverse, Washington, in a whiteout, when solid tour plans are paramount.*

big days out when efficiency becomes crucial (fig. 14-6).

SELF-ARREST TECHNIQUES

While it's less important than practicing the technical aspects of crevasse rescue or anchor construction, you'll still want to revisit and rehearse the classic self-arrest positions—sliding on your back feetfirst, sliding on your back headfirst, and sliding on your stomach headfirst (taking extra caution)—to be well prepared when the time comes (fig. 14-7).

REAL-LIFE RIGGING PRACTICE

While it is incredibly helpful to do dry-land practices in parks or other convenient locations, at some point you *must* perform

Figure 14-9. *Skiers should practice both roped and unroped crevasse rescue. Anywhere with a good wind lip will do.* (Photo by Josh Cole)

crevasse rescue on snow and with the load of a real person. Even for experienced professionals, a backup to the system should be mandatory—you're practicing to gain proficiency at a technique to reduce your overall risk, but if you practice without backups, you are definitely *not* reducing that risk.

Follow these steps:

1. Back up both the anchor and the person in the crevasse. With a little planning, you can pull this off with a single 60-meter rope.
2. Start with the backup anchor, which should be around 15 or 20 feet from whatever "crevasse lip" you are working with; take the time to make this anchor robust.
3. Now measure the distance from the backup anchor, plus around 10 to 20 feet

Figure 14-10. *Taking a course from a professional can be a great way to improve your skills. If you are considering hiring a guide, seek out courses taught by people trained or certified through AMGA or ACMG. Here, IFMGA guide Jeff Ward instructs an AMGA alpine guides course near Ingalls Peak in Washington's North Cascades.*

to put your "victim" in the crevasse. Tie an overhand knot on a bight—this is where the fallen climber is going.

4. From the fallen climber's knot, pay out the approximate distance from where they'll be hanging in the crevasse to the rescuer's anchors, which will be roughly 5 to 10 feet closer than the backup anchor. Compare the rope distances to confirm this.
5. Now, have the rescuer take up the remainder of the rope in whatever fashion they normally travel.
6. You can lower the "fallen" climber into the crevasse and back up the rescuer's anchor once it has been constructed.

PRACTICE FOR SKIERS

Just as avalanche educators, avalanche professionals, patrollers, and many backcountry skiers practice companion rescue, using a beacon, shovel, and probe to save someone who's been buried in an avalanche, it's a good idea for skiers to refresh their crevasse-rescue skills as well. For example, while all mountain enthusiasts traveling on glaciers should create solid tour plans that are loaded (or built) onto their phones as a navigational aid, this holds particularly true with skiers, who tend to travel on glaciers earlier in the season when the weather isn't as stable (fig. 14-8). Below are key skills to drill and practice:

1. The different methods of roping up—If you don't practice and aren't familiar with these, you are unlikely to use them.
2. How to perform crevasse rescue efficiently if someone falls into a crevasse unroped (fig. 14-9).
3. How to perform crevasse rescue by doing a weighted transfer with skis on your feet.

Figure 14-11. If you are looking for a course or a guided trip, seek out programs run by certified professionals or reputable clubs with established organizations. (Photo by Paul Koubek)

HIRE A PROFESSIONAL TO HELP

Hiring a professional guide to teach you many of the skills in this book can be a great way to jump-start or refine your skills. While this book is an excellent resource for learning and revisiting the techniques required to climb snow- and glacier-covered mountains the world over, like most skills, there's undeniable value in hands-on practice and getting first-hand coaching and feedback from a qualified professional (fig. 14-10).

The American Mountain Guides Association (AMGA) and the Association of Canadian Mountain Guides (ACMG) train and certify guides to both lead climbs and teach all the skills presented in this book. There are dozens of reputable guide services and climbing clubs across North America that offer quality snow-climbing, glacier-travel, and crevasse-rescue courses. Seek out courses with AMGA or ACMG-trained or alpine-certified guides, fully certified IFMGA mountain guides, or reputable clubs with experienced trip leaders (fig. 14-11).

THINKING OUTSIDE THE BOX

The techniques described in this book are the most common solutions for the most common problems glacier mountaineers and skiers face. However, if you ever run into unexpected or unusual challenges—as you most certainly will—it's okay to think critically about unusual or less common solutions, and even to create your own. After all, these techniques have all been invented over the many decades that people have been going to the mountains. They are in a constant state of change as people refine them, tools are updated, and knowledge continues to evolve.

Acknowledgments

Thanks to my sons, Henry and Hayden, and my wife, Rebecca Schroeder, for their support of this project. Thanks to everyone I have been lucky enough to share a rope with but particularly my longtime climbing partners Andy Dahlen, Graham McDowell, Ryan O'Connell, Tino Villanueva, and Graham Zimmerman.

Thanks to Larry Goldie, Chris McNamara, Dale Remsberg, Matt Schonwald, and Jeff Ward for their endless mentorship and inspiration. Thanks to Sharon Birchfield, Sarah Janin, Alexis Kane, Micha Lewkowitz, Chris Marshall, Zack McGill, Hannah McGowan, Grant Price, Neil Satterfield, Mike Soucy, and Tino Villanueva for posing for photos. Huge thanks to Brooke Warren for the cover photo and to Max Bond, Josh Cole, Jared Drapala, Juliana Garcia, Dallas Glass, Jon Griffith, Bryce Hill, Joshua Jarrin, Brian Muller, Mikey Schaefer, and Jonathon Spitzer for their spectacular photos featured throughout the book.

Thanks to Conrad Anker, Willie Beneges, Dan Corn, Emilie Drinkwater, Juliana Garcia, Clint Helander, Kyle Horner, Joshua Jarrin, Michael Kennedy, Paul Koubek, George Lowe, Sam Luthy, Jackson Marvell, Lyra Pierotti, Alan Rousseau, Evan Stevens, Jonathon Spitzer, Rob Smith (AKA Uncle Rob), Mike Soucy, Jeff Ward, and Graham Zimmerman for their contributions. Their excerpts, insights, and expertise added depth to this book and elevated it to another level.

I would like to acknowledge the great alpinist Michael Gardner, who had planned to contribute to this book before his untimely passing on Jannu East in Nepal. In *Alpinist*, Gardner described how he felt about climbing, "An indescribable awareness of place and peace takes hold."

Thanks to my family and friends Debbie Black, Josh Brewer, Alex Chew, Jonathan Nicholson, Mackenzie Nicholson, Detmar and Susan Schroeder, Jussi Tahtinen, and my mom Megan Nicholson. Additional big thanks to other people who have influenced my life, including Arthur Baines, Tracey Bernstein, Oliva Cussen, Mark Gunlogson, Dave Haavik, Paul McKinley, Sue Nicholson, Jaime Pollitte, John Race, Matt Schonwald, Greg and Paula Shaw, Ago (Agnes) Sykes, Sheila Walsh, Peter Webb, Dan Whitmore, Steve Whittaker, John Yarnall, and many, many others. Thank you to everyone I've had the privilege of sharing a rope or skin track with—whether during courses or while guiding. There are too many individuals to name, but please know how deeply grateful I am. Each of you has played a role in shaping me into the person I am today.

Lastly, thank you to Kate Rogers and Laura Shauger at Mountaineers Books for their invaluable assistance and influence on the project as well as for trusting me to create the best book I possibly could on this topic. Huge thanks also to Matt Samet and Sarah Breeding for their edits, to John McMullen for creating illustrations, and to McKenzie Long for laying out the pages, gracefully handling my endless requests, and helping bring this project to life.

Suggested Reading

HOW-TO MANUALS

Chauvin, Marc, and Rob Coppolillo. *The Mountain Guide Manual: The Comprehensive Reference—From Belaying to Rope Systems and Self-Rescue*. Falcon, 2017.

Coppolillo, Rob. *The Ski Guide Manual: Advanced Techniques for the Backcountry*. Falcon, 2020.

House, Steve, and Scott Johnston. *Training for the New Alpinism: A Manual for the Climber as Athlete*. Patagonia, 2014.

House, Steve, Scott Johnston, Kilian Jornet. *Training for the Uphill Athlete: A Manual for Mountain Runners and Ski Mountaineers*. Patagonia, 2019.

Houston, Charles, David Harris, and Ellen Zeman. *Going Higher: Oxygen, Man, and Mountains*. 5th edition. Mountaineers Books, 2005.

Jones, Jeremy. *The Art of Shralpinism: Lessons from the Mountains*. Mountaineers Books, 2022.

Mountaineers, The. *Mountaineering: The Freedom of the Hills*. 10th edition. Mountaineers Books, 2024.

Nicholson, Ian. *Climbing Self-Rescue: Essential Skills, Technical Tips & Improvised Solutions*. Mountaineers Books, 2024.

Rebuffat, Gaston. *On Ice, Rock, and Snow*. Oxford University Press, 1971.

Richardson, Alun. *Mountaineering: Essential Skills for Hikers and Climbers*. Skyhorse, 2015.

Samet, Matt. *The Climbing Dictionary: Mountaineering Slang, Terms, Neologisms & Lingo: An Illustrated Reference*. Mountaineers Books, 2011.

Stock, Joe. *The Avalanche Factor: Understanding and Avoiding Avalanches*. Stock Alpine, 2024.

Tremper, Bruce. *Staying Alive in Avalanche Terrain*. 3rd edition. Mountaineers Books, 2018.

Twight, Mark and James Martin. *Extreme Alpinism: Climbing Light, Fast, and High*. Mountaineers Books, 1999.

Tyson, Andy. *Glacier Mountaineering: An Illustrated Guide to Glacier Travel and Crevasse Rescue*. Falcon, 2009.

UIAA Alpine Skills Summer Handbook. 4th edition. UIAA, 2024.

Volken, Martin, Margaret Wheeler, and Scott Schell. *Backcountry Skiing*. 2nd edition. Mountaineers Books, 2025.

Wilkerson, James, Ernest Moore, and Ken Zafren. *Medicine for Mountaineering and Other Wilderness Activities*. 6th edition. Mountaineers Books, 2010.

MOUNTAIN LITERATURE

Beckey, Fred. *Fred Beckey's 100 Favorite Climbs of North America.* Patagonia, 2013.

Blanchard, Barry. *The Calling: A Life Rocked by Mountains.* Patagonia, 2014.

Bonatti, Walter. *The Mountains of My Life.* Translated by Robert Marshall. Modern Library, 2001.

Child, Greg. *Mixed Emotions: Mountaineering Writings of Greg Child.* Mountaineers Books, 2012.

———. *Postcards from the Ledge.* Mountaineers Books, 2000.

———. *Thin Air: Encounters in the Himalayas.* Mountaineers Books, 1998.

Cordes, Kelly. *The Tower: A Chronicle of Climbing and Controversy on Cerro Torre.* Patagonia, 2014.

Davidson, Art. *Minus 148°: First Winter Ascent of Mount McKinley.* Mountaineers Books, 2013.

Harrer, Heinrich. *The White Spider: The Classic Account of the Ascent of the Eiger.* Harper, 2005.

Herzog, Maurice. *Annapurna: The First Conquest of an 8,000-Meter Peak.* 2nd edition. Lyons Press, 2010.

Hornbein, Tom. *Everest: The West Ridge.* Anniversary edition. Mountaineers Books, 2013.

House, Steve. *Beyond the Mountain.* Patagonia, 2009.

Krakauer, Jon. *Into Thin Air: A Personal Account of the Mount Everest Disaster.* Vintage, 1999.

Messner, Reinhold. *Fall of Heaven: Whymper's Tragic Matterhorn Climb.* Mountaineers Books, 2017.

Powter, Geoff. *Survival Is Not Assured: The Life of Climber Jim Donini.* Mountaineers Books, 2024.

Rébuffat, Gaston. *Starlight and Storm: The Conquest of the Great North Faces of the Alps.* Random House, 1999.

Roberts, David. *The Mountain of My Fear and Deborah.* Mountaineers Books, 2012.

Roper, Steve, and Allen Steck. *The 50 Classic Climbs of North America.* Sierra Club Books, 1982.

Simpson, Joe. *Touching the Void: The True Story of One Man's Miraculous Survival.* Harper Perennial, 2004.

Steck, Allen. *A Mountaineer's Life.* Patagonia, 2017.

Swenson, Steve. *Karakoram: Climbing Through the Kashmir Conflict.* Mountaineers Books, 2017.

Terray, Lionel. *Conquistadors of the Useless: From the Alps to Annapurna.* Mountaineers Books, 2008.

Viesturs, Ed, with David Roberts. *K2: Life and Death on the World's Most Dangerous Mountain.* Crown, 2010.

———. *No Shortcuts to the Top: Climbing the Worlds' 14 Highest Peaks.* Crown, 2007.

Wickwire, Jim, and Dorothy Bullitt. *Addicted to Danger: A Memoir about Affirming Life in the Face of Death.* Pocket Books, 1998.

Zimmerman, Graham. *A Fine Line: Searching for Balance Among Mountains.* Mountaineers Books, 2023.

Index

Page numbers in *italics* denote figures.

D

E

F

About the Author

Rebecca Schroeder

An internationally licensed IFMGA mountain guide, **Ian Nicholson** has been climbing glaciers for more than twenty-five years and guiding full-time for the better part of two decades. A veteran of more than twenty-five expeditions, he has climbed all over the world and has more than a dozen first ascents to his credit.

Nicholson instructs and examines as part of the American Mountain Guides Association's (AMGA) National Instructor team and serves on AMGA's technical committee. He also works for the American Institute for Avalanche Research and Education (AIARE) as both an instructor trainer and a pro instructor. In these roles, he trains the next generation of mountain guides and avalanche professionals. Nicholson is also the recipient of two Denali Pro Pin Awards for assisting other climbers in dire need in the Alaska Range.

Nicholson is the author of *Climbing Self-Rescue* and *Washington Pass Climbing* and a contributor to *Climbing* magazine, OutdoorGearLab.com, and WildSnow.com. He lives in Seattle with his wife Rebecca and their sons Henry and Hayden.

recreation • lifestyle • conservation

MOUNTAINEERS BOOKS including its two imprints, Skipstone and Braided River, is a leading publisher of quality outdoor recreation, sustainability, and conservation titles. As a 501(c)(3) nonprofit, we are committed to supporting the environmental and educational goals of our organization by providing expert information on human-powered adventure, sustainable practices at home and on the trail, and preservation of wilderness.

Our publications are made possible through the generosity of donors, and through sales of 700 titles on outdoor recreation, sustainable lifestyle, and conservation. To donate, purchase books, or learn more, visit us online:

MOUNTAINEERS BOOKS
1001 SW Klickitat Way, Suite 201 • Seattle, WA 98134
800-553-4453 • mbooks@mountaineersbooks.org • www.mountaineersbooks.org

An independent nonprofit publisher since 1960